Teaching Nonfiction Revision

Teaching Nonfiction Revision

A Professional Writer Shares Strategies, Tips, and Lessons

Sneed B. Collard III • Vicki Spandel

ILLUSTRATIONS BY BRAD SNEED

HEINEMANN
Portsmouth, NH

Heinemann

361 Hanover Street

Portsmouth, NH 03801–3912

www.heinemann.com

Offices and agents throughout the world

Excerpt from *A Platypus, Probably* by Sneed B. Collard III. Text copyright © 2005 by Sneed B. Collard III. Illustration copyright © 2005 by Andrew Plant. Used with permission by Charlesbridge Publishing, Inc., www.charlesbridge.com. All rights reserved.

Author photo of Sneed B. Collard III by Braden G. Collard and author photo of Vicki Spandel by Lynn Woodward, www.lynnwoodwardphotography.com.

Cataloging-in-Publication Data is on file at the Library of Congress.
ISBN: 978-0-325-08777-1

Acquisitions Editor: Katie Wood Ray
Production Editor: Sean Moreau
Cover and Interior Design: Suzanne Heiser
Cover and Interior Illustrations: Brad Sneed, www.bradsneed.com
Typesetter: Gina Poirier Design
Manufacturing: Steve Bernier

Printed in the United States of America on acid-free paper

21 20 19 18 17 PAH 1 2 3 4 5

For Amy, Braden, and Tessa: The best revisions I ever made.

—Sneed

∾

I would like to dedicate this book to all those students and

teachers who have asked me the important question:

"What do writers actually do when they revise?"

I hope this book provides some answers for you.

—Vicki

CONTENTS

 This icon indicates that an online reproducible is available to download.

Teaching Nonfiction Revision **Online Resources**

To access the online resources for *Teaching Nonfiction Revision*, please go to **www.heinemann.com** and click the link in the upper right to **Log In**.

(If you do not already have an account with Heinemann, you will need to create an account.)

Register your product by entering the code: **TNFREV**.

Once you have registered your product, it will appear in the list of **My Online Resources**.

ACKNOWLEDGMENTS

From Sneed . . .

It's no small challenge to properly acknowledge the many people who contributed to this project—by far the largest and most involved of my career. The obvious place to start is with my wonderful colleague, Vicki Spandel, and our amazing editor, Katie Wood Ray.

This is the first book I have ever coauthored, and Vicki rendered the process both pleasurable and incredibly educational. Not only was she instrumental in conceptualizing the project, but she added depth and insight I could only have imagined before I began. She also put up with my grumbles and—choose all of the above—inspired, provoked, and goaded the best out of me. And did I mention she's a lot of fun? Thank you, Vicki!

And Katie? Well, that's easy. She simply delivered the most productive, insightful, and enjoyable editorial process of my career.

I also want to add my thanks to the teachers and students who provided their help and writing samples for us to work with. I am especially grateful to Judy Mazur and her incredible class, and Elizabeth Fessler and her terrific students, with a special shout-out to Jack Clark. I was touched both by these teachers' willingness to help, and by their students' passion for writing and learning. I would also like to thank Keegan Clarke and send one last "thank you" to my own Miles City writing camp students, especially Anna Carlson. I'm waiting for your first book, Anna!

Thank you, too, to Vicki's and my author and artist friends who were willing to add a well-timed quote or two to our message, and to the consummate artist, my "cousin" Brad Sneed, who helped bring this book alive. As all writers do, Vicki and I stand on wide and mighty shoulders.

As always, I could not have tackled this project without the complete support of my family. My wife, Amy, never flagged in believing that I not only could, but *should* write this book. My son Braden and daughter Tessa both took more than a casual interest, and provided me with just the right writing samples at just the "write" times. I love you. You are the best!

—*Sneed B. Collard III*

From Vicki . . .

First and foremost, I want to thank the students who shared their writing with us, knowing full well that Sneed and I planned to pick it apart to illustrate revision opportunities. I'd love to bottle your fearlessness and share it with writers everywhere.

I also want to thank the teachers whose expertise helped me, over time, deepen my understanding of writing workshop, revision, and the art of conferring with students. They include Judy Mazur—who also helped us procure diverse student writing samples for this book—as well as Megan Sloan, Billie Lamkin, Jeff Hicks, Steve Peha, Andrea Dabbs, Leila Naka, Jeff Anderson, and Rosey Dorsey.

It's no secret to anyone who's been in one of my workshops that I've admired Katie Wood Ray's work for years. My copy of *What You Know by Heart* is so "loved" it can no longer travel with me because the pages are literally falling out. When I learned Katie would be our editor for this book, I knew we had won the publishing lottery.

Katie believed in this book from day one, embracing our goal of bringing professional-level revision strategies right into everyday writing workshop. She brought her years of classroom experience to bear on the project, helping us zero in on revision mysteries that plague both students and teachers—and her approach was consistently hands-on. She cautioned us from the outset that she would be reading our manuscript perhaps more closely than anyone had ever read our work before. Some writers might find that intimidating; we loved it. Katie's insightful and persistent questions, comments, and suggestions continually awakened fresh ideas, pushing us deeper and deeper into the revision process, and helping us make the book all we wanted it to be.

For me, working with Katie was like having a one-on-one conference with the writing mentor who had inspired me for years. What a rare privilege. Our deepest thanks to you, Katie.

Naturally, I need to say a word about my coauthor.

A couple years ago I was beachcombing outside Port Douglas in Queensland—hoping not to bump into the neighborhood crocodile—when I got an email from one of my favorite nonfiction authors: Sneed Collard. Sneed was considering writing a book to help young writers revise their own nonfiction effectively, and asked me, "What do you think of that idea?"

What did I think? Why, it was the most exciting news I'd heard since my husband announced we were going to Australia. When Sneed invited me to be part of the project, I was overjoyed.

It's an understatement to say I appreciate the chance to work with Sneed, whose humor, knowledge, compelling voice, and meticulous research have made his many books such a delight to read. But most of all, I want to thank Sneed for involving me in an approach I'll call "team writing."

Our process for putting this book together made for one of my finest writing experiences ever. I'd draft or revise a section and send it off to Sneed for his review and comments—and he would do the same, sending his latest copy to me. Something about ongoing immediate feedback electrifies the whole revision process.

Of course, I've worked with numerous coauthors in the past. This time, though, it was different. Why? For one thing, I was both writer and reader *all the time*—and that's about as much fun as someone who loves writing the way I do can have. Moreover, the revision was recursive. We had time to reflect. And to change our minds—repeatedly. That difference taught me something important. While a one-time revision focuses all our energies on the document at hand, ongoing revision *with a partner* teaches us deeper lessons about the act of revision itself—in particular, about how our words affect readers.

Thank you, Sneed, for giving me the chance to be part of this project; for making revision enlightening, rewarding, and outrageously fun; and most of all, for sharing what really goes on in a writer's head. From now on, whenever I struggle with an unwieldy nonfiction passage, I will just listen for your voice echoing in my head—"You could cut this part, Vicki . . . Here's another sentence that could go . . . You really don't need this word . . . or this one . . ."

—*Vicki Spandel*

INTRODUCTION

The Rosetta Stone

You've just put on the original Broadway soundtrack to *Les Misérables* and settled into that comfy, leather reading chair you picked up at a garage sale last summer. On your lap sits the latest pile of papers from your seventh-grade language arts class. The students' assignment? To revise a short report they had written two weeks ago. Feeling hopeful, you reach for the top paper, "The Rosetta Stone," by Allie—one of your more promising young writers. Allie has stapled her original draft to the revision, so you begin by reviewing that:

> The Rosetta Stone was discovered by French captain Pierre Bouchard. At the time, the pharaoh Ptolemy V's reign, he told the priests to carve it to calm down a revolt and publicly state he was the rightful pharaoh of Egypt. The Rosetta Stone is written in 3 different scripts in 2 different languages (hieroglyphic, demotic, and Greek). Thomas Young identified Ptolemy's cartouche and figured out the hieroglyphs for p, t, m, y and s. Jean-Francois Champollion figured out the 7 demotic symbols. Without this stone, we never would have deciphered Egyptian hieroglyphs. It is now considered the most important archeological artifact in the world.

Though Allie's original draft ended up vague and confusing, you thought it had potential. She had chosen a compelling topic and included interesting information about this important artifact. To help her improve the piece, you had advised her to create a timeline, clarify the roles played by Ptolemy V and Pierre Bouchard, define terms like "hieroglyphic," "cartouche," and "demotic," and help readers understand why scientists consider the Rosetta Stone so important. Did she do these things? To find out, you turn your attention to Allie's revision:

> The rock called the Rosetta Stone was discovered in 1799 by French captain Pierre Bouchard while he and his soldiers were rebuilding Fort Julien during the Napoleonic wars. Earlier, in the pharaoh Ptolemy V's reign, the Egyptians were totally out of hand. He told the priests to create the stone to stop the revolt and state publicly he was the rightful pharaoh

of Egypt. The stone elucidated all the really good deeds Ptolemy did for
Egypt and his people. The Rosetta Stone is written in 3 different scripts
(hieroglyphic, demotic, and Greek) and 2 different languages (Greek and
Egyptian). In 1814, an Egyptologist, Thomas Young recognized Ptolemy's
cartouche (his name) and discovered the hieroglyphs for p, t, m, y and s,
as well as which way to read them. In 1822, Jean-Francois Champollion, who
knew Greek and Coptic (demotic script), figured out the same 7 demotic
symbols. Using them to translate the hieroglyphs, Champollion completely
deciphered the stone. Without this amazing stone, we never would have
begun to read Egyptian hieroglyphs in a million years. It is now considered
by far the most important rock in the world.

You lift your pen to respond, then lower it and sigh. Where do you begin? Though
Allie has made a serious attempt to revise, it's difficult to detect any significant improvement. Yes, she's made her report longer, introduced new facts and vocabulary, worked
on the timeline, and tried to define words readers may not be familiar with. Despite her
efforts, Allie's report tells us next to nothing about Ptolemy V and the other major play-
ers in this drama. She also has yet to explain why decoding hieroglyphs was so important, how an Egyptian artifact came to be called the "Rosetta Stone," or why experts
consider this ancient message the "most important rock in the world." Worse, given
the weak transitions, unclear references, and parenthetical remarks, the writing bumps
along like a Model A on a washed-out road.

Unfortunately, revision like Allie's is all too common. Despite decades of emphasis
on writing, revision remains, for many students, as mysterious as ancient hieroglyph-
ics. Not knowing what else to do, students plug in extra facts, make sentences longer, fix
spelling, change fonts, swap one word for another—or maybe insert an adjective, adverb,
or exclamation mark for emphasis.

Experienced writers approach revision very differently. For us, revision involves
taking rough text and transforming it into something clear, fluent, informative—and
yes, engaging.

Reconciling these two sets of expectations may seem as achievable as, say, jumping a
bicycle over the Grand Canyon. And actually teaching kids to revise? Well, why not just
march ourselves right off the edge?

Like most things, revision carries with it both bad and good news. The bad news is
that it does indeed take years of practice to develop an intuition about where to take a
piece of writing that isn't working. The good news is that most revision is methodical.

Professional writers consistently apply proven strategies to hammer and reshape nonfiction until it becomes something that educates and excites readers. These steps are not only definable, they are *teachable*.

That's why we've written this book—to demystify the revision process and provide simple strategies you can readily teach your students. Think of these strategies as a Rosetta Stone of nonfiction revision. Students may not master every strategy on the first try, but they will make huge strides toward understanding the revision process. Given practice, they will write words you will actually look forward to reading.

We have organized this book into seven sections. "Part I: Setting the Stage" comprises seven short chapters that examine the nature of revision, foundational beliefs about teaching it, and early steps your students can take to promote effective revision later. These chapters, written in response to common questions from teachers, provide a critical context for the instructional strategies that follow.

Parts II through VI contain nuts-and-bolts teaching strategies designed to strengthen students' nonfiction revision skills. These strategies proceed from "big" to "small," and follow specific approaches many professional writers use to revise their work. We first tackle whole-manuscript issues such as content, organization, and the writer's vision. After that, we gradually work our way down through scenes, paragraphs, sentences, and words.

Part VII concludes by offering final revision suggestions along with firsthand perspective about the entire revision process.

You can read strategies to yourself—or share them aloud with your students. In many instances, chapters may spark important and useful classroom discussions. The strategies in these chapters are pulled directly from Sneed's extensive experiences writing and revising nonfiction—so when you see the word "I" in the main text, that is Sneed talking!

Following each strategy, Vicki has added two or more special features to help you teach and communicate that strategy to your students. Vicki has pulled these suggestions and exercises from her years of experience as a teacher, author, writing coach, writing workshop facilitator, and journalist. The "I" in these features is Vicki.

We want you to be able to travel through this book quickly, so we've kept each strategy as short as possible. Still, some revision concepts demand more attention than others, so we've allocated our word count accordingly.

Although our approach and exercises primarily target grades 4–8, teachers of both younger and older students can readily adapt lessons to fit their classroom needs. Whether you are a regular classroom teacher, a literacy specialist, or a writer yourself, this is *your* book, and we know you'll figure out the best way to use it. So have fun—and get ready to launch!

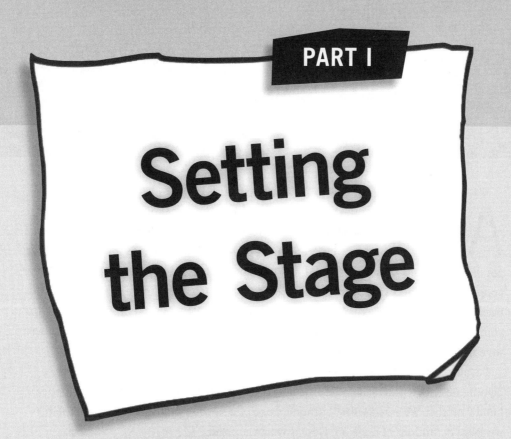

PART I

Setting the Stage

I can list a host of reasons why I would never attempt a serious repair of my 1986 Toyota 4Runner. Sure, I like cars and might even enjoy working on my soon-to-be-classic vehicle. The problem? I am totally ill-equiped to contemplate any task beyond replacing a lightbulb or adding windshield wiper fluid. I don't have the proper tools. I don't have an adequate work space. Worse, I have only a vague idea about how to approach a repair—which things to do first, what precautions to take, and how to make sure my efforts don't lead to an even bigger mess than I started out with.

Revision is a lot like automotive maintenance. It can make all the difference, before you begin, to make sure you have the tools and environment you need and an understanding of how to proceed. The chapters in Part I are your "garage." Vicki and I wrote them to help you pinpoint what revision is, define what you and your students are trying to achieve, create an environment that supports your goals, and offer key advice on getting started. You *could* skip straight to the revision strategies in the subsequent sections, but we believe that some thoughtful "shop setup" now will pay handsome dividends when you and your students begin tearing apart manuscripts down the road.

1

What Nonfiction Revision Is—and Isn't

As Allie's assignment in the introduction demonstrates, expectations for revising nonfiction can vary dramatically between teachers and young writers. It can vary among experienced writers, too! Before Vicki and I wrote this book, I rarely pondered the word *revision*. Through my years of writing, I'd developed and refined approaches for improving my work, and as my experience grew, these approaches became more and more exhaustive. Rarely, though, did I say to myself, "Okay, now I am going to sit down to revise." That word conveyed only a vague significance or usefulness to me, and I'm guessing this may be true for your students as well.

So, a first step in bridging the expectation gap between teachers and students is coming up with a practical consensus on what revision actually means. To get a better handle on that, we asked fellow authors of both fiction and nonfiction to share their personal definitions of revision. Here is what they said:

> The art of rereading what you've written to mine and polish the gems and discard the gravel.
>> —Lola Schaefer, author of *Lifetime: The Amazing Numbers in Animal Lives*

> I think of revision as LOOKING AT SOMETHING AFRESH. Editing is what I do AFTER I'VE LOOKED AT SOMETHING AFRESH.
>> —Larry Dane Brimner, author of *The Rain Wizard* and *Birmingham Sunday*

> I wrote a book about eyeballs. As I was finishing the book I had a new idea to include a fish that has no eyes. That's a revision.
>> —Jerry Pallotta, author of *The Incredible Crab Alphabet Book*

> First draft: digging up the clay. First revision: shaping the clay into something useful.
>> —Kate Barsotti, artist

*A search for perfection, when I choose to do it; the labors of Hercules when
my editor asks me to do it.*

> —Gary Blackwood, author of *The Shakespeare Stealer*

*Revisiting your first thoughts, rereading your last words, rewriting to
find clarity.*

> —Lester Laminack, author of *Cracking Open the Author's
> Craft: Teaching the Art of Writing*

Revision is not a straight line: It erases, retraces, and replaces.

> —Jeff Anderson, author of *Revision Decisions* and
> the Zack Delacruz series

An opportunity to improve perfection.

> —Eric Kimmel, author of *The Runaway Tortilla*

As you can see, revision means different things to different people. Yet together, these responses move us toward a workable definition—one that applies to both nonfiction and fiction. Combined, these various perspectives give us a strong sense that revision isn't so much about fixing technical details, but instead tackles the soul of writing. According to these authors, revision shapes the message, voice, flow, and clarity of a piece. It is *deeper* work, requiring careful thought and decision-making.

Forming a good definition also requires us to extrapolate what revision is *not*. Revision is not:

- adding *really, very, extremely, pretty,* or *humongous* to sentences
- trying to impress readers by replacing everyday words with more complicated words
- ending sentences with exclamation marks!!!
- putting words in CAPS for EMPHASIS.

Such window dressings are usually made by beginning writers hoping for quick fixes to more fundamental problems.

Revision also is not correcting spelling and punctuation. These changes fall more under the category of editing, not revision. Which brings up a key question: just what *is* the difference between revision and editing?

Again, you'll hear different viewpoints on this, and there's no doubt the two overlap. Author and teacher Barry Lane says, "Editing is adjusting the tie. Revision is deciding which tie to wear" (Lane, pers. comm.). In their book *Because Writing Matters* (2003), The National Writing Project and Carl Nagin suggest that while revision involves "structural changes" to text, editing is something different:

> *For some teachers and writers, editing is synonymous with revision. For others, it is micro editing—that is, line edits and proofreading . . . focusing on mechanics, spelling, punctuation, and other conventions. Editing prepares a piece of writing for its final or published form. (26–27)*

This is a lot to take in, but together, these comments and definitions provide us with a solid compass heading. For the purposes of this book, we can consider editing largely as a process of correcting mistakes in conventions and grammar, while revision focuses on making a work more readable, meaningful, enjoyable, useful, inspirational, and yes, artistic.

With this definition in our pocket, let's take a quick look at when and how writers choose to revise nonfiction.

When and How Writers Revise

My dad enjoyed writing about as much as he enjoyed operating on his ingrown toenail. Both activities caused him pain, aggravation, and frustration. As a biology professor, my father's biggest literary obligations were to generate grant proposals to obtain funding for his research and to write scientific papers detailing the results of that research. I remember one summer watching him sit down to write the first sentence of a scientific paper. Five days and ten packs of cigarettes later, he still anguished over that first sentence! He literally could not move on to the next sentence until he had perfected the first. Compare that to my nine-year-old daughter, who will sit down and furiously scribble out a three-page story while barely taking a breath. Revision? She'll tackle that later—if she gets around to it at all.

The majority of writers fall somewhere between these two extremes. Although most of us recognize that we need to improve early drafts, just when and how we do it varies enormously. Some, like my daughter, charge through an entire draft before they turn their attention toward improving it. Others revise continually as they work.

I didn't even think about how I revised until I'd been writing professionally for about fifteen years. One day I sat listening to a presentation by the wonderful writer Pam Muñoz Ryan. She described how she continually revised as she worked, moving forward in fits and starts, but frequently returning to the beginning to run through the entire manuscript. She even had a name for this style of writing. She called it "recursive writing."

Her talk got my attention because I realized that I write in the exact same way. Each day, I start from the beginning of my manuscript—or at least from the beginning of the last major section—and work my way through everything I've written before, making changes and adding fresh material. I find that working in this way helps me create the greatest consistency in voice and style, and keeps me on track for where I want to take a particular project. As my wife will happily tell you, I also have a low tolerance for uncertainty. I prefer to resolve emerging problems as I go along instead of trying to fix them later!

In contrast, many writers—especially writing students—find it easier to complete an entire draft before trying to improve it. They don't want to get caught up in reworking details before getting that first draft completely under their belts. Here's the thing: *there is no one right way to revise.* Each writer eventually comes up with his own method, a method that works best for him.

That said, in organizing this book, we are assuming that your students will hammer out a first draft before they turn their attention to revision. This is actually how most students work, and it's probably most efficient to teach revision from this standpoint. If you find that you've got some recursive writers in your class, don't panic. The strategies will work just as well for them as for your other students. Even recursive writers need to step back, look at the big picture, and revisit the other revision steps that we detail in this book. Encourage these students to keep working in their own ways, but incorporate the revision lessons that you teach as they go along. Revision is method, but it's also art, and each "author artist" should be free to create his own particular way of doing it. This acceptance also plays a key role in our next topic . . .

Creating an Environment That Supports Revision

Remember the scene in the movie *Alien* where the baby alien bursts out of the crew member's chest cavity? The same horror we felt watching that monster erupt onto the screen is what many students experience when facing revision. Really, who can blame them? They just finished sweating over a writing assignment—and that was hard enough. Now you want them to go back and revisit that very same piece? *Have you lost your mind?*

Student resistance to revision often comes from a perception that revision is not only tedious, but an indication that they have done something wrong. After all, if they had not failed in some way, why would they need to revise?

Professional writers view the process differently. For us, revision reflects a deep commitment to both audience and message. While an early draft provides a beginning point, good writers are driven to refine that draft until it conveys their thinking as precisely, completely, and compellingly as possible.

In *The Story of Charlotte's Web* (2012), biographer Michael Sims tells us that author E. B. White "kept revising, crossing out, starting over" throughout

And look, I completely revised the tone by changing the font from Times New Roman to Arial Rounded MT Bold.

the many days it took him to write his best-selling book. White spent hours "wrestling to get sections right," often drawing large Xs across whole pages, framing sentences in multiple ways to see which one sounded best, and writing himself marginal notes such as "Fix" or "Make this better" (194–205).

Sharing these kinds of anecdotes with students helps show them the pains top writers take to create something people actually want to read. But how do we encourage E. B. White's kind of determination and experimentation in students? One way is by creating an environment that presents revision not as an ordeal or threat, but as an opportunity.

What would such an environment look like?

Well, obviously, writers who are revising need tools—a comfortable workspace, highlighters, tape and scissors, resource books, and with luck, computers. But an environment that truly supports revision goes beyond the physical. Below are six steps you can take to turn your classroom into a safe, rewarding—even exciting—"revision ecosystem."

Choice

Give students opportunities to choose their own topics, at least some of the time. Granted, there can be sound reasons for assigning writing topics, but students are nearly always more passionate about subjects they have chosen, or at least refined, themselves.

Collaboration

Provide writers multiple chances to share and confer with one another. Small writing groups of four or five provide an intimate, nonthreatening atmosphere where writers learn to offer and receive constructive feedback on shaping content, filling informational holes, and clarifying fuzzy passages. Though the makeup of the groups can and should vary throughout the year, students should be allowed to stay together long enough to develop trust. (See "A Note to the Teacher" for ideas on helping writing groups work well together.)

Modeling

Model revision often. Do you feel shy about this? No worries. It isn't as hard as it sounds. Think small. Rewrite a lead that falls flat, brainstorm a better title, search for the just-right phrase to describe those inedible *hors d'oeuvres* from a recent party, cross out a redundant line. Small lessons work well because they make one point that students will remember. You don't have to aim for a Pulitzer Prize. It's the process students need to see.

Helping Students Make Choices

Students gain confidence and independence by making their own writing decisions. You can support a student's independence during a conference by asking one or more questions like these:

- *How far along do you feel you are with this draft?*

- *What's the next thing you plan to work on?*

- *What's the most important thing you've learned about this topic?*

- *Do you feel you'll need to do more research? Do you have a plan?*

- *Here's a question I still have: _____?*

- *What else will readers want to know that you haven't told them yet?*

- *Have you listened to this piece as someone else reads it to you? What did you think as you were listening?*

- *What kind of voice do you want readers to hear? What helps create that voice?*

- *Do you have a favorite part you could read to me? What do you like about that part?*

- *I sometimes struggle to keep my writing concise. As you work on this piece, is there anything you're finding especially hard?*

Ownership

Let students own their writing.

Raise your hand if this sounds familiar: while reviewing a piece of writing with a student, you spot three or four places begging for attention. The student, however, sees no need for revision, so you ask yourself, "What's to become of this piece if I don't choreograph the revision plan?"

Actually, that's up to the writer. You can and should offer suggestions and insights, but as hard as it might be—and it can be one of the hardest things we do as teachers— resist the temptation to make revision choices for the writer. Instead, be patient. With careful instruction and coaching, students will begin to come up with their own revision ideas. Remind yourself that it's not the particular piece of writing that matters. It's the student's growing ability to take charge of her own revision process.

Risk-Taking

Timid revision is about as effective as whipping cream with a noodle. Nothing exciting happens. To revise effectively, students must be willing to take risks—often, big ones. They must write a sentence three or more ways before settling on one that works, axe a paragraph if it wanders off topic, turn an ending into a lead if that's a better fit, or even start over if a topic just isn't working.

What if students fear losing something good while trying to make it better? A trick I use is to copy the section of text I am working on into a new blank document. In that new document, I can safely tinker with it, try different approaches—even mess it up beyond all recognition. If my efforts result in disaster, no problem! I still have my original in another file so that I can start over. If your students seem hesitant to revise, share this simple technique with them. It may free them up to take the risks required for bold, effective revision.

Examples

Fill your classroom with the best nonfiction writing you can find. (See our list of recommendations in the back of this book.) Don't just stick books on a shelf. Read selections aloud and invite students to respond. If you have a document projector, share photos and diagrams and talk about how those features enhance the texts. Examples show students how nonfiction writers handle special challenges like organizing complex information, achieving the right voice, making statistics interesting, explaining technical terms, knowing when and how to use graphics, and a host of other things.

All of the above steps share a common goal: to make your students feel comfortable taking charge of their own writing. A supportive environment doesn't guarantee that students will start pounding on desktops, demanding more revision time. It *will* help them view revision as a dynamic, exciting process—one that, with practice, will let them achieve their full writing potential.

Helping Writing Groups Work Effectively

Read these suggestions aloud to students, then post them and add to the list as your students discover additional ways of helping each other as writers:

- *Always remember that you are there to help your group members reach their goals with their work. Spend more time listening and thinking than talking.*

- *Let someone else read your work aloud occasionally. Many writers find that hearing their words in someone else's voice helps them identify both strengths and problems.*

- *Always express something positive about someone else's work before tackling things that aren't working.*

- *If you have a negative comment, combine it with a helpful suggestion for improvement.*

- *Take turns. Be aware of how many people are in your group and divide your time accordingly, allowing everyone a chance to speak. Hint: It's useful to set a timer.*

- *When sharing your own writing, let your group know what kind of feedback you need—general responses to the piece as a whole, comments on voice or wording, thoughts on organization, suggestions about missing information, and so on. Remember, though, to stay open to the group's other comments as well.*

- *In offering feedback, be specific. A comment like "good job" is fun to receive, but not especially helpful. Did the writer create a striking image or phrase you remember? Did she teach you something or help you see things in a new way? Did you have questions? Let the writer know exactly what worked—or confused you.*

- *Pay close attention to which kinds of feedback are most helpful so you can work on improving your own responses to your classmates' work.*

- *If you need it, don't hesitate to seek advice even before you begin writing. If you just can't seem to get started, your writing group might have suggestions about topic selection or research. You don't need to take their advice verbatim, but perhaps their thoughts will spark helpful ideas.*

Balancing Expectations

> Almost anybody can sit down and write something—once.
> But the real writer, the committed and potentially successful
> writer, will write and revise and write and revise until whatever
> she is writing . . . works.
>
> —**Lee Gutkind**, *You Can't Make This Stuff Up* (2012)

So . . . write and revise, write and revise until it works. *Until it sings!* Makes sense. But can you picture it in your classroom? Okay, let's keep it real. We do want students to improve as revisers, but they are not professional writers. Some may *become* professional writers, however, and most will eventually write on the job—so while we strive to be realistic, we don't want to lower expectations too far, either. Here are some guidelines for keeping expectations high, yet still grounded on Planet Classroom.

First, let students choose which pieces they want to revise—every other piece, perhaps, or every third piece they write. They might choose something meaningful to them personally, or something that's going to go public, say, in the school newspaper. Why is choice important? Because while professional writers will revise almost everything they write—including Facebook posts, emails, and graffiti on freeway underpasses—students don't usually share that revision zeal. Choice, though, sparks motivation. In addition, students need to write as much as possible in order to become proficient. If they are forced to revise everything, they may be tempted to keep their writing as short and simple as possible. Letting them pick what they will revise helps keep their writing juices flowing through *all* of their assignments.

Second, help students understand what the concept of multiple revisions really means. In his classic book *On Writing Well* (2006), William Zinsser suggests that "most rewriting consists of reshaping and tightening and refining" (84). This kind of fine-tuning requires multiple *rereadings*, but it rarely means *rewriting* the whole piece multiple times. You can model this liberating concept using either of the approaches described in "A Note to the Teacher."

Third, celebrate small victories. For a student who has never done much real revision (remember, fixing spelling or punctuation doesn't count), changing even one sentence is a breakthrough. Don't be afraid to linger in the moment and pop open that bottle of Dom Perignon 2003 (or at least a can of Sprite), helping the student appreciate the impact of revision on a reader. You might say something like, "When you changed the words 'huge snake' to 'seven slithering feet of muscle,' you put a whole new image in my head. That was one terrific revision."

At the other end of the continuum, you may have writers—including recursive writers—who produce remarkably readable first drafts through skill, continual revision, or both. Do such writers even need to revise further or for that matter, need coaching? Yes—and yes. Rereading unearths new revision possibilities in *any* piece of writing, no matter how clear or engaging. Dare your strongest writers to elevate their work from good to memorable.

Fourth, allow enough time for careful reading and reflection. Not too much time, though. When deadlines appear far off, many students procrastinate. To help you budget time for the revision process, here is Vicki's *Irresistibly Practical Super-Flexible Four-Day Plan* to share directly with students who have completed or nearly completed an early draft:

- *Day 1:* Leave your piece of writing alone to gain mental distance and perspective.

- *Day 2:* Share your writing with a trusted friend or classmate, and listen carefully to his feedback. Read your writing aloud to yourself to see if you agree with your friend's assessment. Make in-text and marginal notes, using a pencil or the comment option on your computer screen, to remind yourself of things you might want to delete, insert, expand, or change.

A NOTE TO THE TEACHER

Modeling Your Own Revision Process

Many writers prefer to finish a complete draft before plunging into revision. If that's you, show your students what this approach looks like. Read a short first draft aloud when it's fresh, and then put it away for a few days. When you pull it out again, read it aloud once more, letting students know how you hear it differently after a little time has passed. Ask for suggestions, using students' ideas as well as your own to make a few revisions as they look on. Once you finish, read your final version aloud and ask students if they hear improvement.

If you are a recursive writer, read your work aloud *as you write*, asking (yes, aloud) if this will make sense to readers. As you're reading, you might pause to say, "That isn't exactly what I mean. Let me phrase this differently . . ." Take two or three runs at it—whatever it takes to make the writing match your intended meaning. Don't feel compelled to hack your way through a full draft. A line or two will give students the idea, provided you read and revise more than once.

- *Day 3:* Get ruthless. Make that keyboard hum. Insert, cut, rewrite, rearrange (all the things we address in later strategies). Don't forget to quietly read aloud to yourself as you work.

- *Day 4:* Read your entire draft to yourself once more, making any spontaneous changes you didn't think of before. Then, in writer's group, ask another person to read your work aloud. Take note of places that confuse listeners or block the flow of the writing. Ask your group, "Does it make sense? How could I make it more interesting?" Ask yourself, "Am I happy?"

A NOTE TO THE TEACHER

Helping Students Build Stamina for Revision

Like running or weight lifting, revising takes stamina. Here are four ways to help students develop the endurance they need to make it through a round of revision without toppling over or groaning (much):

1. Start with short sessions—five to ten minutes tops—gradually extending revision time to about half an hour. Always congratulate students on focusing, but ask if they can go a little longer the next time. Challenge them to push themselves.

2. If you spend a major portion of your class period revising, provide a two-minute break—a chance to stand, stretch, and think through next steps. As the majority of students return to work, you might use the second half of your revision time to confer with students who need individual help.

3. Encourage students to tackle one manageable portion at a time: the first paragraph, the first page, or whatever feels reasonable. Next time, they can quickly review that revised portion and then move on.

4. Revise with your students. Let them see you read, reflect, and make decisions. Seeing *you* push yourself gives them confidence that they can do the same.

Vicki's *Four-Day Plan* works well for a single paragraph or up to several double-spaced pages. Longer documents require more time and perhaps additional research, so factor that in.

Finally, don't expect students to attend to every last detail that you spot when you read their work. They aren't as experienced as you in reading critically. What's more, some kinds of revision present more challenges than others. Brainstorming good titles is a relatively light, fun task; reworking a paragraph that doesn't make sense can exhaust even a resilient reviser. We revised this chapter almost *twenty times* to produce the version you are reading now. Building up revision stamina takes time. With that in mind, start slowly, remembering that for a struggling student, rewriting even one paragraph may feel like climbing Yosemite's Half Dome. For more ideas on building students' writing endurance, see Vicki's "A Note to the Teacher."

5 Creating a Vision

In many ways, revision is influenced by the writer's initial vision: the picture she creates in her mind of what a given piece of writing might become. In the world of nonfiction, that original vision could take the form of a memoir, journalistic report, essay, analysis, nonfiction picture book, biography, review, or any of a dozen other projects.

Of course, the original vision doesn't always determine how a piece of writing ends up. When I began thinking about this book, I envisioned it as a short handbook of nonfiction writing tips for students. As I brought Vicki into the project, however, and we began discussing it with our editor, Katie, the project began to morph into what you are reading now. This sort of transformation is extremely common. Almost always, in fact, writing projects shrink, expand, and/or change focus as they proceed through the writing and revision process. That's because a writer reshapes the writing continually as she obtains new information and experiments with new possibilities.

Staying open to these kinds of changes takes courage, because changes don't always bring positive results. Writers who *begin* with a clear vision, however, usually struggle less during the revision process. Why? Because they understand what they are trying to achieve.

Four simple but important decisions can help students clarify where they are going—and have an easier time both writing and revising their work.

Decision One: Choose—or Refine—Your Topic

Sometimes, as a teacher, you may assign topics to your students. That can be important if you want to find out what they know about a particular subject, such as alternative energy. If you do it all the time, though, realize that you are doing important writers' work for them. All on their own, writers must learn to come up with topics that are interesting and worthy of exploration. As Vicki has already indicated, choice almost always leads to greater writing enthusiasm.

Just the other morning, I walked my thirteen-year-old son to his bus stop and to my surprise, he rattled on and on about a report he and a friend were working on for social studies.

I asked him, "Did you choose that topic, or did the teacher?"

"We did," he replied.

Recognizing an opportunity to conduct some on-the-spot field research, I asked, "Do you like choosing your topics more than having them assigned?"

His recently changed voice dropped an octave for emphasis: "Oh, yeah."

Even when a topic is assigned, a skillful writer, much like a journalist, will search out the angle, the approach, or unanswered question that will give the assignment fresh appeal. In helping your students sort through the possibilities, remind them that a good nonfiction topic should be something that:

- piques the writer's curiosity
- can readily be researched given available resources
- won't grow too big to cover in the time and space available
- engages readers—either because they need to know about it, or because the writer has endeavored to make the topic especially intriguing.

IN CONFERENCE

Students Choose Their Own Topics

For some students, the very act of choosing a topic can be overwhelming. It's tempting to make things easier for them by just assigning a topic. But you can encourage more independence by holding a topic choice conference with a small group of students who need extra help with this decision. Begin by exploring personal interests and any favorite nonfiction books. Share your own favorites, too. End by brainstorming a list of potential topics, including some of your own, from which students can choose or at least narrow their choices. Alternatively, you can provide a general theme—like "explorers" or "outer space." This gives students guiding parameters without taking the choice out of their hands.

A Writing Secret to Share with Students

Choosing a topic is one of the most important writing decisions you can make. If you write about something you love, your enthusiasm will be contagious, and readers may come to love your topic as much as you do. Remember, though . . . sometimes a subject you aren't crazy about in the beginning can grow on you as you learn more about it. Do a little research before saying "no" to any idea.

Decision Two: Identify Your Readers

Writing for the wrong audience can be like wearing a Denver Broncos jersey to an Oakland Raiders home game. You can expect disgruntled looks—if not empty beer cans sailing toward your head. Anticipating readers' needs and preferences helps a writer figure out what to say and how to say it. Help your students work through this decision by answering questions such as:

- Will anyone other than my teacher read this?
- What sort of content or tone is appropriate for this piece?
- What do readers already know about my topic?
- Are these readers looking for information, entertainment, or both?

When I began working on *Science Warriors: The Battle Against Invasive Species* (2008b), I set out to write an entertaining book about a provocative topic. At the same time, I knew that most of my readers would know very little about the subject. I realized that, step by step, I would have to define an invasive species, explain the tremendous scope of the problem, and document specific examples—such as how a seemingly benign tree from Australia ended up strangling the Everglades or how one snake species single-handedly devoured most of Guam's wildlife.

In contrast, when I wrote *Sneed B. Collard III's Most Fun Book Ever About Lizards* (2012), I targeted readers who would be fans of lizards—or at least animals—and would already know a fair bit about them. That freed me from having to explain lizard anatomy, how lizards differ from amphibians, and the lizard's place in the reptile world. Instead, I could go straight to "sexier" subjects such as how Komodo dragons eat people, chameleons shoot out tongues longer than they are in order to catch prey, and certain horned lizards squirt blood from their eyes to persuade predators to drop them. Knowing that my readers already loved lizards also convinced me to write in the first person in an

A NOTE TO THE TEACHER

How Long Does It Have to Be?

Perhaps, like many teachers, you don't always assign specific numbers of words or pages. That uncertainty prompts many students to ask the question that's become a cliché: "How long does it have to be?" Sometimes you may have guidelines in mind: e.g., "At least two pages—no more than five." Other times, consider challenging students by tossing the question back to them: "I don't know—how much space do you think this topic demands?" Even if you only do this occasionally, you encourage writers to think about factors that influence length, such as the importance and depth of the message, the details involved, and the extent of the research.

entertaining, informal style. This showed readers that I was one of them—a fellow lizard lover.

Decision 3: Narrow Your Topic

Student writers can save themselves a lot of trouble by matching the breadth of their topic to their available space—in most instances, the number of pages or words they have been asked to write.

This lesson reared its head when I was writing my book *Global Warming: A Personal Guide to Causes and Solutions* (2011). Initially, I had intended to make global warming only one of five chapters on five different environmental topics such as pollution, over-population, and warfare. When I roughed out the book, it was a disaster—not just the environmental issues, but my manuscript, too! I was simply trying to cover too much territory in a short space.

After talking it over with my publisher, we agreed that the book needed a tighter focus. Writing exclusively about global warming not only helped me concentrate as a writer, it allowed me to create a satisfying, in-depth treatment of one subject instead of superficial treatments of five different topics.

Even in student writing, scaling down a topic is often one of the most important and useful steps a writer can take. Unfortunately, it often requires *starting* a manuscript to recognize that your focus might be too large or small. Remind students that this, too, is a valuable part of the writing—and revision—process.

A Writing Secret to Share with Students

One good way to whittle down an oversized topic is by making a list from big and general to small and specific. As you work your way down, imagine yourself bringing an image into focus through a microscope. Let's say I'm a sports enthusiast and want to write about my passion. Great—only "sports" is such a huge topic, I could be writing forever! So I ask myself questions like, "What sport in particular? What about that sport interests me—or would interest readers? Do I want to focus more on training or on competition? Is there a particular person readers are curious about?" The result is a list in which the topics get more and more specific:

- *sports*
- *swimming*
- *Olympic swimming competition*
- *Olympic freestyle races*
- *what makes Olympic champion Michael Phelps so good at freestyle.*

Decision Four: Picture Your Writing in Its Final Form

Envisioning a manuscript as a biography, memoir, report, picture book—even a Power-Point narrative—renders it more real. It also helps a writer more easily make decisions about content and approach.

When I began formulating my book *Animal Dads* (1997), I knew that I was going to write a picture book. Because of that, I understood right off that my information had to be conceptually simple and concise. I struggled mightily to come up with just the right voice and beginning that would accomplish that. After about thirty tries, I wrote the opening line, "Dads do many things."

Immediately, I knew that I had it! That opening line established the voice for the book as well as the breadth and depth of material I would include. From there, I wrote the main text of the book in about half an hour. One reason I could write it so quickly is that I understood my picture book parameters. Having restrictions on length and audience actually made writing the book easier. Of course, another reason I was able to knock out the main text so quickly was that I had already done most of my research on the subject. And, what do you know? That just happens to lead to our next topic about setting the stage . . .

The Rewards of Research

nexperienced writers often consider research a waste of time. Rather than reading books, watching a documentary, or talking to an expert, they prefer to dive into writing like a penguin chasing a sardine. The problem with this approach is that a writer may dash off a rousing first paragraph only to find she doesn't know enough about her topic to add even one more good line. Thoroughly investigating a topic can solve this problem—and do much, much more.

I guess he already knew what he was after!

Carefully researching a topic also helps the writer:

- discover important questions to answer in the manuscript

- uncover the most interesting facts, quotes, and events to share

- make personal observations or have experiences that can dramatically enrich the text

- become enough of an expert to write with a compelling voice.

Research is so important that it plays a key role both *before* writing begins and *during* the revision process. That's why we also include it as one of our revision strategies later. Even before you have your students begin writing, it's important to encourage them to do as much research as possible. The best way to do that is to show them just how much fun the process can be.

Nowadays, students and adults alike equate research with getting on the Internet or, we all hope, checking out books from the library. Internet research, however, has inherent problems. One is that no one checks most information on the Internet to make sure it's true. Government websites tend to be pretty good, and I love Wikipedia, but it is only as good as the people who happen to work on individual subjects—and they do so with very little oversight. Most other websites are not checked at all. They teem with incorrect data, hearsay, and opinion masquerading as fact. Students don't know that, of course, so you have to tell them. Have them find out who created a website they wish to use for research. If it's an expert or group with an established reputation in a particular field, chances are that it will be trustworthy. If, on the other hand, it's an advocacy group, an enthusiastic amateur, a company trying to sell something, or a political party—in other words, most websites— advise them to steer clear.

Something to try
Checking the Need for More Research

How do students know when they've done enough research to begin writing? Here's a quick way to find out: Group students into teams of two. Ask them to summarize their information orally, walking their partners through the main points they plan to cover. When they finish, they should invite their partners to raise questions or point out informational gaps. If writers can't answer their partners' questions, or find it hard to converse about their topics for more than a few seconds, more research is almost certainly needed!

The greatest problem with Internet research may be the least obvious: *it robs writers of the genuine joy of discovery.*

Recently, in eastern Montana, I taught a week-long writing camp for underserved youth. After focusing on the writing process for a couple of days, one afternoon I led my students, armed with notebooks and cameras, on a field trip. Our first stop: a small-town art museum that had been created from an old waterworks building. Next, we visited one of the town cemeteries.

"Look all around you," I instructed them. "Notice what you see, how you feel, the different senses you experience. Whenever you notice or see something that may be useful in your own writing, jot it down in your notebook or take a picture of it."

The students ate it up. They raced around both venues scribbling notes, taking photos, and reading art descriptions and gravestones.

The next day, I led them in two different writing exercises. First, I projected pictures of some of the museum artworks and asked the students to write a story that was inspired by each image. Then, I had them craft a compelling narrative using their notes and photos from the cemetery. Here is a first draft from one of the students:

> Hundreds of gravestones lined the cemetery, cut from the same stone and arranged uniformly, a testament to the uniform lives of the soldiers that lay beneath them. Though at one time the white marble pillars had been arranged neatly, they now leaned every which way, like a set of teeth badly in need of orthodontia. Unlike the gravestones in the rest of the cemetery, no flowers graced these; they had been forgotten. Instead of individual people, the stones now represented the tolls of war on mankind—not fame, glory, nor the immortality of memory, but death, cold and absolute.

These two writing exercises turned out to be the most successful of the entire week. Equipped with their own observations and perspectives, students forged pieces brimming with insight and passion, and often touched on the profound. The quality of their writing leaped, too. Why? Because they were writing from their own research, inspiration, and choice.

A NOTE TO THE TEACHER

Encouraging Field Research

As Sneed points out, local research can be just as rewarding as exotic adventures. Below is a list of ways to get students "out in the field" where original research happens. Keep in mind that writers may need to head in different directions since they're likely to be researching a range of topics. Also note that some of these research ideas may require initial "set-up" from you:

- *Interview a family member or friend.*
- *Tour a nearby police station, firehouse, or courthouse.*
- *Talk to a local store owner about her business.*
- *Interview your mayor or other city or county official.*
- *Check out a documentary film from your local library.*
- *Visit a water treatment plant.*
- *Interview someone from a local band or theater group.*
- *Follow a local story in the newspaper for five days in a row.*
- *Visit a public or university library and have your students look up old newspaper or magazine stories stored on microfiche. (Old technology can fascinate young students!)*
- *Attend a city council meeting.*
- *Browse an old family photo album.*
- *Visit a local museum, TV studio, art gallery, nature observatory, zoo, historical site, or botanical garden.*
- *Attend or participate in a class on cooking, fitness, theater, or dance.*
- *Invite an expert on any topic to visit your class and prepare for that visit by discussing note-taking and the art of asking good questions.*

Ready, Set, Write!

Getting started is often the hardest part of writing. One way to spur the process is to have students list questions—maybe three to five for a start—that an interested reader might want answered. Unlike an outline, which can sometimes feel rigid, a list of questions remains totally flexible. The writer can add, delete, reword, or reorder questions at any time. What's more, questions feel *inviting*, as though the writer is conversing with future readers—which in a sense, she is.

Here are four questions one young writer posed for an article on vegetarianism:

1. What does it mean to be vegetarian and is it different from being vegan?

2. What are some advantages to being vegetarian?

3. Are there disadvantages—or even dangers—to a vegetarian diet?

4. Does the growing world population have implications for the vegetarian way of life?

Questions such as these provide a starting point for the golden rule of early drafts: *get it down*. No matter how skeletal a rough draft may be, completing it buoys a writer's confidence by giving her tangible evidence of progress. Remind your writers that their drafts do *not* have to be conventionally perfect or include every pertinent detail. Students will have time to address those things during the revision process.

A NOTE TO THE TEACHER

Unlocking the Door to Drafting

When a writer just cannot seem to get started, the problem is often lack of information. Reading—or chatting with an expert—raises questions that unlock the door to drafting, and you can model this for students. For example, let's say I'm writing about octopuses, but I have no strong sense of direction yet. I read the first two pages of Sy Montgomery's book *The Octopus Scientists* (2015) and encounter this quotation about the octopus' camouflage capabilities: "As well as changing color to match its surroundings," Montgomery writes, "it can instantly spout little projections all over its skin called papillae (pa-PIL-ay) to make it look exactly like a piece of algae or coral or rock" (2). This passage, I tell students, gives me a question to guide my writing: "If the octopus is so adept at hiding from predators, what other amazing skills might it possess?" I make sure students see me write this question at the top of my note page, telling them it will propel my research, thinking, and writing as I move forward.

Helping Students See Their Topics Through Readers' Eyes

During drafting, carefully timed conferences can be catalysts for new thinking. The student bent over her work, writing madly, probably doesn't need (or want) to talk to anyone just then. But that student chewing through his pencil or eyeing the clock might benefit from discovering a new angle to explore, one readers would find fascinating. You could say to him, "I see you're writing about playing the drums. What an intriguing topic. Does it ever bother anyone when you practice? Yes? I'd love to read more about that. Write a bit, and I'll stop back."

Another student writing about the skills needed for softball pitching might have trouble getting beyond generalities. She almost certainly knows more than she realizes, and your questions help her tap into this knowledge: "You say practice is critical, but let's say I've never pitched a softball in my life. If you were coaching me, what specific things would you tell me to do with my eyes, my hands, or my feet? Pretend I'm on the mound, with you right there beside me. How can I strike out the batter?"

Something to try
Modeling Marginal Reminders

It takes only moments to show students how helpful quick reminders can be. Share a brief piece of your writing aloud and talk about one or two changes you would like to make. Then write yourself marginal notes to jar your memory for the next draft. For example, underline a sentence you're not happy with and write in the margin, "Reword this." Keep your marginal notes short and specific. Use a pencil to mark the exact section of text—a circled word, a paragraph with a vertical line beside it—that you want to revise. Explain to students how these marginal assignments will save time by helping you dive right into revision when you come back to this piece. Incidentally, though you can't see them any longer, the book you are reading was once filled with marginal notes that Sneed and I wrote to ourselves—or to each other. My notes were particularly insightful, I thought. Just kidding, Sneed.

Early writing should be adventurous, a time for exploring questions and selecting and piecing together details.

As they write, have your students leave plenty of white space on their pages. Whether they are writing by hand or on a computer, they should double-space lines and leave big margins. That will make it easy to jot down thoughts and questions or add new information as it turns up.

As much as possible, students should turn off the editors in their heads during the drafting process. Now is not the time to run to a dictionary to look up the spelling of *deteriorate* or check the thesaurus for other ways to say *exciting*. It's critical not to interrupt the flow of ideas, so encourage them to quickly circle words they want to check or revise later, and move on. Of course, keep in mind that your recursive writers may need to revise as they go along, so try to accommodate this while still coaxing them forward.

Once writers have finished that first draft, they can read it through and even give themselves little assignments in the margins—*little* being the key word: *Add more detail here. Change this wording. Find a quotation that supports this point.* When students come back to revise, these notes tell them where and how to dive back in—and make starting the revision process much less intimidating.

A NOTE TO THE TEACHER

Creating the Right Workshop Atmosphere

A student may finish a short draft within one class period and even move on to revision—if she's working in an atmosphere that speaks to her inner writer. Though it's hard to please everyone, giving writers variety and choice helps keep them happy and engaged. Some like complete quiet—always hard to attain. Others prefer the hum of workshop chatter, or enjoy working to music. Students brought floor pillows to my friend Rosey's writing classroom, while others perched on the window ledges. On warm days, my own students sometimes wrote outdoors. Sitting at a desk seemed to be everyone's last choice. Also remember that in writing workshop, not all writers work at the same pace; some may be revising or doing additional research while others continue working on early drafts. Regardless, it's almost certain that most will need to do some work after school hours. Encourage them to search out a personal writing space they can make their own, whether that's a comfy chair, desk, tree house, basement corner, or back step. The "perfect" spot speaks to a writer. It says, "You're home. Let's begin."

PART II

Big-Picture Revision

Big-picture revision is a lot like getting a fifty-year-old house ready for sale. For the first time, the writer must step outside herself and see her writing—all of it—the way a reader (or buyer) would. The results can be unsettling.

More often than not, an early draft just doesn't capture everything a writer means or wants to say—or say it the way the writer would like. The only solution? Pick up a wrench—sometimes a sledgehammer—and rip into the manuscript's core. Content, voice, organization—these structural elements form the foundation of any written work. Tinkering with smaller elements before making this foundation rock-solid is like spackling and priming the walls of a house that is tilting like a drunken sailor and has a roof threatening to cave in on you. Touching up the paint just ain't gonna do it!

Because big-picture revision often requires extensive modifications, writers simply cannot rush this step. Urge students to be patient as they read through their first drafts. Assure them that extra time spent refining a topic, reshaping the central message, or reordering information will will make smaller "fixes" much more effective down the road.

1

Isolate Your Main Idea

An effective piece of writing says one dominant thing.
—**Donald Murray**, *A Writer Teaches Writing* (2004)

A common problem with many early drafts is that they contain more than one competing subject or main idea. That's not surprising. In researching a topic, a writer often discovers a host of fascinating facts or stories he'd like to include in his manuscript. These can vie for attention to such an extent that they leave readers asking, "What is this piece really about?"

I had this problem when researching one of my favorite nonfiction picture books, *1,000 Years Ago on Planet Earth* (1999a). The book surveyed twelve ancient civilizations and tried to encapsulate what they were up to a millennium ago. In many ways, it was like writing twelve short books on separate subjects. My problem? My publisher gave me only 200 words for each civilization and my first drafts ranged from 400–800 words each! Even worse, they contained an inconsistent hodgepodge of information.

In this case, my word count cap became a blessing. Why? Because it forced me to focus on one idea for each civilization. Instead of presenting a fairly random collection of information, I chose one powerful thrust to showcase each society. For the ancestral Pueblo people, I focused on their engineering skills; for the Mayans, their religious and celestial beliefs; for South Africans, their cattle culture. This focus turned each spread, or two-page section, into a concise, forceful narrative that drove the book forward.

As I did when writing about ancient civilizations, young writers often wander into a variety of topics in their early drafts. A paper that starts out talking about Gettysburg might swerve into a biography of Robert

A NOTE TO THE TEACHER

Discovering a Topic

Writers often do not find their real topics until they begin writing. It does not mean they have done something wrong. On the contrary, they have done something very right, which is to explore ideas until the question that interests them most bubbles to the surface. That's the time to sharpen focus, turning all drafting and research attention on that most intriguing question.

E. Lee. A report about the Amazon rain forest might get caught up in the habits and behavior of jaguars. What to do?

Probably the easiest approach is to counsel a writer to pick the idea that most interests him. My son, for instance, would probably pick jaguars over the entire Amazon. I would probably pick the battle of Gettysburg over Robert E. Lee. Once a writer has made that choice, it's fairly straightforward to either delete competing subjects, or pare them down to make sure they are subordinate to—or merely enhance—the main subject.

What if a student doesn't even realize he has competing subjects? One thing my editors have done with me is simply count up the number of sentences, paragraphs, or pages devoted to various topics and write down the totals for each one. You can have your students perform similar "accounting." Tell them, "Okay, write down all the subjects you have in your draft. Now, go through and count the lines you have devoted to each subject." One of two things will happen: the main topic will naturally emerge from the totals, or the student will realize he's got too many competing ideas in his paper and, perhaps with nudging from you, he'll pick one to focus on.

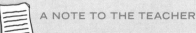

A NOTE TO THE TEACHER

Discussing How Students Revise Now

We are just beginning our adventure into the world of nonfiction revision. Before we get too far down the path, it might be instructive for you and your students to find out how they approach revision now. Ask your students, "What is the very first thing you do when you revise?" Record their answers, offering no judgments or comments. Then compare them with the answers they give to this same question several months from now, after practicing revision strategies in this book. That comparison is likely to reveal a whole new approach for many, one that shows what strong nonfiction revisers they have become.

A Writing Secret to Share with Students

Just because you drop a topic for now doesn't mean you can't return to it later. Sneed and I keep writer's notebooks—places to record observations, favorite quotations, writing ideas, book titles and authors we admire, and much more! If you haven't started a writer's notebook yet, this is a good time to think about doing so. As your first entry, start a running list of subjects worth returning to down the road.

2

Research Your Topic—Again!

I deally—as we discussed in Part I—most research occurs *before* writing begins. However, almost all writers end up doing important additional research during the revision process.

Why?

One reason is that after isolating or refining your main idea, you may find yourself writing about new topics or new angles of topics that you hadn't originally anticipated. This almost always requires digging up more information. Even if the main focus of your piece remains the same through your intitial draft, roughing out a manuscript unearths fresh questions that a writer simply cannot predict at the beginning of the writing process.

Recently, for example, I worked on a short book about Balto, the famous sled dog who helped deliver medicine to Nome, Alaska during the diphtheria epidemic of 1925. I did my basic research about Balto and began writing. As I drafted and referred back to my research materials, however, I kept running across references to other dogs that had participated in the great relay. After finishing my first draft, I realized that to do the story justice, I needed to describe at least some of these dogs in more detail. That required going back and learning more—especially about a dog named Togo, who led one of the other relay teams and performed just as heroically as his more famous contemporary.

A second reason to do more research is to add more detail to a piece. Sticking to a doggie theme, before writing my nonfiction "dog-ography" *Shep: Our Most Loyal Dog* (2006b), I read all of the available literature on Shep, and proceeded to rough out a draft of the book. Reading it over, though, I felt that the book needed more substance. To rectify this issue, I traveled to Shep's hometown, Fort Benton, Montana, to try to find people who knew the famous dog.

A Writing Secret to Share with Students

Variety is vital to good research. Have you already done some reading on your topic? Great! Now think about adding another approach: watch a documentary film, interview an expert, or make a site visit. Having multiple sources enriches your understanding of any subject, helping you write with confidence.

Testing Audience Interest in New Topics

As Sneed discovered when writing about the sled dog Balto, research sometimes unearths new, intriguing topics. How do students know which of these to explore? As they conduct their research, have students list new ideas or questions that emerge, then share these for discussion within their writing groups. For example, a student writing about the Amazon rain forest might start out researching deforestation, then uncover intriguing details about how deforestation affects medical research or how new roads bring miners into conflict with Brazil's indigenous people. Sharing these topics in her writing group gives a writer a chance to ask which topics readers want to know more about. But—caution! Trying to cover too much can make any writing unwieldy and lead to thin research as writers run out of time. Twig George, author of *Seahorses* (2003), put it best in her author's note from that book: "As I write, many facts get left along the way, like film clips on a cutting room floor" (32).

I ended up interviewing a man named Steve McSweeney, who grew up just down the railroad tracks from where Shep lived. He knew Shep well and recounted many anecdotes that had never been published. One of my favorites was that the stationmaster used to feed Shep Life Savers candies as dog treats! I also learned that far from being the morose character portrayed in many magazine articles, Shep was actually quite a happy fellow, even after his master died. If I hadn't met Steve, I would have missed these gems—and struggled mightily to put together Shep's story. Even more important, Steve's account provided a solid backbone for the book and made the subsequent revision process much easier.

In each of the above cases, research makes writing better. It not only helps revision. In many cases, it *allows* revision. What do I mean by that? I mean that without a rich fund of information at his fingertips, a writer can't possibly choose the best structure for his manuscript, know how to place details in relation to each other, or sometimes, even identify the most important points of a piece. Research provides that expansive overview that a writer needs—and in doing so gives writing a direction or foundation that it often lacked before.

And did we mention that research is fun? Even a decade later, I treasure my memories of traveling to Fort Benton, interviewing Steve McSweeney, and seeing where Shep had lived. Other research projects have proved equally rewarding. Writing *Science Warriors* (2008b) gave me the opportunity to visit Florida and go airboating through the Everglades. Working on a book called *In the Deep* (2005a) landed me an invitation to dive 3,000 feet deep to the ocean floor in a tiny submersible. All of these experiences not only led to better books, they helped shape me as a person—just as your students' research will shape them.

 A NOTE TO THE TEACHER

Taking Research Question by Question

"Ongoing research" can sound to some students like a never-ending assignment. Show students how to manage research by focusing on only one key question at a time.

Recently, I wrote a piece on humpback whales (2005a). I had the information I needed to write about the birth of calves off Maui, and the whales' migratory journey to their feeding grounds in Alaska. Then I hit a wall. What did they eat once they reached Alaska—and how did they find their prey? One article mentioned the term "bubble-net feeding" and presto, I had a question to guide my research: "How does bubble-net feeding work?"

Staying focused on my one key question, I scanned additional articles until I'd gathered enough information to describe how circling humpbacks create an enormous cylinder of air bubbles that tightens around their prey, trapping them. If I had allowed myself to get sidetracked by too many other questions all competing for my attention, I might have wound up floundering in an informational bubble net of my own.

Add Missing Information

don't think I have *ever* completed a first draft of a book without discovering that I had left out vital information. To wit: as I was roughing out this very tip, I received an email from one of my editors. Together, we were working on a photo-illustrated picture book about gliding animals titled *Catching Air: Taking the Leap with Gliding Animals* (2017a). In his email, my editor asked, "Sneed, do you think we should include a little more explanation of lift?" Well, guess what I added during the next round of revision?

Both beginning and veteran writers frequently leave out details, descriptions, or explanations that a reader requires to fully understand or appreciate a subject. One reason this happens is that by the time a writer sits down to write about something, she has become something of an expert on it. She mistakenly takes for granted that readers understand what she understands.

What's the solution?

This is one of those cases in which a writer's group, or at least other outside readers, can be more valuable than ever. Especially when someone else reads a work aloud, it

A Writing Secret to Share with Students

It's never possible to include every smidgeon of knowledge our research uncovers. So how do writers decide which information makes the cut? They start by asking what's critical to a piece's central topic. For example, in his book on lizards, Sneed spends a good bit of time discussing what lizards eat and how they avoid becoming another creature's lunch—core topics for any group of animals. Next, writers look for striking details that surprise, startle, amaze, and/or inform readers. In her essay "Tarantula Heaven" (from *Guys Read: True Stories* [2014]), science writer Sy Montgomery managed to uncover many such details including, "Tarantulas can regrow lost legs, and at times, when a leg is injured, they will pull it off and eat it for energy—a trick many a human athlete would envy." (38) Now that's a striking detail.

quickly becomes apparent where a piece of writing needs to be enhanced. Certain passages will elicit scrunched eyebrows and blank stares—sure signs of confusion. Others might generate an anxious restlessness, which could be the mark of burning curiosity about an unanswered question or—less happily—dissatisfaction with a proffered explanation.

IN CONFERENCE

Unveiling Your Own Curiosity

As they're drafting, help students focus on missing information with comments or questions that say, "Here's what I'm still curious about." For example, you might tell a writer, "You've taught readers so much about Harriet Tubman and the Underground Railroad—but I'm still wondering how Harriet managed to elude capture for so long." Or, "It would be fascinating to know how much artificial intelligence will affect the everyday life of a person like me." Questions or comments often prompt further research. Even more important, they help the writer see that her topic choice was a good one because—guess what?—she's got a reader hungry to learn more. Students don't realize how exciting it might be for us to discover that kangaroos can leap thirty feet or that the moon's thin atmosphere makes objects appear more distinct. They often imagine we know such things, and more, already. That *aha* moment when the student recognizes that she is the teacher helps her feel the power of writing nonfiction.

I fondly remember listening to a new story by Hanneke Ippisch a number of years ago. Before she died, Hanneke was a member of my writer's group. She had already written *Sky* (1998), a highly acclaimed account of her time working for the Dutch resistance during World War II. Now, she was writing a new memoir about her life after the war, when she moved to Sweden to work as a servant for a branch of Sweden's royal family. As we all sat around in a circle, another member of our group, Jeannette Ingold, began reading aloud a chapter in which Hanneke mentions "making out" with the prince of the family. Then, abruptly, the story moved on to another topic. After a few pages, we all said, "Wait a minute, Hanneke. What happened to the prince?"

Hanneke looked at us in her matter-of-fact way. "Oh," she said. "I married him."

We all burst out laughing and one of us asked, "Don't you think that's a little detail you just *might* want to include?"

A totally clueless expression spread across Hanneke's face, and she asked, "Do you think I should?"

Of course, you may be asking yourself, "What if my students can't always work in a writer's group? How will they recognize when something is missing in their drafts?"

To be honest, both beginning and experienced writers have trouble with this. Of course, your guidance as a teacher will prove extremely valuable in pointing out missing information. Having students read their work aloud to themselves also can call attention to missing information. My favorite tool, though, is simply letting a draft rest.

After working intensely on a draft, writers—*all* writers—simply become too close to a project to recognize things that may be missing. Resting drafts for a time and looking at them with fresh eyes always helps me in this regard. When I was roughing out *Catching Air* (2017a), for example, I focused solely on land animals. One day, while the manuscript was "resting," I had a conversation with my daughter in which flying fish came up. That thought must have lodged in my brain because when I glided back into the manuscript, I suddenly realized, "Oh, flying fish are gliding animals, too. I'd better include them in the discussion!"

Don't you love how our brains work?

! Something to try
Modeling the Addition of Information

Searching out missing information provides an ideal opportunity for modeling. Pick one of your early drafts for this exercise—so it's more likely to have a few informational holes. Then ask the whole class to be a writing group for you. Be specific about the kind of help you need: e.g., "I need to know if I've given readers enough information about my topic. As you listen, think about what questions pop into your mind. When I finish reading, we'll list those questions and choose the most important ones to answer." Hold on—important? Yes. Because a writer isn't obligated to answer every possible question that occurs to listeners. Some questions are better than others. The most helpful inquiries get at information that the writer would most certainly have included had she only thought to do so! Other good questions seek to satisfy readers' curiosities, detangle confusing points, provide little-known details, or expand readers' understanding of a topic.

4 Cut, Cut, Cut!

I have a confession: I *love* to cut. Almost nothing pleases me more than to read through a manuscript and find a sentence, a paragraph, a page—*entire chapters*—that can be placed under the guillotine and dispatched into history once and for all.

Cutting is definitely my favorite part of writing!

My general rule of thumb? If I can't cut at least a quarter of my first draft then I'm not doing my job.

Fortunately, the majority of early drafts contain more fat than Iowa-raised bacon. We will focus on paring down sentences later, but right now let's talk about *Texas Chainsaw Massacre*-style cuts—you know, hacking off large sections of your manuscript to make it better. How do you know where to begin?

All nonfiction writing has a purpose. It might be to explain how to perform a task. It might be to introduce readers to a fascinating place or convince them to act in a certain way. It might be to tell an inspiring story or recount an important event—or it might be a combination of several things. Understanding this purpose provides a key to guiding the revision process—especially when it comes to cutting.

Armed with a clear understanding of purpose, a writer can read through her draft, constantly asking herself, "Is this helping me achieve what I want with this piece? Does it relate to my main idea?" If the answer ever comes up "no," then baby, that section needs to go!

I ran up against a host of difficult cutting decisions while revising *Snakes, Alligators, and Broken Hearts: Journeys of a Biologist's Son* (2015b). While roughing out this memoir of my childhood, I incorporated dozens of events and anecdotes into my early drafts. The result was a narrative that often felt bloated and lost its thread. I knew that the manuscript needed trimming, but how could I possibly know which stories and events to keep and which ones to throw out?

My first guide was to keep reminding myself of my purpose. I had decided early on that this book would focus on my experiences with my father. As I went through each chapter of the book, I asked myself, "Does this particular anecdote provide a key insight into the relationship with my dad? Do people *have* to read about this event to understand the big picture of my story?" The answer often came up "no."

> ## 🔑 A Writing Secret to Share with Students
>
> The first time you cut words from your writing, it can feel like a very big deal. But as you learn how much better concise writing sounds, cutting grows easier and easier—until, like Sneed, you even ponder ways to shorten the writing on road signs. If you aren't sure whether to cut a sentence or longer piece of text, try this: Using a pencil or strikethrough key on the computer, draw a line through the passage in question. Then, read the piece aloud without those parts you crossed out. If it's sharper, snappier, and more direct, the cross-outs can go! Still not sure? Then have a friend read the paper aloud *to you*, omitting any cross-outs you've marked. Ask yourself, "Did I miss those cross-outs?" If not, you didn't need them!

Growing up, for instance, I had a close relationship with one particular family. The mom often watched me after school, and her daughters essentially became my sisters. I felt an emotional pull to include them in my memoir, but guess what? They had little to do with my relationship with my dad, so out they went.

Another story recounted my dad dressing up as Santa Claus and coming to my nursery school. The story had everything. It was warm and funny and sweet. It also stopped the narrative in its tracks. Why? Because it simply didn't contribute any new insights or drama to my story. Worse, as a reader, it left me impatient to move on.

Snip. Snip.

These are just two examples of the kinds of cold-blooded choices I and other writers have to make during big-picture revision. But what about a more factual manuscript such as, say, an informational article?

Suppose a student has written a paper on Blue-footed Boobies. If she went through and made a list of the information she included, it might look something like the following:

- lives in the Eastern Pacific Ocean

- half of all breeding pairs live in Galápagos Islands

- the first scientist to visit the Galápagos was Charles Darwin

- is one of six species of boobies

- bright feet come from pigments in diet

- eats mainly sardines

- Nazca Boobies also eat sardines

- Nazca Boobies have whiter feathers

- Nazca Boobies have brown feet

- females choose male partners with the brightest feet

- many other birds live in the Galápagos

- thousands of visitors come to the Galápagos each year

- numbers of Blue-footed Boobies going down in the Galápagos.

Something to try
Cutting Text in Half

When I worked for *The Willamette Week* newspaper in Portland, feature articles had to fit inside two-inch columns, and we writers rarely knew in advance how many columns the editor would allow us. When you're paid by the word, it's pretty disappointing to hear, "Sorry! You'll need to cut this in half!" The good news? Extreme cutting, like cleaning the closet, forced me to focus on what mattered most, and the resulting articles were always more readable.

Try this with students who are typically writing pieces at least two pages in length. Have them write 300–400 words on any topic. Then, ask them to cut the length by half without altering the main message. If they're anything like me, they'll protest—vehemently! But they will also discover that trimming nonessentials dramatically improves both writing and revision skills.

It's important to note that these are not actual sentences or phrases from the paper. Instead, each line is a summary of an important point or piece of information the writer included.

Looking over the list, did you spot anything that doesn't contribute directly to the student's purpose and main idea? Sure. The writer went off on tangents about Nazca Boobies and about visitors to the Galápagos Islands. To be fair, these topics might fit into a larger, more expansive paper. In fact, Charles Darwin's visit to the Galápagos might be an effective lead into the subject of Blue-footed Boobies. But for a short, concise paper, her list clearly spotlights several chunks that can be left on the cutting room floor.

Now, I can see some of you waving your hands out there saying, "I can hardly get my students to write a paragraph or two, and now you want me to have them cut something? They won't have anything left!" Well, obviously you have to use your own judgment about where your students are as writers and what they are ready to do. The kinds of big cuts we're talking about in this tip apply more to longer pieces of writing than to shorter ones. Even in a two-paragraph essay, however, chances are that a student will throw in at least one sentence that doesn't relate to his purpose.

Snip. Snip.

IN CONFERENCE

Helping Writers Make Good Choices

To cut or not to cut needs to be the writer's decision. Your questions, however, can nudge her toward a good choice: "Does this third paragraph support your message? Let me read it aloud so you can focus on your purpose as you listen . . ." A writer may understandably resist any suggestion framed as an edict: "This part needs to go!" But most writers respond positively to questions that frame alternatives: "If you ended the piece right here—and cut the final paragraph entirely—you would close by describing the consequences of not opening the new dog park instead of adding general comments on the pros and cons. Which ending strikes you as more powerful?"

Modeling Cutting

Cutting unneeded scenes, paragraphs, and sentences is a perfect thing to model. Students need to see and hear you weigh your own words—keep or cut?—then bravely slice off what needs to go. Be very specific about your reasons for keeping or deleting something. Students cannot read your mind, and need to hear you *think out loud*—like this: "I've already made this point and I don't want to repeat myself." Or, "I'm getting away from the main point here. This needs to go."

If you're reluctant to dispatch a favorite section but your ear tells you it's the right move, let students know you're struggling, then slash away. When students suggest a cut, listen—even if you disagree at first. Read the passage aloud both ways to help spark a class discussion on whether the cut would improve the passage. Only then decide if you should hold your ground or go along with the suggestion. You'll be interested to know that Sneed and I have enjoyed suggesting cuts many times—especially in the other person's work. It's been enormously helpful. Sneed's writing has gotten far more concise.

Check Your Organization

As a rough manuscript is still emerging, events and topics often wind up organized in ways that render them more confusing or less effective than they could be. This isn't a bad thing or a mistake. It's simply a normal part of the writing process. Getting organizational issues resolved in the early stages of revision, however, can save a lot of time and trouble later on.

In revising my book *Birds of Prey: A Look at Daytime Raptors* (1999b), I ended up moving a chapter on common raptor behaviors and anatomical features from the back of the book all the way to the front, where it fit much better. I'm not sure why I put it in the back originally. Maybe I hadn't eaten enough chocolate that day! After letting the manuscript sit for a couple of weeks, however, I realized that readers needed to first learn what eagles, hawks, and falcons have in common before finding out about individual species.

In this case, I reorganized my project to create a more logical learning sequence. Logic isn't the only reason to organize topics or events in a certain way, however. Sometimes, putting *a* before *b* creates more drama or tension in a manuscript. Other times, it emphasizes the most important points or topics a writer wants the reader to pay attention to.

Creating and playing with an outline before drafting begins can facilitate strong organization. Before beginning to draft this book, Vicki and I created a detailed outline of our topics and how we thought they should be organized. We shifted things around—sometimes radically—and tried them out in our heads before settling on a final plan. This proved invaluable in wrapping our minds around the entire project and providing a rough-cut idea of what we wanted to include. It also provided a working document that we could refer to and make notes on when discussing and refining the scope of the book.

The problem is that when a writer sticks too tightly to an outline, the results can end up stiff and devoid of spontaneity and expression. Sometimes, another useful approach is to make what I call a reverse outline. How does it work? First, the writer finishes his rough draft. Then, he creates an outline of *main topics* and events based on what he has already written. He uses this not to cut information, but to provide a conceptual snapshot of the entire manuscript—and especially as a tool for spotting problems with order and organization.

Not long ago, I wrote an article for *Highlights for Children* (January 2017) about a large weight called a "damper ball" that had been installed to reduce the swaying in Taiwan's tallest building, Taipei 101. Below, I have reverse-outlined an early draft of the article (initially titled "The Damper Ball Rocks!"). Take a moment to read through the list as if you were reading the actual manuscript. Do you see anything that could be put in a better order? If so, swap points around to create a better sequence.

1. Intro: superficial description of the "damper ball" in Taiwan's tallest building, Taipei 101

2. Explain how a damper works

3. Define what a damper ball or "tuned mass damper" is

4. Present problem #1 for tall buildings in Taiwan: people's comfort

5. Present problem #2 for tall buildings in Taiwan: earthquakes

6. Present problem #3 for tall buildings in Taiwan: typhoons

7. Solution? A damper ball

8. Explain how the damper was installed

9. Add in-depth details on the damper ball's immense size and weight

10. Explain how the damper reduces movement in the building

11. Recount the damper ball's performance during a large Chinese earthquake

12. Explain how the damper ball has become a tourist attraction

Something to try

Reordering Using Sneed's Reverse Outline

Share Sneed's reverse outline for his "The Damper Ball Rocks!" article with your students, using a document projector so they can see the outline as they respond. Have students work with partners to reorder the twelve points so the sequence will create a stronger piece of writing. Discuss the results as a class, asking students to justify any revisions they have made to the order. Then share Sneed's revision on page 45 and compare it to what your students came up with. You may also want to read Sneed's discussion of his reorganization aloud so students can understand the reasons behind his changes.

You probably spotted several opportunities for improvement. One is that I explain how a damper works before I define what a damper is. This could leave readers flailing because without knowing what a damper is, they would lack the correct context to understand how a damper functions.

A second, more subtle ordering issue arises from my list of three "problems" to constructing a building so tall. In my initial draft, I list people's comfort first—but actually their comfort is more of a side benefit of the damper. For engineers, the most urgent issue is to keep the building from falling down! Different writers might make different choices on this, but I decided that to keep readers interested, I should tackle the most life-threatening issue first—a pure judgment call on my part.

The final order issue has to do with describing how workers installed the damper ball before I describe its enormous dimensions. That renders the damper ball's eighteen-foot height and 1.5 million-pound weight less dramatic—almost an afterthought. If I describe how immense the damper ball is first, however, that ratchets up tension for the problem of hoisting this monster to the top of Taipei 101.

After tackling all of these order problems, here is the new outline I came up with for the article:

1. Intro: superficial description of the "damper ball" in Taiwan's tallest building, Taipei 101
2. Define what a damper ball or "tuned mass damper" is
3. Explain how a damper works
4. Present problem #1 for tall buildings in Taiwan: earthquakes
5. Present problem #2 for tall buildings in Taiwan in Taiwan: typhoons
6. Present problem #3 for tall buildings in Taiwan: people's comfort

7. Solution? A damper ball
8. Add in-depth details on the damper ball's immense size and weight
9. Explain how the damper was installed
10. Explain how the damper reduces movement in the building
11. Recount the damper ball's performance during a large Chinese earthquake
12. Explain how the damper ball has become a tourist attraction

Do you agree that this organization works better? I think it does, but if I hadn't employed a reverse outline as a tool, I may never have spotted these organizational problems—or been able to effectively revise the article's organization.

One thing to add is that in articles like this, and in chapters as well, writers often use subheadings—often called A-Heads—to help group related points or stories and make it easier for the reader to process them. A-Heads, though, can also be a great organizational tool for student writers. Just for fun, ask your students to insert A-Heads into their next nonfiction draft. Ask them, "Did this help you organize your thoughts and your writing?"

A Writing Secret to Share with Students

Even when we craft them ourselves, outlines can feel rigid—like a set of rules we need to follow *or else.* The truth is, the more flexible your outline, the more useful it will be to you as a writer. Almost no one can organize information effectively on the first try. So control your outline— don't let it control you. Add to it, delete elements, and move things around until it becomes a kind of map to guide readers through your thinking.

Something to try
Having Students Reverse-Outline Their Own Work

Have students try reverse outlining for themselves, focusing on their own recent drafts. Once they finish, have them study their reverse outlines carefully to see if any parts seem out of order. Then have them revise their organization—rearranging, combining, or even deleting some elements—based on what the reverse outline reveals. When you finish, talk about using reverse outlining as a tool for revising organization. Is it effective? Do students find it more helpful than simply reading through their drafts? Why?

Something to try
Looking for Drama

Sneed tells us that drama sometimes trumps logic in deciding which information to present first. Let's put that theory to the test. Check out this reprint of an introductory scene subtitled "Inferno" from Sneed's book *Fire Birds: Valuing Natural Wildfires and Burned Forests* (2015a):

If you do not have a copy of the actual book to show students, make sure they understand that this section is *the very first thing* readers see. Read it aloud and ask students what sort of mood it creates. Is it fair to describe this writing as dramatic? If so, talk about where the drama comes from. Then share the following paragraph, which opens Chapter One:

> *University of Montana professor Dick Hutto walks through a pine, larch, and Douglas-fir forest. Like any self-respecting bird biologist or ornithologist, he wears binoculars around his neck. As he ambles along a trail surrounded by wildflowers, he calls out a list of bird species.*

This, too, could make a strong, engaging lead for Sneed's book. It could have come first—but is it as captivating as the scene titled "Inferno!"? Did Sneed make the right choice in putting "Inferno!" first? Why? Which lead do your students find more compelling? Does beginning the book with a more intense scene give students more patience while reading the quieter scene that follows?

Inferno!

A dry summer in Montana. Warmer-than-usual spring weather melted the snowpack early, and by July soaring temperatures have turned the mountain landscape into a tinderbox. The heat stirs up enormous, boiling thunderheads. Like a ravenous beast, the storm sucks up warm, humid air from the ground below until finally, the sky splits open. Thousands of lightning bolts launch toward earth. Most fall harmlessly, but one strikes an especially rotten, dead log, setting the wood aglow.

Within hours, the log erupts into flames. By the next morning, the fire has consumed a couple of acres of forest. Then, dry winds spring up, whipping the flames out of control. Firefighters can do nothing. As they watch, the inferno devours hundreds, then thousands of acres. The fire rages for days, then weeks. It reduces green mountain ridges and valleys to charcoal. Thick smoke chokes local communities. Ash falls on cities and towns a thousand miles away.

Finally, in late August, a break in the weather brings cooler temperatures. Rains arrive, quenching the flames, but the damage is done. Government and timber industry officials join the public in proclaiming the fire a total disaster. Living forests have been replaced by dead, blackened trees. It will be decades, perhaps longer, before the forests grow back. Nature has been devastated, leaving behind a vast wasteland.

Or has it?

Introductory scene from **Fire Birds**

6 Unleash Your Voice!

> Writing with real voice has the power to make you pay attention and understand. The words go deep.
>
> —**Peter Elbow**, *Writing with Power* (1998)

Voice.

Almost nothing in writing is more difficult to discuss, let alone *teach*. One reason is that while almost everyone agrees that it is important, few people agree on what voice actually is. For some, voice is concrete and well defined. For others, it is more abstract. Before discussing how to improve voice, we'll need to define what we're talking about here—and specifically in terms of writing nonfiction. Fortunately, over the years, I've come up with a definition that I like. To me, strong nonfiction voice is:

> *The quality of the narrator that not only makes a reader want to listen to him,*
> *but accepts his authority to be writing on a given subject.*

As a teacher, you've undoubtedly noticed that some students write with strong voice: e.g., "When Captain Cook felt *Endeavor*'s hull crash into the reef, he leaped into action." Others stumble along with little or no voice: "Captain Cook's boat hit some rocks. Something had to be done." Improving weak voice can be challenging. The plain truth is that strong voice usually develops from writing regularly over a period of years. It emerges naturally—*if* it's encouraged. And by that, I don't mean telling your students, "Add more voice!" Encouraging voice requires a deep look at the student's whole writing process—beginning with research.

If you glance back at "The Rewards of Research" and "Research Your Topic—Again!," you'll note that one of the advantages of thorough research is that it strengthens a writer's voice. That may sound surprising, but it's easy to understand. The more a student knows about a subject, the more forcefully and confidently she tends to write about it.

As a working writer, I often take jobs from publishers needing books on particular subjects—subjects I may have little knowledge about. In the past few years, I've written about cubism, military drones, patriotic music, and a host of other topics. Often, as I begin roughing out a book on a brand-new topic, my writing is tentative. Not only am I feeling my way along through what's important, I lack the knowledge to write with conviction.

As I continue my research and get comfortable with the subject, my voice grows more confident. I better understand how the topic's pieces fit together. I can include better details and descriptions. I even toss in amusing anecdotes. This gives my voice authority and expression. If some of your students struggle with voice, the problem

A Writing Secret to Share with Students

Nonfiction voice isn't an add-on, like frosting on cake. It grows out of the writer's genuine wonder at the fascinating information her research reveals. Passages with strong voice share other common qualities as well:

- *confidence that comes from knowing a topic well*
- *enthusiasm for that topic*
- *strong, active verbs*
- *showing instead of telling*
- *absence of qualifying expressions like "sort of" and "somewhat"*
- *use of present tense to create drama*
- *specific words and phrases, not generalities ("falcon" instead of "bird")*
- *suspense, action, or humor*
- *sensory descriptions (sights, smells, sounds, feelings)*
- *use of similes and metaphors*
- *fresh, original wording (avoiding overused words like "special," "awesome," or "wow")*
- *sentence variety—different lengths, different beginnings, an occasional question*
- *strong, direct statements ("the orangutan is intelligent" versus "many people consider the orangutan rather intelligent").*

What do you think contributes most to the voice in your own writing? Talk about this next time you meet with your writing group.

Reading Aloud to Teach Voice

Almost nothing helps young writers understand nonfiction voice as much as hearing good writing read aloud. You don't need to read a whole book. Open writing workshop with a short voice-filled passage like this one from *A Black Hole Is Not a Hole* by Carolyn Cinami DeCristofano (2012): "From the headlines, you'd think that black holes were beasts with endless appetites, lying in wait for the next meal. By some reports, they are 'runaway,' out-of-control 'predators' that 'feed' on galaxies, only to 'belch' and 'spit out' what they don't eat" (2).

Our list of recommended nonfiction books for students (Appendix B) will give you more ideas for captivating read-aloud moments. As you share each example, ask students, "What creates the voice in this passage?"

may not be voice per se, but the lack of confidence that comes from not fully understanding what they are talking about. Suggest that they do more research into their topics and discover the enticing details that help voice blossom.

Which leads beautifully into a second point about voice: *writer choice* helps draw out strong voice. Vicki hammers this point home again and again, and she's made a convert out of me. My son (isn't it convenient having a teenager?) recently showed me a story he wrote about one of his major passions, birding. As I read it, my first thought was, "Oh my god, this has incredible voice!" He wrote with enthusiasm, confidence, humor—everything you'd like to see in a manuscript. I stopped after three paragraphs and asked myself, "Where did he get this voice?"

Well, duh—choice.

In this case, my son's strong voice came from two main things: knowledge about his subject and *enthusiasm* for his subject. That made him write more authoritatively and more passionately. A fun exercise is to have your students compare the voice they come up with in a subject you assign versus one they choose for themselves. Having them do the analysis should generate a chorus of useful *aha* moments—insights that will come in handy during the revision process.

One last point about voice and revision has to do with *keeping voice consistent.* Voice can drift because writers tend to get very excited about starting a piece and put a lot of effort into it. We discover, however, that it takes too much energy to sustain that enthusiasm and focus. As a result, our writing—and voice—settle into "hard labor." Some common ways voice can shift unintentionally include:

- starting out light and playful, and settling into a more serious, plodding style

- opening with an action-packed "hook" or intro, and then following up with a more passive, less-inspired approach

- changing from one point-of-view to another during a manuscript.

To help correct the problem, I read through my first draft, taking note of sections that have the most enthusiasm or passion. I then go back and try to match my voice in other sections to that "choice cut." This proved especially important when working on my humorous science book, *Sneed B. Collard III's Most Fun Book Ever About Lizards* (2012a). The success of the book depended on maintaining a light, playful approach throughout the manuscript. As I read over the early drafts, though, I realized that some sections were laugh-out-loud funny while others drooped into a more plodding "just tell the facts" voice. To fix the problem, I consciously read each section, revising to match my favorite funny parts in tone and style. Under the chapter "Falling in Love," for instance, I wrote:

> *Female lizards usually do the choosing in the mating game. During courtship, males put themselves on display. They drive fancy cars or flash wads of cash. Sometimes they wear gold jewelry.*
>
> *Just kidding. (30)*

Under the A-Head "Gila Monsters," I wrote:

> *Gila monsters live in the deserts of the American Southwest. They spend most of their time in underground burrows that they dig with their sharp claws. This allows them to avoid extremely hot and cold temperatures—and to keep the glare off their television screens while they watch reruns of Saurian Idol. (12)*

By making similar revisions throughout the book, I ended up with a manuscript that maintained a consistent voice—one that accomplished my goal of entertaining while informing.

Of course, writers have to learn to recognize what kind of voice matches their subject and intent for a passage. Do they want to be funny? Dramatic? Conversational? Precise? Persuasive?

I faced this decision while writing *Hopping Ahead of Climate Change: Snowshoe Hares, Science, and Survival* (2016). The book explores the vulnerability

> ## Something to try
> ### Highlighting Moments of Voice
>
> As students share their writing with partners, have them exchange papers and read each other's work silently, twice through, pencils (not pens!) in hand. On the second pass, ask them to draw a light vertical line in the right margin beside any passage where the writer's voice blossoms. They do not need to write suggestions or make any comments. When they trade back, have writers compare their partners' responses to their own perceptions and talk with each other about both agreements and surprises. Did they hear the writer's voice in the same spots? What created each moment of voice?

of snowshoe hares in the face of shorter winters with less snow cover. While writing the book, one subject that came up again and again is that snowshoe hares die. They die *a lot*. On the very first page of text, in fact, I describe an owl that has spotted a hare and swoops in for the kill. I had to ask myself, "How should I write about this?" One option was to go action-packed and graphic à la *Game of Thrones*:

> *The owl swoops in and impales its prey with its deadly talons, dismembering the hare and spreading its entrails across the ground.*

Another was to employ an *As the World Turns* approach, tearful and maudlin:

> *As the owl pounces, the defenseless hare lets out a pitiful cry.*

! Something to try
Devoicing a Passage

> *At full throttle, a large red kangaroo can cover almost thirty feet with each leap. It can cruise between fifteen and twenty miles per hour, with bursts exceeding forty miles per hour. High fences? Not a problem. Dingoes or other predators? Eat my dust. (27)*

That quotation from Sneed's book *Pocket Babies and Other Amazing Marsupials* (2007) rings with voice. Read it aloud to your students and talk about where the voice in this passage comes from. Is it the writer's attitude? The words he chose? The details or imagery? The way the sentences are crafted?

Now try this. Have students work in pairs to rewrite the passage, only this time bleeding as much voice *out* of it as possible. They can make any changes at all, so long as they do not alter the basic meaning. Ask them to keep going until not a drop of voice remains, reading aloud as they work. When they've wrung the passage dry, talk about the changes they made. Expect to discover myriad tiny things that contribute to voice. Make a list! You may also want to give an award for the revision with the "least" voice!

I had other choices, too, but few would have satisfied my purpose. And what was that purpose? To objectively present the gravity of the situation without getting caught up in taking sides or trying to manipulate the reader. For this particular passage, I settled on:

> *The predator pounces on its prey, making a quick kill. For the owl, it is an easy meal. For the hare, it's a disaster—one that casts doubt on the species' future survival (5).*

To me, this set just the right tone—impactful, but unemotional. That gave me more credibility as a writer, and would help make skeptical readers more open to any arguments that I might make later.

7

End with Something to Say

Read the following essay about the central character of Jack Gantos' *Joey Pigza Swallowed the Key* (1998):

> *What's a well-rounded character? A well-rounded character has good and bad qualities that make him believable. Instead of being flat and all the same, Joey Pigza is a well-rounded character.*
>
> *One thing that makes Joey Pigza a well-rounded character is that he's out of control. He does crazy stuff all the time, but at the same time he understands that he's doing it. That makes him well-rounded. Something else that makes him well-rounded is that he gets really mad at people, like his mom and grandma. He also forgives them. Another example is that he causes trouble, but also helps people, like when he kills all the spiders in class and makes sure the mice are in their cage.*
>
> *Joey is made up of good and bad things. He isn't all the same. That makes him a well-rounded character.*

I confess that I wrote this essay myself. However, my inspiration came from almost identical essays I have read from middle school language arts students. These essays were based on prompts that the teacher provided. Why did I include this example here? Well obviously, this essay needs work on multiple levels. For now, however, I want you to reread both the first and last paragraphs, the introduction and conclusion. If you ignore grammar and punctuation, what do you notice?

Answer: the conclusion simply rehashes the introduction—if not repeating it almost *verbatim*.

The blame for this kind of rehashing cannot be laid at the students' feet. Why? Because students are being *taught* to do this. You may even teach this in your

A Writing Secret to Share with Students

A conclusion is the last thing a reader sees—so it's your final chance to make an impression. Be sure it's a good one!

I love to collect good endings. Here are two that caught my attention because they inspire new thinking and bring the writer's discussion to a close without being repetitive. The first is from Elaine Scott's book *Our Moon* (2015):

It will be difficult for us to return to the moon—almost as difficult as it was to get there in the first place. But as Neil Armstrong said, human beings are built to face challenges and surmount them. Our moon has more to tell us, and we humans will never stop exploring. It's the way we are made. (63)

This second ending is from *The Boy Who Harnessed the Wind* (2015) by William Kamkwamba and Brian Mealer:

Think of your dreams and ideas as tiny miracle machines inside you that no one can touch. The more faith you put into them, the bigger they get, until one day they'll rise up and take you with them. (290)

Ask students to collect conclusions they like from nonfiction books and articles, and add them to their writing journals. You may also want to display some of the endings you collect. Read favorites aloud and describe the various purposes they achieve—to resolve a situation, solve a mystery, inspire, raise a new question, and so on. How many purposes can your students identify?

own classroom because it's what *you've* been taught to teach. Come to think of it, my high school English teacher taught *me* to do this five years ago (okay, maybe it was more like forty years ago, but who's counting?).

My point here is not to condemn anyone. However, like Kennedy facing down Khrushchev during the Cuban Missile Crisis, Vicki and I feel compelled to take a stand: the philosophy that endings should simply regurgitate introductions is *bad, bad, bad*!

We know what some of you are going to say: "Giving students this kind of structure at least helps provide a framework for learning how to write an essay."

No, it doesn't. Instead, it gives young writers a false perception about the purpose of endings and cripples their ability to write good ones.

And that's a tragedy, because endings are hard enough to write without slogging through outdated concepts of what an ending should be. Crafting a good ending is a struggle for every writer, including Vicki and me. However, not one of us could write a satisfying ending to a nonfiction book, essay, or report without first understanding the ending's true purpose.

At the risk of beating this rug until its stitching falls out, the first thing to get straight is that the function of an ending, or conclusion, is *not* to rehash the introduction. In first drafts, many writers *do* essentially do this. In my own case, it's because I really don't know what the ending should be, and this "rehashing" serves as a kind of placeholder. When it comes time to revise, though, good writers laser in on what the ending's true purpose should be: *to draw new meaning and insight from whatever information the writer has presented—ideally, to offer fresh wisdom that can extend to the world at large.*

! Something to try
Creating a New, Meaningful Conclusion

Ask students to take a close look at both the lead and ending from any recent piece they have written, without reading what comes in between. Does the conclusion offer a new perspective or important point to think about—or does it merely restate information from the lead? If it's the latter, invite writers to revise their endings by considering Sneed's advice: to draw new meaning or insight from the content of the piece. This is the time to reread the middle, paying close attention to detail and asking what they want readers to gain from the information presented. In crafting a new conclusion, a writer can ask herself questions like these:

- *What is the most important impression I want readers to walk away with?*
- *What do I hope my readers have learned?*
- *Do I want my readers to see the world differently now—and if so, how?*
- *How does this information affect readers personally?*
- *Does the information raise a new question to explore at some point?*
- *Does my conclusion offer readers wisdom—or at least something to think about?*

Have students share before and after endings within writing groups, and ask each group to choose a "best revision" to share aloud with the class. After listening to their choices, talk about what it takes to make a conclusion truly satisfying for readers.

What's more, this new insight should show that the author has not only made her case—whether it's proving a point, writing about a historical figure, or explaining how to do something—but has also reflected on it and learned something from it. In wrapping up the essay on Gantos' book, for instance, the author might have presented us with the idea that Joey's complexity mirrors the complexity of all real people. The author could have reflected on how some of Joey's speech or actions affect readers by triggering sympathy, surprise, or admiration. Perhaps, wearing his critic's hat, the writer might have noted ways the book would be different if Joey were indeed a "flat" character instead of the authentic character he is.

In my book *The World Famous Miles City Bucking Horse Sale* (2010), I spend the bulk of the book describing the action and history of a well-known regional rodeo event. According to the model of endings being taught to many students, my conclusion should have read something like, "The Miles City Bucking Horse Sale is an action-packed, fun-filled, historic event."

Hit me with a horseshoe, right? If I had presented this kind of ending, I would have been run out of the Authors Guild.

What I really did in my early drafts—and what I often do (though don't tell anyone)—was leave the last paragraph blank. Instead of rehashing, I took time to process. I stepped back and thought about everything I had observed and learned. I pictured the crowds lining the opening parade down Main Street. I read through my interviews with the cowboys I had spoken to. I reviewed the histories I had read and flipped through the hundreds of photos I had taken, and I used all of this to formulate new insights and conclusions. One insight is that given its history and economic importance, the sale has become a glue that helps hold the Miles City community together. Another is that the sale has come to mean different things to different people. A last observation is that the sale is not a relic, but a living thing with a promising future.

After several tries, I wrote:

> *All of these voices make it clear that there's not any one thing that makes*
> *the World Famous Miles City Bucking Horse Sale work. Its success lies in a*
> *rich blend of history, adventure, sport, agriculture, business, and more than*
> *anything, people. In a region of the country that is often overlooked and*
> *ignored, the Bucking Horse Sale remains part of a vibrant present—and a*
> *promising future. That, more than anything, will help it keep its reputation as*
> *one of the most interesting and entertaining celebrations in the West. (60)*

Although the body of the book provides evidence for everything in this final paragraph, this ending ties the book together with new, slightly different insights that the reader can think about and digest.

Teach this to your students!

Your kids are smart. Why have them write an essay or a report if it doesn't put their minds to work? Coming up with satisfying endings, those that reveal fresh ideas and insights, is the perfect opportunity for kids to use their brains. It also helps them understand that writing is not a rote activity, but one that can add depth and meaning to their lives.

8

Give It a Rest

I tend to pursue writing projects like a dachshund digging after a badger. I want to *get the badger* and then sit back with a sense of accomplishment. Unfortunately, this impatience always backfires.

When a writer has been working hard on a manuscript for a period of hours, days, or weeks, she is simply too close to the work to be able to evaluate it objectively. Students and veteran writers alike need to turn their minds to other projects and forget about what they've been working on for a while. I like to let my manuscripts sit for several weeks, but even a day or three can let a writer view her piece with new eyes (again, see Vicki's *Irresistibly Practical Super-Flexible Four-Day Plan* in "Balancing Expectations," page 13).

A break allows two things to happen. It lets a writer look at a piece more objectively, and therefore recognize what is and isn't working. It also gives a writer the mental space to allow fresh ideas and insights to form. When a writer is focusing too intensely, it often blocks new ideas. Look away for a while and new ideas and thoughts seem to creep in of their own accord.

The book you are reading perfectly demonstrates the importance of letting a manuscript rest. After roughing out the first half, Vicki and I let it sit for almost three months while we worked on the second half. When we came back to this "chunk," we spotted numerous areas for improvement. We added—and subtracted—several strategies. We replaced numerous examples with others that offered more insight. We axed paragraphs that didn't seem to be earning their keep—and more. Without that three-month rest, we wouldn't have been able to recognize the need for these "upgrades" nearly as easily.

Something to try

Using a Checklist of Reminders

Revision is not just one thing. It's a whole collection of possibilities, like a menu. When a writer is trying to recall everything, it can help to have a list of reminders that say, "Did you think to give this a try?" We have put together such a list, and you will find it in Appendix A. Once students are ready to continue revising, have them refer to this list, focusing for now on things we have already touched upon. They can return to the list every now and then as we—and they—tackle additional revision strategies. Be sure to modify or expand the list as you and your students develop your own approaches to revision.

I go through this with virtually every trade book that I work on, sometimes doing extensive overhauls after the "fallow period." Take the woodpecker book I'm working on now. I originally organized it by species, telling about each, one at a time. After setting it aside, however, I realized that this approach wasn't likely to hold a reader's interest. Instead, I rewrote it by topic, much closer in organization to my humorous books on lizards and insects.

Time away from a draft will give your students those same opportunities for fresh insights. After the break, have your students carefully read through their drafts to see what's working, referring to Vicki's "Checklist of Revision Possibilities" in Appendix A. This is also a great opportunity to have students share their work in a group. Chances are your students will find additional big-picture work that needs to be done. It's important to allow time for revision at this stage. A common misconception is that a first draft is the most time-consuming step in creating a manuscript, but the opposite is true. It's revision that requires the most time, so if possible, build that into your time budget.

Something to try
Evaluating Anonymous Writing

What will you do for those couple of days while students take a break from their writing? How about having the whole class work together to critique anonymous writing samples? This activity is fun and nonthreatening, and helps students prepare for their own revisions to come. Their comments during discussion are often surprising, insightful, and helpful to classmates.

You can pull short samples to review from nonfiction books, periodicals, or newspapers, or download student papers from multiple online resources. Just type in *student sample writing* to begin your search. Many nonfiction examples from various grades are available. Read each piece aloud, then discuss what works or doesn't and why. Ask students, "How would you revise this piece if it were yours?"

A Writing Secret to Share with Students

Right now you're letting your writing "rest" so you can see it with fresh eyes when you return. What's the first thing to do as you resume revising? *Read aloud!* Almost nothing makes you a better reviser than hearing your words, whether read by you or by someone else who reads expressively. Try to find a place that is reasonably quiet and free of distractions. Take your time and really tune in to your voice. Is it a confident voice? Does it sound like you? By the way, when it's your turn to read, don't be shy, don't rush, and don't read in a monotone. Give it your all! Bring out every ounce of voice the writer put into the work—whether that writer is you or someone else. Later, pencil in hand, write notes about anything you want to change or add. Draw arrows to show where you want to move words, sentences, or whole paragraphs. Sentence by sentence, ask yourself, "Does this support my message?" Be merciless in cutting anything that doesn't!

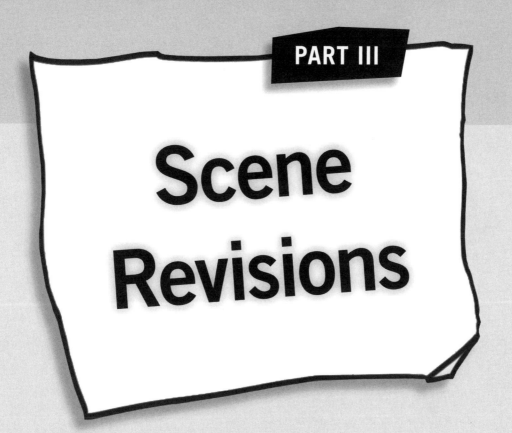

PART III

Scene Revisions

N ovelists, screenwriters, and playwrights often discuss the importance of developing a scene in a book, movie, or play. However, most people—including many writers—are astonished to learn that building an effective scene also plays a vital role in a work of nonfiction.

What exactly is a scene? Definitions exist for fiction and so-called creative nonfiction, but for regular ole nonfiction? To tell you the truth, I've never actually read one. So let's break some new ground and define a nonfiction scene as:

> *A section of text in which something important happens or something crucial is revealed through a sequence of actions (including exchange of dialogue), set of facts, or arguments.*

Please don't get hung up on the word *scene* itself. If you are more comfortable with the word *section*, go with that. The important point is that *a scene is a self-contained unit with a beginning, middle, and end.* It is a ministory, miniessay, or argument that is related to a larger whole. Studying good nonfiction picture books is especially helpful in grasping the concept of a scene. Here's a short example from my picture book *A Platypus, Probably* (2005b):

> *Waving its bill back and forth,*
> *And using its wonderful webbed feet to swim,*
> *The platypus explores eucalyptus-lined streams.*
> *When its bill touches another animal,*
> *Or feels the electricity from its body,*
> *The platypus attacks.*
> *Worms, mussels, shrimps, tadpoles,*
> *Even the larvae of insects found walking around the river bottom—*
> *The platypus stuffs them all in its cheek pouches*
> *And carries them to the surface.*
> *With no teeth for chewing,*
> *The platypus crushes its food*
> *On hard grinding pads inside its bill.*
> *Meal finished, it swallows,*
> *Takes a breath,*
> *And dives again. (9–11)*

The subject of this scene? Simple—how a platypus obtains food. Here's another scene, from Laurence Pringle's *Owls! Strange and Wonderful* (2016), that offers an explanation for an owl's appearance:

> *Throughout history, owls have inspired superstitions, myths, and legends. An Inuit tale explains how the first owl was created. By magic, a young girl was changed into a bird with a long beak. Frightened by this sudden change, she started to fly frantically. She flew face-first into a wall! Her face and beak were flattened. She became an owl. (4)*

Because scenes may be a new concept to many readers, let me include one more example—this one, from my book *Catching Air* (2017a). Unlike the previous two examples, this scene does not tell a story but instead presents a set of closely related facts:

Almost 50 species of flying squirrels live in Asia, but only two species inhabit
North America.

Both are nocturnal, active at night.

Both are also omnivores, feeding on nuts, berries, insects, and other foods.

For flying squirrels, the main advantage of gliding is probably to escape
predators.

Owls, snakes, and larger mammals all hunt flying squirrels, but when they're
in danger, the animals can glide up to 150 feet (45 meters) to reach safety.

Want to see a flying squirrel for yourself? Try shining a light on a bird
feeder at night. (12–13)

Although all three scenes are short, can you see how they each form a discrete unit, with beginning, middle, and end?

In contrast, a simple line such as "Joe ran into a door" is not a scene. Nor is a blanket statement of fact such as "Saddam Hussein goofed up by invading Kuwait." In a scene, any result or conclusion must be earned, or backed up, with facts, arguments, and events—just as it must be earned in an entire essay or book. If a student is going to state that Saddam Hussein "goofed" by invading Kuwait, for instance, she's got to back that up by explaining the outrage and response from the international community. This might form one scene in an entire paper about the first Gulf War.

Other examples of nonfiction scenes might be:

- *a short description of Mount Everest*

- *an account of a key "at bat" in an essay on the 2001 World Series*

- *an explanation of ways that elephants are like humans*

- *the capture of a German decoding device as part of a paper on cracking Nazi*
  codes during World War II

- *a recounting of Rosa Parks' famous "bus encounter"*

- *a short summary of types of clean energy in a report about climate change.*

But by now, you are probably asking yourself, "What is the difference between a scene and a chapter?"

Glad you asked!

Although chapters often are composed of a single scene—and at times can be treated as one—to me, chapters usually tend to be more arbitrary divisions imposed on a longer work. In many books I read, authors insert chapters mainly to give readers breaks at regular intervals.

A scene, on the other hand, has a more fundamental unity and purpose, and can assume almost any length. In student writing, a scene often consists of a single paragraph, but a scene can also be a section under a subheading (or A-Head) within a chapter, an entire chapter, or an event that extends across multiple chapters. The previous platypus scene extends across three pages in the published book. The take-home lesson is that like the platypus example, the scene forms its own little unit that adds something essential or new to a manuscript.

That said, it's important to recognize that scenes are intimately related to an entire piece of nonfiction writing. In fact, *they are its building blocks*. I like to compare them to those five-foot-long cement squares in a sidewalk. Each square leads to the next square, but they are all required for me to complete my journey. Scenes, therefore, must do a lot of work. They have to:

- *establish the importance of a topic*
- *present essential information about a topic*
- *propel a narrative forward*
- *build and develop characters*
- *maintain a manuscript's tension and conflict*
- *and do much more.*

Not all nonfiction books contain scenes. Short photo or illustrated books may consist of collections of facts. But the top nonfiction writers I read write in scenes—whether they realize it or not.

Which brings up a last important point: learning to write effective scenes can take years of practice, and of all the types of revision in this book, I consider scene revision the most advanced and, perhaps, challenging. Just notice how long this introduction is! You probably will want to pick and choose which of the following scene revision strategies you share and study with your students. If something looks too advanced or difficult, skip it! When you are tackling scene revision, though, remember to be patient with both yourself and your students. Understanding and perfecting scenes, like cooking an omelet, takes preparation, ingredients, and practice. You're going to flub a few, but the more you do it, the more often you'll sit down to a good meal.

I just keep getting better and better at this!

1 Make Sure Every Scene Contributes

When revising scenes, a logical first step is to make sure that every scene belongs in a manuscript. Almost always in first drafts, writers include scenes that do not contribute to the writer's main goal, whatever that might be. As with all "extra text," drafting extra scenes is not necessarily a mistake. It is a natural consequence of trying to present a large volume of information to an audience. Many times, a writer has to see a scene on paper before she can fully evaluate whether or not it's needed. I delete multiple scenes from almost every book that I write!

Having a student read through a manuscript, or work within a writer's group, often helps identify scenes and sections that don't belong. Reverse-outlining a manuscript (Part II, "Check Your Organization"), listing each scene as one line, also helps.

Let's say your student has written a five-page report about Benjamin Franklin's role during the Revolutionary War. A first step is to identify the scenes in the report. This can be easily done making horizontal marks in the margins where each scene ends and a new one begins. For a report like this, each scene will most likely be a paragraph, maybe two, so the job should be easy. Using these scene markers, your student can create a reverse outline of the report, listing the scenes in the order that they appear:

> ## A Writing Secret to Share with Students
>
> Think of a scene as any chunk of text that could come under a subheading. Even if you don't use subheads (A-Heads) in your own work, you can ask yourself, "Where would I put them?" This will help you separate scenes from chapters—which can be more random divisions of text, often intended, as Sneed points out, just to give readers a break.

- Ben, one of seventeen children, was born in 1706 in Massachusetts, a colony of Great Britain.
- His father didn't believe in school and sent him to be a printer's apprentice under his brother, James.
- At age seventeen, Ben ran away to Philadelphia and started his own print shop and newspaper.

- At age forty-two, Ben turned his attention to science and invention.

- Ben discovered that electricity has two charges, invented the first battery, and "pulled" electricity from a storm cloud.

- Relations between Great Britain and the Colonies became poor.

- In the 1750s, Ben tried to improve the relationship between the American colonies and Great Britain.

- Once war started, Ben designed defenses for American cities.

- Ben appointed the first postmaster general.

- He helped write the Declaration of Independence.

- During the Revolution, he traveled to France to get military and economic aid.

- Ben helped negotiate a peace treaty with Great Britain.

- After returning home, Ben helped write the Constitution.

Just a reminder—the above lines are not actual lines from the student's draft. They are one-line *summaries* of the different scenes. And while all of them may be interesting, you've undoubtedly spotted several that do not contribute to the main topic—Franklin's role in the Revolutionary War. In fact, the first five scenes listed have nothing to do with the war. Is the solution to axe them? Given my passion for cutting, that might be your first guess! In this case, however, simple cutting may not be the best solution.

One of the purposes of scenes is to develop characters that will interest the reader. Before diving into the Revolution, one of the writer's jobs is to establish Ben as a character worthy of our interest. Instead of chopping the entire first five scenes, the writer might condense them into perhaps two scenes, one about his childhood and early adulthood, and one about his life as a scientist and inventor. This would give us an appreciation for Ben as a person, and help establish his credentials for his wartime efforts.

A NOTE TO THE TEACHER

Exploring Scenes in Film

Like books, films have scenes, and because films are visual, they can be helpful in teaching how scenes begin and end, what they include, and what they achieve. Watch any short documentary film together, or assign a film on public television for viewing, and ask students to watch for clues that tell viewers when the focus is moving from one scene to another. As students are likely to notice, transitions from scene to scene on film are usually marked by noticeable changes in time or setting, and often by a shift in focus as well, say from one character or event to another. Studying scenes visually helps many students define the concept of "scene" in their minds and understand how this concept applies to writing.

! Something to try

Identifying a Scene's Purpose

Sneed tells us that a scene should be cut unless it achieves some key purpose—such as one of the following:

- *establishing the importance of a topic*
- *presenting essential information*
- *propelling a narrative forward*
- *developing a character*
- *maintaining tension or conflict.*

Share the following scene from Sneed's book *Reign of the Sea Dragons* (2008a). As you read this scene aloud, ask students to identify the purpose (or purposes) it achieves, referring to the list above. Does it accomplish anything beyond what's on the list?

The Last Hurrah

By about 85 million years ago, mosasaurs outnumbered plesiosaurs by more than ten to one. Life was not perfect, of course. Large fish and other marine reptiles preyed on young mosasaurs. Enormous sharks up to thirty feet long probably even attacked adult mosasaurs. One of the most fearsome fishes was the ginsu shark, Cretoxyrhina manteli *(kreh-tox-ee RINE-uh-man-TEH-lye). Reaching the size of today's largest great white sharks, the ginsu shark came armed with hundreds of razor teeth two inches long. Paleontologists have found these teeth embedded in the bones of many mosasaur fossils.*

Even with large sharks swimming around, however, Mesozoic life was probably pretty good for the mosasaurs. During the time that Tyrannosaurus rex *(tye-RAN-oh-sohr-us rex) terrorized the land, mosasaurs ruled the ancient seas. They had plenty to eat. Their enemies were few. To paraphrase the title of a popular song, their future was so bright they had to wear shades.*

But then, in a geological instant, it all came to an end. (46)

How many purposes did your students identify? Once they wrap up their discussion of "The Last Hurrah," ask those who have written longer pieces (more than one page) to identify individual scenes in their own work. How many do they find? Does each scene fulfill one or more of the purposes listed above? If not, the writer may need to cut it. Students who are not sure about keeping or cutting a scene may want to discuss this decision in their next conference with you.

One other scene you may have flagged for possible deletion is the scene about Ben's role as our nation's first postmaster general. Although his postal work probably contributed to helping out the Continental Congress and perhaps our military operations, it seems less important than his other activities. Especially if space is a concern, this might be a good scene to cut. Alternatively, the writer might be able to modify the scene so that it *does* contribute to the main message—adding one or two concrete details about how this position helped Ben advance the cause of the Revolution.

Whether you are cutting scenes or filling them out, this kind of scene work usually leads to a more readable, tightly focused manuscript. It helps the work move along at a satisfying clip and, by deleting unnecessary material, simplifies more detailed revision down the road.

2

Craft for Cohesion

Once a writer has winnowed out unnecessary scenes, revision of individual scenes can begin. Again, going through and marking the beginnings and ends of each scene is a useful first step. These marks provide easy reference points—like highway mile markers—for examining each chunk of text. What is a writer looking for in each marked-off scene? Several things.

A Lead or Thesis

We're used to thinking about leads or thesis statements for an entire piece, but each scene or section must provide readers with a map of what to expect in that section. Leads of beginning writers may be obvious and deliberate—e.g., "George Washington faced three major hardships at Valley Forge." As a writer improves, however, readers will barely notice that they've been introduced to a new scene or section.

Here are some scene leads from my book *The World Famous Miles City Bucking Horse Sale* (2010). Just for fun, share each one aloud and have your students predict what each scene will be about:

> *The bareback rider adjusts his grip on the rigging one last time, then gives a nod to the men handling the gate. (5)*

> *The great grasslands that dominate the center of our continent have always provided ideal forage and habitat for grazing animals, including horses. (12)*

> *Friday is when the Bucking Horse Sale kicks into high gear. (19)*

> *A love for bull riding, though, doesn't explain how someone rides a bull. (21)*

> *In recent decades, Miles City has suffered through the same struggles as other rural farming and ranching communities throughout the West. (31)*

> *As soon as a rider rides or gets bucked off a bronc, the auctioneer begins auctioning off that horse. (48)*

My guess is that both you and your students found it fairly easy to figure out each scene's topic. In fact, if I added in every lead from every scene, they would together form a pretty good outline or synopsis of the entire book. This is what your students should strive for in crafting the beginning of each scene.

A Supporting Middle

Of course each lead needs to be supported or validated by the sentences or paragraphs that follow. Sometimes, this support reads like a formal argument. Consider this lead from a scene in *Insects: The Most Fun Bug Book Ever* (2017c): "Insects have three major advantages over most other animals" (8). Obviously, after a statement like that I'd better make darned sure I describe or list these advantages to defend or prove my statement!

Often, though, the support for a lead takes the form of a description rather than a proof for an argument. In the fourth chapter of *The Prairie Builders: Reconstructing America's Lost Grasslands* (2005c), I open with, "Dr. Diane Debinski is on a mission. It is a warm July day on the refuge, and Diane climbs a hill, butterfly net and notebook in hand" (47). What follows is a description of Professor Debinski's search for a rare butterfly, the Regal Fritillary. This description doesn't read like a formal argument, but it fulfills the promise of the lead just the same.

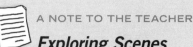 A NOTE TO THE TEACHER

Exploring Scenes in Picture Books

Nonfiction picture books can be invaluable in teaching students how scenes work. Their brevity makes it easy to share several scenes within a class period, discussing as you go how various scenes begin and end, and what each scene achieves. You may notice that scenes in picture books are often (though not always) conveniently formatted to fit a two-page spread—and some fill only one page. Many have A-Heads to identify the main focus of the scene, and this can offer students a clue about the scene's primary purpose.

Recommended for use in this context: Sneed's *A Platypus, Probably* (2005b); *One Night in the Coral Sea* (2006); *Neighborhood Sharks* (Roy 2014); *Ubiquitous: Celebrating Nature's Survivors* (Sidman 2010); *If . . . A Mind-Bending New Way of Looking at Big Ideas and Numbers* (Smith 2014); and *Moonshot: The Flight of Apollo 11* (Floca 2009).

An Effective Ending

Sometimes, a nonfiction writer will simply end a scene when the necessary material or story has been presented. I did this several times in my *Buckinghorse Sale* book—especially when I recounted the life of a particular cowboy or other character. I'd tell his story and stop, and the next scene would tackle a brand-new topic.

Something to try

Checking Scene Cohesion

For the first part of this activity, you'll need a collection of nonfiction writings. (See our book recommendations at the end of this feature.) You can use chapter or picture books, periodicals, or any other nonfiction resource. Have students work with partners to explore these sources and mark off two or more scenes, noting when, where, and how they begin and end. You might have them use Sneed's "mile marker" technique, putting one-inch horizontal pencil lines in the margin to show where each scene begins and ends—or if they cannot write in the margins, use removable tabs. Ask them to notice how each scene opens and ends, as well as how the middle "fulfills the promise of the lead" by answering readers' questions or providing important details.

Once students have a good grasp of how scenes begin and end, have them focus on one particular scene *in their own writing*, asking themselves three questions:

1. Does the scene have an effective lead?

2. Does the middle support or expand on that lead?

3. Does the ending either guide the reader to some closing point or encourage her to keep reading?

Students who can answer yes to all three questions can feel confident they have written a scene that has real cohesion. If they cannot, they know what revisions are needed.

Recommended for the first part of this activity: Sneed's *The World Famous Miles City Bucking Horse Sale* (2010); *The Cod's Tale* (Kurlansky 2001); *Most Dangerous: Daniel Ellsberg and the Secret History of the Vietnam War* (Sheinkin 2015); *A Black Hole Is Not a Hole* (DeCristofano 2012); or *Extreme Animals: The Toughest Creatures on Earth* (Davies 2006).

A more satisfying way to end a scene is to create momentum or suspense for the *next* scene. In my book *Science Warriors: The Battle Against Invasive Species* (2008b), I devoted one scene to describing how University of Texas biologist Larry Gilbert and other scientists began releasing parasitic phorid flies to control invasive fire ants in Florida and Texas. After describing how the flies had spread over thousands of square miles, I wrote:

> *And that leads to a big question: Will phorids finally break the fire ants' grip on the Southeast? For Larry, the answer is "possibly"—but not just yet. (17)*

These last lines form a cliffhanger. They get the reader wondering, "Well, are these phorid flies going to obliterate fire ants or aren't they?" Naturally, readers have to dive into the next scene to find out. We'll explore scene endings more in the section, "Lead into the Next Scene."

3

Create and Use Unforgettable Nonfiction Characters

Have you ever watched a film that you enjoyed, but afterward had trouble describing—or, worse yet, never thought about again? Unfortunately, many Hollywood movies fall into this category.

They seem well-constructed and crackle with gee-whiz action, yet leave the audience empty and disappointed. Most often, the problem boils down to one issue: there's no person or thing in the movie that we actually care about. Instead of being *character-driven*, these movies are *plot-driven*. They are defined by events instead of characters that we actually identify with.

Character-driven movies and books are almost *always* more engaging than their plot-driven counterparts. Even if you're an action movie fan, as I am, it's almost guaranteed that you will enjoy an action film with complex, well-rounded characters more than one populated by cardboard stereotypes. This is as true for nonfiction as it is for fiction. The next time you're in a bookstore, take a look at the nonfiction shelves. You'll see that most of the best-selling books are biographies or memoirs. That's no accident. People love reading about other peoples' lives. We want to learn about their passions and experiences. Mostly, we want to learn about their struggles and how they did or didn't overcome them.

That doesn't mean that all nonfiction manuscripts have to be about people. Characters can be almost anything—places, events, buildings, animals. And a writer doesn't have to stick to just one character. Most nonfiction books switch between a number of different characters to tell a story. My book *Fire Birds* (2015a) contains several major characters, including:

- Professor Richard Hutto, a biologist at the University of Montana
- wildfires
- birds that prefer living in burned forests
- Forest Service experts on fires and forests.

With a few exceptions, each scene in *Fire Birds* is driven by one of these characters. In order to hold readers' attentions, therefore, I have to make sure these characters engage readers right off the bat. Following are some strategies I and other writers use to make readers care about our nonfiction characters.

Introduce the Character in a Surprising Setting

In *Fire Birds*, I introduce Professor Hutto out birding, calling out one bird species after another. The reader assumes Hutto is hiking through a lush, green forest. At the end of the first scene, I pop the surprise: Professor Hutto is birding in a forest that has recently been devastated by a severe wildfire. This creates a curiosity in readers, making them want to find out more about Professor Hutto and about what other characters (the birds) are doing in this charred landscape.

Place the Character in a Hopeless Situation

Unbroken (2010), Laura Hillenbrand's popular biography of Louis Zamperini, opens with Zamperini near death, floating in a small life raft surrounded by hostile Japanese, ravenous sharks, and thousands of square miles of open ocean. This scene makes us care about—and root for—Zamperini, but also makes us want to learn his entire story, including how he ended up in that life raft. It also carefully describes the sharks and the ocean itself, establishing them as important characters that will play roles later.

Establish a Character Through a Memorable Anecdote

The opening of my biography *Benjamin Franklin: The Man Who Could Do Just About Anything* (2006a) shows Ben wondering whether or not a kite could pull him across a pond. He performs the simple experiment and it works! This curiosity and inventiveness helps readers identify with him and ask, "What else will this guy come up with?"

A Writing Secret to Share with Students

Drama not only provides a welcome mental break from fact-dense text, it actually helps readers recall what they read. Behind every good fact is a story—if we teach ourselves to look for it. As author and teacher Tom Newkirk reminds us in *Minds Made for Stories* (2014), "Photosynthesis is a story; climate change is a story; cancer is a story, with antecedents and consequences. To the extent these phenomena can be told as stories, readers will have a better chance of taking in the information" (11).

Present a Character as a Foe or Challenge

In my book *The Deep-Sea Floor* (2003), the deep ocean is the main character, and I develop that character through humans' relationship, history, and thoughts with and about it:

> *For most of history, the geography and animal life of the deep-sea floor have remained a total mystery. As recently as the mid-nineteenth century, many people believed that the ocean was bottomless or that no life existed in the deep. Others felt sure that the deep sea was filled with terrifying sea serpents or animals that had disappeared from shallower waters millions of years before. (9)*

These kinds of passages place humans in their proper, minute context, akin to minnows swimming through an awesome, vast landscape—exactly the effect I wanted.

Show a Character in Opposition to Another

In *Hoover Dam: An American Adventure* (1990), author Joseph E. Stevens opens with a scene that introduces one of the dam's chief engineers, William H. Wattis, dying of cancer. We might think Wattis would be thinking mostly about his impending demise, but his mind is focused on one overriding task: conquering the Colorado River by building the largest dam in the history of the world. In this scene, the author sets up three giant characters—the engineer, the river, and the dam. Readers want to find out what drove this man on his obsessive pursuit, but also just how on earth his team will "conquer" this unprecedented project.

All of these methods *introduce* characters, but they do something more important. They make us *care* about the characters. Even when the subjects are

Exploring Characters in Nonfiction

This chapter introduces us to a way of thinking about "characters" that may be new to many students. As we see from Sneed's examples, characters in nonfiction are not always people. They may be animals, dams, forest fires, medieval trebuchets—or almost any creature, place, or concept that makes the writer's information important and fascinating to us as readers. In his memoir *Farewell to Model T* (2003), author E. B. White talks about the iconic car as if it were more horse than horse-powered machine: "I can still feel my old Ford nuzzling me at the curb, as though looking for an apple in my pocket" (17). After sharing this or other examples, have students identify characters from any nonfiction they are currently reading. Discuss their new perspective on nonfiction characters either as a class or within writing groups.

the ocean and Hoover Dam, the authors give us enough detail, drama, and "personality" to develop strong feelings about them. Without these kinds of characters to care about, nonfiction writing often degenerates into a collection of facts that not only bores the reader, but finds little relevance in his life.

Simply establishing the characters is not enough, however. Once a writer has created and introduced strong characters, she needs to go through each scene and ask herself, "Is one of my characters driving this scene?" If the answer is no, the writer should consider whether recasting the scene from one of the characters' vantage points might lead to a stronger, more compelling narrative.

Take a moment to reread the scene on hunting that I recounted from *A Platypus, Probably* (2005b):

> *Waving its bill back and forth,*
> *And using its wonderful webbed feet to swim,*
> *The platypus explores eucalyptus-lined streams.*
> *When its bill touches another animal,*
> *Or feels the electricity from its body,*
> *The platypus attacks.*
> *Worms, mussels, shrimps, tadpoles,*
> *Even the larvae of insects found walking around the river bottom—*
> *The platypus stuffs them all in its cheek pouches*
> *And carries them to the surface.*
> *With no teeth for chewing,*
> *The platypus crushes its food*
> *On hard grinding pads inside its bill.*
> *Meal finished, it swallows,*
> *Takes a breath,*
> *And dives again. (9–11)*

Now note that I could have easily written that same scene as follows:

> *To find food, a platypus waves its bill back and forth.*
> *When it touches another animal,*
> *Or gets close enough to feel the electric charge from its body,*
> *The platypus moves in.*

A platypus can catch worms, mussels, shrimps, tadpoles,
and insect larvae.
It puts this prey into its cheek pouches and carries it to the surface.
The platypus has no teeth for chewing.
Instead, it mashes up its food on pads inside its bill.
Then it keeps hunting.

Competent—but dull, right? Instead of going that route, I used this wonderful character I had already created and showed readers *her experience* of hunting. This helps readers see the platypus not as a species, but as an individual—and keeps them engaged and rooting for her. More specifically, here are some techniques I used to make this character come alive:

- I focused on a particular platypus, not a generic one.
- I wrote in the present tense to give a sense of immediacy to the situation.
- I used dynamic verbs such as *attacks, stuffs,* and *crushes.*
- I varied the pacing and rhythm of the scene to build drama.

Full disclosure: this approach may not work for every subject or scene. If your students have to write a paper on how to build a trebuchet, well, even your most creative thinkers may not come up with characters for that. Then again, they might. Right off the bat, I can envision turning the inventors of this medieval catapult, the victims, and/or the device into characters. Just for fun, let's tackle the most difficult of the three: the trebuchet itself. If I were writing about this—and had the research to back it up—I might open my paper by describing how this character would appear through the eyes of medieval citizens seeing it for the first time:

When sunrise greeted the defenders of the fortress, a shadow fell across them.
It was cast by a tall tower made of wood and fitted with stones of monstrous
proportions. The defenders had never seen anything like this terrible machine,
but even before it swung into action, it filled the defending army with dread.

Not every scene in a book needs to be character-driven, of course. Even in *Fire Birds* (2015a), two or three of my scenes simply present background information that the reader needs to know. After dispensing this information, however, I quickly revisit my main characters to push the book forward—an approach you should encourage with your students.

Something to try

Making Readers Care About Your Characters

In this chapter, Sneed presents five ways to make readers care about nonfiction characters:

1. Put the character in an exciting, unusual, or even hostile setting.

2. Confront the character with a hopeless situation.

3. Tell a memorable anecdote.

4. Put one character in opposition to another.

5. Give the character an unassailable challenge.

As a way of reviewing these five strategies, see if students can identify which of the five—and there could be more than one—each of the following authors is using:

- *Jon Scieszka's memoir* Knucklehead *(2008) is filled with recollections of treehouses and raccoon hunts, broken collarbones resulting from an invented game called "Slaughterball," awkward moments spent attending school where his father was principal, and other tales about growing up as one of six brothers.*

- *In* Extreme Animals *(2006), author Nicola Davies takes readers from the frozen Arctic to the lethal heat of the desert to show how bears, frogs, camels, Arctic musk oxen and other impressive creatures endure conditions most of us could never survive.*

- *In* Case Closed? *(2013), author Susan Hughes pits an eighteen-foot bamboo raft against weather, insects, and the ocean itself to see if it can make the 7,500-mile journey from Hong Kong to Japan to America.*

- *In Laura Hillenbrand's* Seabiscuit *(2001), the fabled thoroughbred meets his nemesis—the legendary, Triple Crown winner War Admiral—in a grueling match race "still widely regarded as the greatest horse race in history" (264).*

- *In his memoir* The Boy on the Wooden Box *(2013), author Leon Leyson recounts his struggle to survive in a German concentration camp: "My first impression of Plaszów as hell on earth never changed" (113).*

After reviewing these five strategies, have students go through their own drafts, choosing one character to focus on, then asking, "How can I make readers care more about this character?" Give them time to revise, using one or more of Sneed's five strategies.

4

Check Consistency in Tense and Pronoun Reference

One thing I notice a lot in student work—and sometimes my own—is that the tense changes midstream. For example, read the following passage:

> The jaguar sneaks up on his prey, a forest bird called a tinamou. The tinamou is eating seeds on the ground. It is unaware that the jaguar is near. The jaguar creeps forward, getting closer and closer. Then, it leaped! He grabbed the tinamou in his jaws and tore him apart for his next meal.

Uh, did you notice anything there? Halfway through the scene, the writer suddenly shifted from present to past tense. Surprisingly, writers do this a lot without being aware of it. This kind of shift may even be a subconscious experiment to see which tense they like best, and as such, it can be a valuable part of the writing process. Nonetheless, it does have to be resolved in favor of one tense or the other.

What if the writer has trouble choosing?

There are no hard and fast rules about when to employ a certain tense, but writers usually employ the present tense when they want to create a more immediate, tension-filled atmosphere. I did this in the platypus example from the previous tip. When I describe a scientist at work in the field, I also almost always go with the present tense. Here's a humorous example from one of my early science books, *Monteverde: Science and Scientists in a Costa Rican Cloud Forest* (1997):

> A ripe fig comes whizzing out of the tree and smacks into the mud next to Bob Lawton's feet.
>
> "Ah, missed!" Bob shouts at his attackers—a troop of white-faced capuchin monkeys. But the monkeys aren't through with their

A NOTE TO THE TEACHER

Referring to Other Works

Explain to students that present tense is also used when a writer is referring to a publication. For example, if I were to quote from Sneed's book *Monteverde*, I would set up the quotation using the present tense, like this: "In his book *Monteverde*, author Sneed Collard tells us . . ." Even though Sneed finished writing the book years ago, it is appropriate to use present tense ("tells" us) rather than past tense ("told" us).

target practice. Soon, other figs follow the first, striking uncomfortably close to their human targets. Bob isn't fazed. He seems to be enjoying the show.

"They're all up there in the upper crown," he says, peering into the tree. "They got the lay on us, but at least they're not trying to pee on us. Sometimes they do." (15)

In this case, the present tense helps amplify an exciting, dynamic scene, pulling readers right into the plot.

Past tense, though, often works better for recounting well-established historical events—the discovery of a cure for polio, for example, or a pivotal showdown during a workers' strike. Here's an example from Larry Dane Brimner's wonderful book, *Strike! The Farm Workers' Fight for Their Rights* (2014):

> *Support for the boycott mushroomed across North America and even into western Europe, where growers now were trying to sell their crop. More housewives joined college students and farm workers on the boycott lines to pressure markets to remove California grapes from their stock. (123)*

Here, the past tense just seems to fit this historical reconstruction of well-documented events. What's more, moving to present tense would have been awkward and risked distorting the actual facts.

A good exercise to do with your students would be to have them rewrite each of the above passages in a different tense and discuss the results. This will give them insights into which tense to choose for their own work.

Before moving on, I want to tackle one more topic—pronoun reference. Take another look at this tip's opening paragraph about the jaguar and the tinamou. You will probably note a second problematic issue in the paragraph: Both the jaguar and the tinamou changed from "him" to "it" or "it" to "him." Which is

A NOTE TO THE TEACHER

Teaching the Basic Verb Tenses

This lesson will only make sense if students know the difference between present and past tense. Often, we assume they do—only to discover that they're actually not sure about it. While the following explanation doesn't address all possible tenses, it will help students sort out the basic three:

- *Something* happens *(or is happening) now:* present tense
- *Something* happened *(or was happening) yesterday:* past tense
- *Something* will happen *(or will be happening) tomorrow:* future tense

For additional helpful—and often humorous—information on verb tenses, along with examples, I recommend *Woe Is I* (2009) and *Woe Is I, Jr.* (2009) by Patricia T. O'Conner, *Mechanically Inclined* (2005) by Jeff Anderson, *Sin and Syntax* (1999) by Constance Hale, and *The Deluxe Transitive Vampire* (1993) by Karen Elizabeth Gordon.

correct? That depends on what the writer is trying to achieve. "It" gives the impression that a jaguar is just any jaguar, putting more emotional distance between the reader and the animal. The writer, though, could opt to use "him" or "her" to present the jaguar as an actual character and create a closer connection with the reader. Again, once the writer chooses "him" or "it," she needs to stay consistent—something your students should check for when revising each scene.

! Something to try

Checking for Inconsistencies

Have students look for inconsistencies in the following four examples. As they make corrections, ask them to think about which tense creates the right mood for the scene: the drama of something happening right now, or the historic ring of something that happened before. Have them also watch for jarring shifts in pronouns, and choose which they would commit to:

1. The glaciers are melting at a rapid rate, and as a result, oceans continued to rise.

2. A crow lands on the feeder as the scientists looked on. It seems to know they are watching. She snatches a cracker, then stretches her wings and sailed away.

3. The shark circled slowly. It approached the boat, then appeared to leave. Moments later, however, he returns, this time rising from the deep in an explosive burst of energy.

4. By the time he finishes his second term as president, George Washington felt exhausted. Though there were no term limits in those days, he does not want a third term in the White House.

Once you've had a chance to review and revise these short samples, ask students to read their own writing aloud, looking for any unintentional shifts in verb tenses or pronouns. If they find any, have them share those examples in writing groups, talking about which tense or pronoun works best and why.

Nail Those Transitions!

5

Others will disagree, but I think of transition words and phrases as falling into two categories. One class of transitions deals with time. These transitions include phrases such as *next*, *then*, *afterward*, *soon*, *immediately*, *at the same time*, *while*, *once*, *before*, etc. . . . Use of these is pretty straightforward and simply keeps a sequence of events straight in the reader's mind.

A second class of transition words connects, well, everything else. These transitions can be used to add information, clarify, compare, conclude, contrast, emphasize, show location, summarize, and introduce. Examples include, but are not limited to, words and phrases such as *however*, *though*, *as well as*, *in fact*, *additionally*, *for example*, *honestly*, *for instance*, *actually*, *most important*, *remarkably*, *ironically*, *first*, *second*, *third* . . . and many more. Instead of providing time sequence, these transition words and phrases serve as guideposts to aid a reader's understanding of a writer's message by showing how ideas connect.

Both categories of transitions are essential to good writing. Not only do they help control the flow of a piece but, wisely chosen, they create wonderfully precise detail in meaning. I debated discussing transitions in the next section, "Paragraph Revision," but a writer really has to look at transitions through an entire scene—and, indeed, an entire manuscript. If you use *however* in three consecutive paragraphs, for example, it can stunt the writing and even get the reader thinking that you're negating what you just said in the previous paragraph!

Vicki has cooked up some good transition activities for you, but I'd like to add a couple of thoughts that may be useful when working with students. The first is that transitions connecting two ideas or events are often more powerful in the middle of a sentence than at the beginning. Compare these two sentences:

1. However, the rabbit posed a greater threat than the bulging can of beans.

2. The rabbit, however, posed a greater threat than the bulging can of beans.

In the first version, the *however* almost stops the action—not what you want. In the second version, the *however* keeps the narrative flowing more smoothly. The second version also alerts the reader to the subject of the sentence before she has to deal with the contrast set up by the transition. That makes the sentence easier to assimilate. Reading these two sentences, my thirteen-year-old son made one more observation. "In the first sentence," he said, "even though there's a comma, you could misread it as 'However the rabbit posed . . .'"—a much different meaning. Maybe I should have him read my work more often, huh?

The second point I want to make about transitions is that during early drafts, it's okay to go a little overboard with them. When in doubt, I almost always stick in a *however* or *though* or *in fact*. This helps reinforce in my own mind what I am trying to say, especially the relationships between sentences in my scene. As I am polishing my writing later, I find that I can remove most transition words without degrading the clarity of

! Something to try
Getting Rid of Unneeded Transitions

As Sneed suggests, writers sometimes go overboard with transitions early on, even putting one at the beginning of every sentence. The result can be comical:

> Without warning, *the snake approached the rat.* Next, *it camouflaged itself in the tall grass.* Then, *the rat moved.* For a moment, *the snake went still.* Soon, *it lashed out at the rat.* After that, *the rat raced for its life.* Luckily, *the rat was faster than the snake.* Finally, *it escaped.*

Display this passage on a document projector as you share it aloud with students, paying special attention to the italicized transitions. Ask students which ones, if any, are essential, and which could go. Could some remaining transitions be revised to make this rat-snake confrontation read more smoothly? Could some sentences be rewritten or combined with other sentences, thereby making transitional words superfluous? When you finish this activity, have students highlight transitions within their own writing and read aloud to see which are important to the reader's understanding and which interrupt the flow without adding meaning.

my message. In fact, I often challenge myself to make my writing flow smoothly without using too many transition words and phrases. That indicates to me that the way I am writing is as logical and natural as possible—in other words, that my statements themselves provide the transitions I need.

! Something to try
Filling In the Transitions

Following is a short passage from a book that Sneed is writing about woodpeckers. I've left out the transitions. Read this aloud as you show it to your students, and see if they can come up with transitions to fill in the blanks. Remember that a transition could be a single word or a phrase. Please note that students *do not* have to replicate Sneed's original text. What matters is for the passage to make sense. As you try various transitions, ask yourself, "What is the author trying for here? Contrast? Emphasis? Or something else?" Tip: Read the entire passage before trying to fill in the blanks. And expect to try several transitions before finding one that works:

> _____ few people have heard of Lewis's Woodpecker, for scientists, the bird is royalty. Why? Because the first scientist to see the bird was a member of the Lewis and Clark Expedition. The bird, _____, is named after the expedition's co-leader, Captain Meriwether Lewis. For biologists, _____, the bird stands out for another reason _____.

After you've talked about your students' tries with this paragraph, show them Sneed's transitions and talk about what each one shows—such as contrast or emphasis. Here is the original passage:

> *Although* few people have heard of Lewis's Woodpecker, for scientists, the bird is royalty. Why? Because the first scientist to see the bird was a member of the Lewis and Clark Expedition. The bird, *in fact*, is named after the expedition's co-leader, Captain Meriwether Lewis. For biologists, *however*, the bird stands out for another reason.

Notice that no transitional word follows *reason* in the final sentence from Sneed's manuscript. If your students added a transition here, that's probably overkill!

6

Lead into the Next Scene

All of us have read books that we "just can't put down." Often, the reason is that at the end of each scene or chapter, the author has effectively dangled a piece of chocolate that we can't resist. What are some ways to do this?

End a Scene on an Uncertainty

Almost every compelling topic has its highs and lows, its breakthroughs and setbacks. Instead of finishing a scene with a final outcome, it's much more effective to end it on an uncertainty. In one scene of my book *The Prairie Builders—Reconstructing America's Lost Grasslands* (2005c), I recount how dozens of volunteers gathered seeds of Iowa native plants and then got together to sow the seeds to create a brand new prairie. Instead of saying whether or not this mass planting worked, I finish the scene with this sentence: "Unfortunately, that spring turned out to be one of the wettest in Iowa history" (24). This uncertainty creates anxiety that can only be relieved by reading the next scene.

A NOTE TO THE TEACHER

Fostering Binge Reading

We are used to teaching students to write endings that wrap things up. This tip seems to call for the opposite! That's because different kinds of endings have different purposes. Remind students that the end of a paragraph, a scene, or a chapter is not always final or conclusive. As you may know well, the cliffhanger ending is one reason fans of *Orange Is the New Black, Better Call Saul,* or *Sherlock* keep coming back for more.

Parse Out Information Gradually

Especially if you're writing about a subject of keen interest, another way to set up the next scene is by withholding information from the reader—at least for the moment. Also in *The Prairie Builders*, I discuss the efforts of scientist Diane Debinski to reintroduce a rare species of butterfly, the Regal Fritillary, onto the new prairie. The scene opens with her looking for and catching the butterfly. The scene wraps up with:

The butterfly Diane holds in her hands is one of America's most beautiful and rare butterflies. This animal species, in fact, has not fluttered over this part of Iowa for more than one hundred years. The only reason it is here again now, after all that time, is because of an idea Diane Debinski came up with more than a decade ago. (48)

These final few sentences not only pump up the significance of the Regal Fritillary, but alert readers that there is an interesting story behind the butterfly's reappearance. This propels them forward to discover just what that story is.

Other ways to launch readers into the next scene tend to be variations of the two methods above. A writer can end a scene by leaving the main character in jeopardy, uncertain what to do next, or eager to discover something just beyond the horizon. This works even if there's not a strong character that we can easily identify with. Let's say one of your students is writing an essay on how to replace a valve cover gasket. Instead of just telling readers what to do, he might finish one scene by writing:

Once you have removed the valve cover and bought the new gasket, you might think it would be simple to just put the new gasket in and screw the valve cover back in place. You'd be wrong!

! Something to try

Separating Finales from the Cliffhangers

To help students understand the difference between the ending to a scene and a conclusion that wraps up a whole discussion, read a few endings aloud. They might be endings to picture books, articles, segments or A-Heads within an article, or chapters in a longer work. Don't share the source before you read. Instead, ask students to focus on purpose. Is each ending's purpose to wrap things up—or to keep readers coming back for more? How can they tell the difference? Next, ask students to review their own work. Does their writing have one ending that concludes the whole discussion? Are there also "read on" lines at the ends of paragraphs or scenes? If not, have them look for a place to add or rewrite a line so that it will coax readers to forge ahead. Once they finish their additions or revisions, have students compare originals with rewrites in their writing groups.

By the way, I just made that up. My only attempt at replacing a valve cover gasket resulted in a major oil spill along Interstate 5 in northern California. My point is how, even in the most routine writing projects, student writers can create tension for their readers—tension that can only be released by reading onward. If this sounds manipulative, well, it is! Fortunately, it's also a whole lot of fun, both for the writer and the reader.

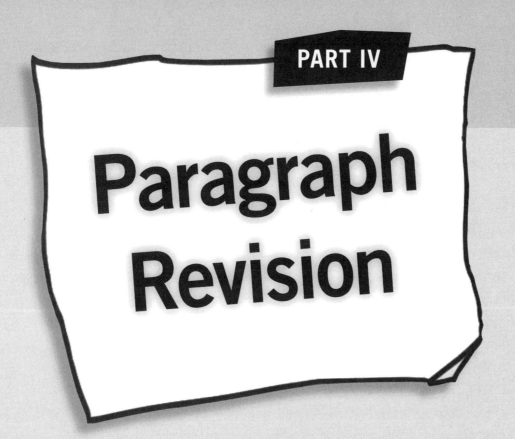

PART IV

Paragraph Revision

Of all the levels of revision I do as a writer, I have to rank paragraph revision as my number one favorite. Perhaps it's because paragraphs are like little works unto themselves, but unlike other, longer works, a paragraph doesn't take too much time to read and consider, and it also doesn't take excessive effort to tear apart and rebuild. That makes a paragraph just the right "chunk" of text to work on without feeling overwhelmed.

Paragraphs, though, are also where the beauty of writing begins to emerge. In his book *On Writing: A Memoir of the Craft* (2010), Stephen King asserts:

> I would argue that the paragraph, not the sentence, is the basic unit of writing—the place where coherence begins and words stand a chance of becoming more than mere words. If the moment of quickening is to come, it comes at the level of the paragraph. (134)

This quickening doesn't happen nearly as much with individual sentences and words, because those are too restricted or isolated to independently convey a broader meaning or action. The different elements of a paragraph, on the other hand, often combine to produce a thought or idea of real significance.

Not surprisingly, a writer who gets good at revising paragraphs will probably get a lot better at revising scenes and entire drafts. Why? Because almost everything that applies to paragraphs—unity, clarity, voice, storytelling—applies to bigger pieces of text as well. That makes the paragraph a perfect microcosm or metaphor for writing as a whole. It also makes the paragraph the ideal place to spend the most time with student writers.

Of course, you can't revise paragraphs without revising sentences and words. In this section, however, we'll do our best to consider the paragraph as a whole before tackling its component parts in more detail in the following sections.

Before we do *any* of that, however, we have to answer the obvious, scratch-your-head question: "What the heck is a paragraph?"

I'm going to punt to The American Heritage® *Dictionary of the English Language* (1976), or AHD, on this one. The AHD team defines a paragraph as "a distinct division of a written work that expresses a thought or point relevant to the whole, but is complete in itself, and may consist of a single sentence or several sentences" (900).

I have to offer my gratitude to AHD for tackling this, because for a definition, this is about as good as we're going to get.

The only problem with this—and all—paragraph definitions is that they only dent the surface of what a paragraph can be, because in the hands of an experienced writer, a paragraph can be and do almost anything. A paragraph can neatly cover one thought or explanation; it can describe a short sequence of events; it can present a line of dialogue from a character—or simply shock the reader with a pointed one-word exclamation. Vicki, in fact, has a nice special feature on all the things a paragraph can do in this section's first chapter.

For our following paragraph discussions, however, we will *generally* treat a paragraph as a unit of text that deals with a short, cohesive explanation, description, argument, or sequence of events. Our paragraphs will generally run several to a dozen sentences, though we acknowledge that paragraphs can consist of a sentence fragment, single line of dialogue, or other text.

Let's begin with the most basic paragraph task of all . . .

Making Paragraphs

1

Several months ago, my third-grade daughter started writing up a storm. I'm not sure why, but I'm guessing it boiled down to three reasons. First, she sees me writing every day. Second, she loves to read. Third, and perhaps most important, we limit her computer game time to a couple of hours a week. "However," we tell her, "you can get on the computer every day if you want to write or do something else creative on it."

A writer is born.

We love what she comes up with. It's crazy, uninhibited, fresh, and completely unpredictable. Beyond that, one of the first things I noticed in her early work was that she didn't break her writing into paragraphs. It wasn't a matter of style. She just didn't have a concept of paragraphs or how to use them. Below is a nonfiction piece she wrote about our recent trip to Taiwan. To help stay on point, I corrected a few distracting spelling and punctuation mistakes:

> I know you LOVE traveling and it can throw you to the tropics, then to
> the beach and (of course) the lovely bodies of water like the ocean.
> But have you ever thought of going to all of those? You'd be excited
> to hear this name: Taipei, Taiwan. Taipei, Taiwan is located right next to
> China. Yes, exactly 20 minutes by plane and by jet. . . . well I don't know
> but probably it goes by really quickly. Taiwan is a small island. Yes it has
> tropical forests, beaches, and lots of bodies of water. Thankfully, lots of
> people speak English. It has (in my opinion) *the* best food like xiao-long-
> bao (Pronounced: Zhow-long-bow) a dumpling with soup and meat. Also
> foods like sesame seed buns. Literally they taste like peanut butter and
> soft bread, though they are really sweet. Also they have the fifth tallest
> building **in the world!!!!!** Taipei 101. Haslea commented on the picture I
> put up on my power point, "That looks so pretty," after I said that it was
> fireworks shooting out of Taipei 101. Jessica also commented that it was
> like fireworks and it was so pretty. Then I said they *were* fireworks so she

laughed. Also they have really, *really fast*, like, *The fastest trains ever!!!* On my birthday I rode one. **IT WAS LIKE A ROLLER COASTER!!! SO, SO, SO FAST!** If you want an adventure, go to Taipei, Taiwan. ✪✪✪✪✪✪✪✪✪✪*!!!!!!*

THANK   YOU   VERY   MUCH!!!!!!!

I found this piece extremely enjoyable to read. Then again, I'm her dad. What you probably noticed right off the bat, however, is that this energetic travelogue could benefit from being broken into paragraphs. As a reader, I found myself itching to group related sentences together. I wanted the general facts about Taiwan to be distinguished from the information on food, and I wanted the information on food to be separated from the dialogue about Taipei 101 and the bullet trains.

Isn't it interesting that I would want that? It gets to the heart of what I will call the "Great Paragraph Mystery": Why we want text broken up and how we know when to do it. I cannot give you hard-and-fast answers to this conundrum, but I can offer educated guesses. Speaking for myself, separating out like pieces of information helps me organize them in my head. A paragraph break tells me, "Okay, put this chunk of data over here. Put this chunk over here" and so forth. This makes everything I read easier to understand and link together.

Paragraphs do more than sort and clarify, however. Each paragraph break gives my brain a little rest to process what I've just read and prepare for the next section of text—like taking a deep breath before running another sprint. Paragraph breaks also guide the pace and flow of my reading, setting up a pleasing rhythm in my head and adding to my reading enjoyment. Sometimes the paragraphs—especially if they are short one-liners—jar or poke me, bringing out sensations of delight, horror, and other things the writer wants me to feel.

From this brief analysis, I conclude that parsing into paragraphs is both a technical skill *and* an art—and I allow for both when I am writing. Specifically, I start a new paragraph when I:

- have presented one subtopic of information and wish to proceed to the next
- move from one event to another
- introduce a new speaker of dialogue
- have made one argument and want to proceed to another.

At the same time, I don't confine myself to these basic uses. I also employ paragraph breaks to create particular emotional effects in the reader. I choose them to please, shock, surprise, satisfy, and intrigue.

In *Fire Birds* (2015a), I often finished the text under an A-Head with a one-line paragraph designed to emphasize a point, arouse the reader's curiosity, or lead into the next section. The last two paragraphs of this A-Head on Black-backed Woodpeckers read:

> *Large, dead trees also provide the perfect homes for the woodpeckers. The birds carve out nest holes in the wood, creating snug, safe places for their babies to grow up. Since the trees also harbor the birds' food source, Black-backed parents can easily bring back a steady supply of beetle grubs to their young.*
>
> *Not surprisingly, other woodpeckers take advantage of this situation too. (24)*

Here, I could have easily tacked that final sentence to the end of the previous paragraph, but by separating it out on its own, I force the reader to pay more attention to it. This helps build curiosity—and momentum to keep reading.

In *Snakes, Alligators, and Broken Hearts* (2015b), I describe my newfound daily routine while spending the summers with my dad in Florida:

> *Conveniently, the post office sat in the basement of the UWF library. After pestering the post office employees, I rode the elevator to the library's top floor. I staked out a comfortable chair next to some floor-to-ceiling windows overlooking Escambia Bay. Then I settled in for one of my favorite activities.*
>
> *Reading. (103)*

Again, I could have placed "Reading" at the end of the previous paragraph, but I wanted to give readers an extra moment, or "beat," for that information to sink in. Why? Two reasons. One is that reading hasn't been discussed much until this point, and I want to alert my audience that I will be discussing it at length now. The second,

A Writing Secret to Share with Students

Sneed tells us that paragraphs help us sort and clarify information. So in an essay on whales, one paragraph might cover feeding, another migration, and another communication. But paragraphs do something else important, too.

Did you ever think twice about reading a book or article because so much unbroken print filled the page that it felt overwhelming? For readers, dense print creates an impenetrable wall. Break up that wall of print by creating space between "chunks" of text, and it's like letting in the light. Next time you pick up a book, newspaper, or article, notice how much of any page is filled with print and how much is open space—sometimes called *white space*. Then, think how paragraphs can make your own writing more inviting to readers.

By the way, skinny newspaper columns can make even short paragraphs look long and imposing. Could that be why editors often limit newspaper paragraphs to a single sentence? How your document looks depends on both paragraphing *and* formatting!

more important, reason is to emphasize that reading wasn't just any activity—it was an activity that would play a large role in my life from then on. The extra paragraph break beautifully accomplishes these goals by making readers pay special attention to it.

Your students may not learn how to do this sort of thing overnight, and that's okay. Deft use of paragraphs develops from intuition and experience. Specifically, it grows from reading, reading, and more reading, and from writing, writing, and more writing. Still, by starting with the four "technical rules" previously mentioned and branching out from there, even a beginning writer can quickly get a handle on basic—and more creative—uses of paragraph breaks.

! Something to try
Testing Students' Intuition

Sneed's reference to the "Great Paragraph Mystery" reminds us that knowing when to begin a new paragraph isn't like knowing when to use a period or question mark. Writers must *sense* when to begin a new paragraph—almost the way conversing friends sense a need to change topics.

Give your students a chance to test their own paragraph-sensing prowess. Take a section of any nonfiction article and type it up without breaks—or use a piece of student writing, if you prefer. Display the piece using a document projector, but let students read it *on their own* so that your reading cannot influence their decisions about where paragraphs should begin. Once everyone has decided how to break up the piece, discuss their choices. How much agreement do you find? Talk about the reasons behind each new paragraph decision.

If you use student writing for this activity, ask the writer to reveal where she began paragraphs and to offer her rationale for each break. If you work with a published piece, you can share the original and compare your students' choices with the author's version.

Following this practice, have students look at their own current drafts, reading aloud and listening for places new paragraphs should begin. Are their choices backed by logical reasons? Feelings? Both? Have students revise as needed, and share their revisions aloud with partners or in writing groups. Writers may find it helpful to have listeners signal—by raising hands, for example—when *they* hear a paragraph shift, just to compare audience response with the writer's own paragraph "sense."

A NOTE TO THE TEACHER

Paragraphs Serve Many Purposes

Some of us were taught to think of a paragraph as a main idea buoyed up by supporting details—but such paragraphs are rare in contemporary nonfiction. Today's nonfiction writers recognize that paragraphs can assume a myriad of forms, depending on the author's purpose. That purpose can range from an in-depth discussion to a one-line announcement: "The eyes of the world were on her—the first woman ever to command a space shuttle" (Stone 2009, 101). As you and your students read various informational texts—newspapers, periodicals, textbooks, trade books, and so on—keep a running list of the many purposes that paragraphs fulfill. Here's a start:

- *providing additional detail*
- *creating a contrast or counter argument*
- *debunking a counterargument*
- *emphasizing a point*
- *giving one striking word or statement "center stage"*
- *presenting new dialogue*
- *posing a question*
- *providing an answer*
- *transitioning into the next point or discussion*
- *presenting an insight or discovery*
- *creating tension*
- *resolving an issue*
- *wrapping things up.*

As your students add to this list, think how purpose influences form. What's the longest paragraph students run across in their reading, and how does length help the paragraph achieve its purpose? What's the shortest paragraph they come across, and what it impact does it have on readers?

2

Make Sure It All Makes Sense

> The pressure to answer such internalized-reader questions as "Why are you telling us all this?" and "What are you getting at?" can help drive an essay, can give it pleasurable suspense and forward momentum.
>
> —**Phillip Lopate**, *To Show and to Tell* (2013, 111)

The absolute minimum bar a nonfiction writer must set for himself is to be understood. If readers can't comprehend his work, a writer may as well drop that work straight into the recycling bin. Unclear writing can be traced to a basket of issues, including:

- too many concepts in one paragraph
- the writer's incorrect understanding of concepts or events
- ambiguous pronouns, adverbs, and other references
- overly long sentences
- information that is out of order
- shifting tense or point of view.

We have discussed the last two issues in other chapters, so right now, let's take a look at the first four stumbling blocks.

Competing Concepts

If you really want to confuse a reader, write a paragraph that has more than one competing point or concept. Consider this paragraph based on my book *Lady Bird Johnson: Keeping America Green* (2009):

Lady Bird didn't like politics and felt uncomfortable in Washington, D.C.
People made fun of her Texas accent and the clothes she wore. When she saw
Lyndon was in trouble running for re-election, she campaigned all across the
country. Crowds loved her and Lyndon got re-elected.

Here, we've got two competing themes—Lady Bird's internal conflicts about being in the spotlight and her role getting Lyndon re-elected. Which is more important? The reader doesn't know—and is confused by how the two themes seem to contradict each other. In the actual book, I avoided this problem by dealing with the themes one at a time. This kept the two issues distinct in the reader's mind and helped show how Lady Bird gradually grew into her role as a politician's wife.

Incorrect Understanding

A writer's flawed understanding of concepts or events is a second major cause of confusion. Take evolution. Despite being around for more than a century, it remains one of the world's most poorly understood concepts. Many—perhaps most—Americans believe that evolution occurs when an organism *needs to change to survive.* I believed this myself as a young person. My high school biology teacher, Mr. Miller, set me straight. He helped me understand that evolution occurs as a result of random genetic mutations that *by chance* give an individual organism a survival—and reproductive—edge.

Unfortunately, a misunderstanding of evolution leads many writers to write paragraphs such as:

Some ocean animals didn't have enough food. Instead of staying in the water,
they evolved into land animals so they could take advantage of the food there.
Later, some land animals decided to evolve back into water animals and
became whales.

In this example, the writer cannot write a paragraph that makes sense because he believes that evolution happens by choice or because of need. Worse, this flawed understanding will probably lead to confusion throughout his entire essay.

When I struggle with an especially difficult paragraph, I step back and ask, "Am I really understanding this correctly?" Often, the answer is "no." Once I do more reading, or consult with an expert, my understanding improves—along with my ability to write more clearly.

Ambiguous References

While we're on the evolution theme, take a look at this paragraph I wrote about Charles Darwin and Alfred Wallace, considered the cofounders of the theory of evolution:

> *Wallace sent letters with his ideas back to Darwin. Darwin shared* them *with other scientists.* Alarm *swept through* there. *Darwin didn't know what to do about* them.

This paragraph attempts to give a narration of events, but a number of ambiguous references confuse the story line. Each of the words in roman typeface could mean one of several things. The first "them" could refer to Wallace's letters or his ideas. "There" could refer to the community of scientists, England, or something else. The second "them" could refer to Wallace's ideas, letters, or the scientists he had shared with. Even "alarm" raises the question, "Alarm at *what*, exactly?"

To fix these issues, a writer has to pin down his meaning. For a first cut, I'd revise this paragraph to:

> *Wallace sent letters with his ideas back to Darwin. Darwin shared* ~~them~~ *these ideas with other scientists* in England*.* Alarm *over Wallace's work swept through* ~~there~~ England's scientific community*. Darwin didn't know* ~~what to do about them~~ how to respond to Wallace*.*

The paragraph remains rough, but its meaning is now clear, paving the way for further refinements.

A Writing Secret to Share with Students

As we see with Sneed's example on evolution, writers sometimes think they have all their facts straight when they do not. While it's always helpful to share writing with a partner or in a group, certain topics—like evolution—call for a reviewer with specialized knowledge. That might be a teacher, friend, or someone in your family. If you cannot talk with such an expert, you'll need to rely on your own reading or hands-on research. Either way, keep in mind that what you learn about your topic as you are writing may contradict everything you wrote in an early draft. Don't let this throw you. Good nonfiction writers always follow where their research leads them.

Overly Long Sentences

Long sentences aren't always run-ons, but they can lead to confusion simply by overloading the reader with information. Take a look:

> *Funding for the space program was in jeopardy because after the explosion of the space shuttle* Challenger, *which killed seven astronauts and stopped space launches for more than two years, people looked at how much NASA cost and asked if it was really worth it to spend all that money when we had so many problems to fix here at home.*

Technically, there's nothing wrong with this sentence. It's simply too complicated and contains too much data. What can we do? Well, first off, recognize that this one sentence contains a paragraph's worth of information. That may not *always* be the case, but it sure is here. With that in mind, a logical fix is to break it into several different sentences, each with its own concise thought. The resulting paragraph might look something like this:

> *Funding for the space program was in jeopardy.* ~~because, after~~ The explosion of the space shuttle Challenger ~~which~~ killed seven astronauts and stopped space launches for more than two years. *During that time,* people looked at how much NASA cost. ~~and asked if it was~~ *They asked themselves, "Is it really worth it to spend all that money when we* ~~had~~ *have so many problems to fix here at home?"*

Something to try
Looking for Confusing Moments

In the essay below, the student writer opens with a brief dramatic paragraph in which she and a camping buddy have a scary encounter with a coyote. Brilliant! But has she thought the situation through carefully enough to write about it clearly? Read and review it with your students—before sharing my comments that follow. See if your students notice any confusing details that would benefit from revision:

"Wake up!" A sudden chill comes down your spine. You hear your tent zipper unzipping. You see your friend yelling at you to get out of your tent. Suddenly you hear leaves rustling and whisper to your friend to get in!! As you look through a hole in your tent, you see a fat coyote—he looks twice the size of a normal coyote. He slowly walks toward you . . .

continues

Looking for Confusing Moments (cont.)

Though this coyote encounter makes for a dramatic opening, problems with logic could make readers less likely to trust the information that follows. Compare your students' own observations with these five problems I noticed:

1. The "sudden chill" happens well before the writer spots the coyote. We don't know yet why the friend is saying "Wake up!" That sudden chill could be triggered by the sound of the tent unzipping, but it's not written that way.

2. "You see your friend yelling at you" doesn't quite work because yelling is something we hear, not see. Further, the friend is yelling at the writer to "get out" of the tent. Why? Just a moment later, the writer tells the friend to "get in." Which is the better coyote-dodging strategy—getting in or stepping out?

3. "Suddenly you hear leaves rustling and whisper to your friend . . ." It seems odd that the friend yells while the writer whispers. Would this really happen? And how can the writer hear leaves rustling when her friend is yelling?

4. "As you look through a hole in your tent . . ." This too seems strange since the tent is now unzipped. Why doesn't the writer just look through the door?

5. "you see a fat coyote . . ." Well, I'm just being picky now. But coyotes aren't fat. They come in two shapes—thin and scrawny. Large? Maybe. Fat? Never.

Once you finish discussing the coyote passage, have students review their own work, looking for any moments that cause confusion. Remind them to check in particular for:

- *confused concepts*

- *flawed understanding of an event or idea*

- *ambiguous references (pronouns like* it *or* they *that do not clearly point to a particular thing or person)*

- *overly long sentences that carry too many ideas.*

A NOTE TO THE TEACHER

Strategies for Eliminating Confusion

Following are six strategies students can use to make sure their paragraphs are easy to understand. Read the list in its entirety, and then consider posting each suggestion's main idea, which is highlighted in bold:

1. **Identify the main purpose or message of each paragraph.** If you can't do this, your reader can't either. A clear message should be as easy to write as a sentence. Examples: "Technology is addictive." "Great white sharks are less aggressive than most people think." "Intelligent life could exist on other planets."

2. **Check for missing details.** What questions are you raising in readers' minds as you write? Answer them.

3. **Replace general words** like *stuff, things, nice, good,* or *wonderful* with language that adds factual information or places pictures in readers' minds.

4. **Check a dictionary or thesaurus to make sure you are saying what you mean.** Using new words or specialized terms is an excellent way to stretch your reader's vocabulary—as well as your own—but it can backfire if you use words incorrectly.

5. **Review your work sentence by sentence.** Sentences in a paragraph form a web of meaning. If even one is weak, the web falls apart. As you read each sentence, ask yourself, "Is this clear? Does it support what I say in other sentences?" If the answer to either question is no, revise or cut that sentence.

6. **Try expressing ideas in different ways.** Revising triggers thinking. The simple act of writing a sentence several ways can often take you closer to your intended meaning.

3 Put Sentences in the Best Order

In early drafts, writers often focus more on content than on style. That makes sense. Writers need to get thoughts on paper before all those original ideas exit the brain cells. But when you rush, events and lists can wind up out of order or sequence, and that can cause confusion.

I already mentioned how I moved an entire chapter while revising my book *Birds of Prey* (1999b), but order also plays a critical role within individual paragraphs. The funny part is that you often don't see a problem until after you write the paragraph. Here's an example from an early draft of my memoir *Snakes, Alligators, and Broken Hearts* (2015b). The paragraph describes a fireworks rocket I watched explode in the air. I numbered the sentences so you can think about how *you* would place them in the paragraph:

> *(1) I felt the shock wave rip through my chest, and even in the morning light, flames streaked out in all directions. (2) The ball exploded with the sound of a battleship artillery shell. (3) Then, as the blast's echoes reverberated through the surrounding wilderness, a thick cloud of smoke began to drift down over the swamp.*

Before you read any further, ask yourself, "Are these sentences in the best possible order to make the paragraph as strong and logical as possible?" If not, jot down your preferred order.

Now let me tell you what I did. I found two problems in this paragraph. I decided the sentence beginning, "The ball exploded . . ." works better as the *first* sentence, not the second. It's powerful, so it's a good place to begin—but it's also the first thing that happens in this sequence of events so it should logically be the first thing I tell the reader. As a classroom teacher, you might call this the paragraph's *lead, introductory,* or *thesis sentence.*

The second problem occurred in the sentence about the shock wave. Notice the order of the two sensations: First I talk about what I *felt* . . . and then what I *saw.* Does that make sense to you? Not really, because light travels faster than sound. Therefore, I would have seen the explosion before I heard or felt it.

To fix these issues, I revised the paragraph to read:

(2) The ball exploded with the sound of a battleship artillery shell. (1) Even in the morning light, flames streaked out in all directions and I felt the shock wave rip through my chest. (3) Then, as the blast's echoes reverberated through the surrounding wilderness, a thick cloud of smoke began to drift down over the swamp.

You'll note that I shifted a few words around to make the sentences fit together in their new arrangement, but do you see and hear an overall improvement? The new paragraph is more logical, and also sounds better when read aloud. Savvy readers will note that both issues in this paragraph have to do with logic. In fact, sequence is *mostly*—but not always—about logic. We'll discuss other sequence issues when it comes time to work on sentences, but for now, let's look at one more example: a paragraph I wrote about the growth of Los Angeles:

In the early 1900s, Los Angeles started growing north. Cities like Van Nuys, Reseda, and Canoga Park were built practically overnight. This was in a place called the San Fernando Valley. These cities needed water to grow, but Los Angeles had already built the Los Angeles Aqueduct to transport enough water from the Sierra Nevada mountain range. They acquired this water by secretly buying up water rights from farmers and ranchers in the Owens Valley.

Do you see any information that could be placed in a better order? Well, yeah. The vital information about the acquisition of water from the Owens Valley should come earlier. Instead, I "backfilled" it into the end of the paragraph. This is a common characteristic of first drafts. As a writer gallops along, he makes statements that need supporting information. Instead of going back and inserting this information where it really belongs, he tacks it on as it occurs to him. Why? One reason is that revision takes effort! Another is that pertinent facts don't always occur to the writer in the same order in which they should be presented to the reader.

Something to try
Revising Sneed's Paragraph

Use a document projector to share Sneed's original paragraph about the explosion. Read the three sentences aloud as students follow along and ask if they can think of a way to improve the original order.

When you finish discussing this passage, share Sneed's revision and his reasons for reversing sentences one and two. How do they feel about this decision? Does it match what they would have done?

A proper revision of this paragraph might look something like:

In the early 1900s, Los Angeles developers wanted to push north. One problem was that there wasn't enough water to support new neighborhoods and stores. Quietly, Los Angeles started buying up water rights in the Owens Valley, near the Sierra Nevada mountain range. They built a huge aqueduct to carry this water to Los Angeles. With water, cities like Van Nuys, Reseda, and Canoga Park sprang up practically overnight.

Swapping the order of information enables me to establish a better cause and effect relationship between the facts, making the paragraph much more logical. It also helps create a better story line, complete with drama and tension. That makes the manuscript easier to follow and more entertaining to read.

A Writing Secret to Share with Students

If your teacher has shared much of this chapter aloud, then you know that Sneed weighs every sentence or word he writes, asking if it says what he wants it to say, if it sounds the way he'd like it to sound, and if it fits where he's placed it. In other words, he is reading like a writer. This kind of slow, careful reading is essential to revising well, and it's unlike most reading we do. Often, we read for information: "How did the Underground Railroad get its start?" Or we read to follow a plot: "What happens if pirates find the missing map?" Reading like a writer is different. It's more active. It requires you to work mentally, to constantly ask yourself questions: *Is this a good place to begin? Are these ideas in a logical order? Should this sentence go here? Does this word say what I mean? Should this detail come here—or later? What have I forgotten? How do I wrap this up?* Next time you review a piece of writing, your own or someone else's, ask yourself, "Am I reading like a writer?" And if you are, how do those questions in your head help you know when to revise? If you're not quite there yet, slow down. Try to think of one question to ask yourself about each paragraph or sentence.

You'll note, of course, that I didn't just "swap pieces" around. As I've mentioned in other chapters, making one improvement often spurs others. In my revision, two other improvements especially stick out. I helped out the reader by making relationships more specific, such as clarifying why water was needed: "there wasn't enough water to support new neighborhoods and stores." I also dropped mention of the San Fernando Valley. Why? Because unless you grew up in southern California like I did, that's a name that won't mean much to you—and may even distract you. Keeping the focus firmly on Los Angeles keeps the point of the story front and center.

! Something to try
Experimenting with Order

Encourage students to experiment with logical order in their own writing. First, have them choose a paragraph that runs about four to five sentences. This provides enough length to make order challenging but not overwhelming. Next, ask them to rewrite the paragraph on a clean sheet of paper in line-by-line format:

- *Write the first sentence on one line by itself, like this.*
- *Write the second sentence on the following line, and so on.*

Have them cut the sentences into strips, and exchange strips with a partner. Students can then play with these sentence strips like a puzzle, trying out different orders until they come up with the one they feel works the best.

The point is not to match the writer's original. That may or may not happen. Students should strive to arrange the sentences in the most logical order possible. Comparing a partner's "best" order with the writer's own text may confirm that the original order made perfect sense. Or—especially if the partner struggles to figure out an order that works—it may raise questions about logical flow or the need for stronger transitions to connect sentences. Tip: Make sure students create a *new copy* before cutting their writing into strips. I learned the hard way that even though they wrote the text themselves, writers cannot always recall the original order once sentences are scrambled!

4 Build Up Hooks

Instructing students to craft engaging hooks, or leads, is SOP for most writing teachers. Everyone knows that a strong hook can pull a reader into a piece of writing. Most young writers get this and begin an essay, report, or memoir with a dash of drama, spice, or action to kick things off. What many teachers and writers don't realize is that hooks aren't just for the beginning of a work. They help maintain momentum and interest *throughout* a piece of writing.

Should never have read that first line!

Where do hooks happen? They happen at the beginning of an entire piece. They happen at the beginning of scenes or chapters. More than anywhere, they occur at the beginnings of paragraphs. Consider the following paragraph from a memoir I am writing about birding with my son:

> *I had to admit to a bit of disappointment at not seeing a Bufflehead on the ponds. We could usually find one here, and they were one of my favorite ducks. Why? Well, uh, I guess I should come clean. They were one of my favorite ducks mainly because* I could easily identify them.

This paragraph probably isn't the worst you've ever read, but it just lies there, doesn't it? Although the entire paragraph has problems, the big one that, *ahem*, quacks out at you, is the first sentence. Sentences just don't come much more limp than this—and that's a big mistake for the writer. Why? Because this first sentence needs to propel the reader forward, not stick like tar to his reading boots. Put another way, this first sentence needs to be a much stronger hook. To improve the piece, I decided to replace it:

> ~~*I had to admit to a bit of disappointment at not seeing a Bufflehead on the ponds.*~~ *The absence of Buffleheads rankled. We could usually find one here, and they were one of my favorite ducks. Why? Well, uh, I guess I should come clean. They were one of my favorite ducks mainly because* I could easily identify them.

Do you think that this first sentence is better? I do. It's snappier, of course, and eliminates unnecessary words, but it also creates a tension that the paragraph didn't have before. Reading it, you begin to feel the angst that I felt. Not only that, it introduces an element of subtle humor missing from the first version.

I hear some of you arguing, "But that isn't a hook. It's just a different sentence." Well, sure, it's not a description of Navy Seals rappelling down cliffs with their machine guns blazing, or an image of John Wesley Powell about to launch himself down the Grand Canyon in a flimsy wooden boat. *But for this paragraph, in this part of the book, this is*

A Writing Secret to Share with Students

Have you ever fallen asleep, literally, while reading something? That document that collapsed on your face could be a treasure. Here's why: If a book or article can put you to sleep, chances are the so-called "hooks" are dull, predictable, or repetitive. In short, that sleep-inducing document is bursting with free lessons on how *not* to write a lead. Check out the paragraph leads in any piece of dull writing. Library series books and (unfortunately) many textbooks—not ours, of course—fit the bill. You'll be amazed how much you can learn about what *not* to do from bad writing!

Revising Hooks

Have students go through their own writing, highlighting or underlining just the hook for each paragraph. Then ask them to identify one to revise. A good choice to focus on? Perhaps a paragraph containing critical information, or the closing paragraph because it makes a lingering impression. Encourage students to write two or more versions of their revised hook, saving each revision for comparison purposes, and jotting down what they hope to accomplish with the version they settle on. Following are some examples of potential goals:

- *creating an image*
- *shocking or surprising the reader*
- *adding humor*
- *making a bold claim*
- *building anticipation*
- *opening with a striking fact or statement.*

When they finish revising, have students meet with partners to share and identify which new hooks work best. Afterward, discuss the impact this one revision had on each piece as a whole. Recall Sneed's comment that revising the hook often lures him into more revision? Did any of your students experience this?

a hook. Why? In this case, because it creates a question that the reader wants answered—and can only *get* answered by reading further.

Others of you may be shouting, "But you hardly changed the sentence at all. How is that an improvement?" Well, I admit that I made only a small change, but that change makes all the difference. By replacing the word *disappointment* with *rankled*, I transformed the entire tone of the paragraph from something languid and impersonal to something charged with emotion—giving the reader a sense of anticipation and setting the stage for something exciting or unexpected to happen. In the process, I also transformed the voice of the narrator. In the previous version, the narrator was just putting in his time describing a situation. With the new lead, he becomes a three-dimensional person with passion and conflict. Specifically, he turns into someone who is capable of getting annoyed—and becomes much more engaging as a result.

The take-home lesson is that revisions don't always have to be extensive and dramatic to be effective. Often, simple changes will do. And once again, these changes often lead to other positive revisions. After changing this paragraph's hook, I no longer felt satisfied with the sentences that followed. I revised the entire paragraph to match that snappiness and voice I introduced at the beginning. Here is the result:

> *The absence of Buffleheads rankled. We could usually find one here, and they were one of my favorite ducks. Why?* ~~Well, uh, I guess I should come clean. They were one of my favorite ducks mainly because I could easily identify them.~~ *Simple*—I could identify them.

These changes won't win me the Pulitzer, but they are an enormous improvement—all set in motion by creating a better hook.

A NOTE TO THE TEACHER

Collecting Hooks from Good Nonfiction

Hooks come in many forms—statements of fact, quotations, questions, humorous quips, shocking descriptions, and so on. Collect them with students to see how many different kinds of hooks you can identify. Here are a few that caught my attention. The first is a book opener. The other four are internal paragraph hooks:

- *"We humans are such a bunch of wimps!"* You have to love any book that kicks off with a wisecrack. And no worries. Nicola Davies has data to back up her claim in *Extreme Animals* (2006, 7), a book about *"The Toughest Creatures on Earth."*

- *"The Atlantic cod is a large and ugly fish."* Mark Kurlansky's unexpectedly frank description from *The Cod's Tale* (2001, 9) lays the groundwork for more explicit detail to come.

- *"Europe was largely deforested, short on fertile land, and prone to famine when Columbus sailed west."* In *Eyes Wide Open* (2014, 103), Paul Fleischman sets the record straight. Columbus wasn't just out for adventure; he was desperately hunting for resources to replenish those Europe was busy exhausting.

- *"Warning: Your sweaters may be seething with life."* In *Buzz: The Intimate Bond Between Humans and Insects* (2004, 26), Josie Glausiusz lets us know that moths—and other insects—are closer than we think.

- *"His wife Mary agreed that Abe should be a senator—she only wished he would act like one."* These words from *Two Miserable Presidents* (2008, 27) by Steve Sheinken open a paragraph that gives us an intimate look at an Abraham Lincoln we rarely see.

5

Pump Up the Action!

Assigned writing—explaining the federal election process or recounting how the Great Recession shaped America—often falls flat because students struggle simply to slog through the required information they must include. Adding conflict or drama is the last thing on their minds. Even when students get to choose their own topics, however, many paragraphs beg for an adrenaline injection.

Here's the opening paragraph in a persuasive essay titled "Smartphones = Smart Kids" by a fifth-grade student:

> Parents, have you ever been so worried about your child when they are home alone? Or so worried that you don't even let your child stay home by themselves at all? Well, if you get your child a smartphone, you won't have to be as worried as you were before. With this smartphone, you can keep in touch with your child whenever you need to.

Now, as a father, I must state that I am *appalled* by this student's line of reasoning. I've told my own kids that they won't get smartphones until they are at least thirty-five years old! That said, this paragraph has a lot of good things going for it. As a hook, the first couple of sentences present a widespread concern that almost any parent will relate to. Even better, the next sentences promise a solution for that concern—and deftly introduce the essay's topic in the process.

What the paragraph *doesn't* do is breathe life into the discussion. As presented so far, the paragraph remains strictly informational, appealing mainly to reason and logic. That's all well and good, but to really engage the reader, a better bet is to take it a step further and also appeal to his emotions. That can be accomplished by introducing more action and suspense into the paragraph. But how?

My first step would be to pump up the lead or hook. (Funny, isn't that what we just talked about?) The writer's first two sentences are already halfway there. Perhaps by intuition, she has taken tentative steps toward creating a dramatic opening situation by asking the reader to imagine something disturbing. The only problem is that she hasn't pushed it hard enough. Let's jack it up:

You're sitting with your husband in a dark movie theater. This is the first time you've ever left the kids at home without a babysitter. "Isn't this great?" your husband Greg asks. You nod and give him a peck on the cheek. But then, as the opening sequence of the movie begins to roll, you have a terrifying realization—you've left your heating pad on at home! The one with the big red "Fire Hazard" warning label on it! "Oh my god!" you think. "The house could be on fire right now! The kids could be turning into screaming marshmallows!" What will you do? Then, suddenly, you breathe a sigh of relief. Why? Because you just remembered something else—last week, you bought your daughter a brand-new smartphone!

Okay, the first thing you'll notice is that I did a lot more than simply changing the lead. I apologize. I had *planned* to only revise the first couple of sentences, but once I did that, I started having so much fun I couldn't control myself. I had to rewrite the entire paragraph. (Remember what I said about the additional benefits of improving the lead?) But since that horse already has left the barn, let's list all the things I did to pump up the action. They include:

- varying sentence pacing to create suspense
- showing instead of telling
- using dialogue
- replacing generalizations with details
- introducing humor.

And probably a few things I'm overlooking. The result? A paragraph that once merely intrigued the reader now sucks him in and rockets him forward.

We'll look at some of these elements in detail in following sections, but the point here is to help students recognize when a paragraph needs more action. How? Well, one sure cry for more action is when you yawn reading your own work! Tell your students, "Okay, pretend you are a random stranger on the street and

A Writing Secret to Share with Students

Drama makes facts memorable. This doesn't mean you should turn your fact-based report into a play (though that's been done with remarkable success—in *Hamilton*, for example). It means using action at the right moments to get readers' attention and show the role those facts play in real-world events.

In *The Wright Brothers* (2015), author David McCullough describes a test flight Orville and Wilbur made in 1902. He could have simply written, "The plane went 120 feet and stayed up for twelve seconds." Those are the facts. But to make sure we remember them, McCullough livens things up: "The Flyer rose, dipped down, rose again, bounced and dipped again like a bucking bronco when one wing struck the sand. The distance flown had been 120 feet, less than half the length of a football field. The total time airborne was approximately 12 seconds" (105).

read what you've written. Does the writing jump out at you? Does it make you want to read more? If you encounter 'dead spots,' those are places that need attention."

The writer, of course, doesn't want to go overboard. Endless paragraphs on full throttle can get just as tiresome as those without a pulse. A good rule of thumb is to save action for places where the writer wants to hook a reader or call attention to a particularly important point (see Vicki's "A Writing Secret to Share with Students").

Just a quick snooze and I'll try to read one . . . more . . . line . . .

Action movies can serve as instructive tutorials. For fun, ask your students what their favorite action movies are and why. I find that the action movies I enjoy most (*Terminator*, the Bourne series, most James Bond movies) deftly alternate action with slower character and story development. That often turns out to be a good strategy for nonfiction writing, too.

A NOTE TO THE TEACHER

Facts Are Not All Equal

How tall was Charles Darwin? You probably don't know—or care. Facts are not important just because they're facts. They only matter if they cause or reshape events, influence a character's fate, or affect readers in some way.

In researching his book *Drowned City* (2015), author Don Brown gathered hundreds of thousands of facts about Hurricane Katrina. But to write his ninety-one-page account, he carefully chose details that would help readers grasp the desperation and terror of that event. In describing the sprawling traffic jams that blocked highways, Brown writes, "One family spends ten hours traveling only seventy miles" (9). In just nine words, he helps us appreciate the anxiety, frustration, and helplessness those trapped evacuees must have felt.

Here is Brown's description of Katrina on August 29, 2005:

The hurricane's strength slips from a category 5 to category 3. But it is still a monster, measuring four hundred miles across, with 121-mph winds (13).

Such daunting facts resurrect the feelings of dread and empathy so many felt watching Katrina engulf New Orleans. As students research their topics, encourage them to search for facts that will remain in readers' minds long after reading.

Something to try
Using Drama to Show, Not Tell

At some point, most writing teachers advise students, "Show, don't tell." In nonfiction, telling means laying out the facts with minimal drama—as if sharing a bus schedule. Here's a "telling" example that's pretty action-free. Ask your students how many would put the book down—and how many would read on—following this passage:

> *The elasmosaur lived in the Mesozoic Period. It had a turtle-shaped body. It had a long neck. It mostly ate squid. It was hunted by the pliosaur.*

Pretty dull stuff, right? Actually, the information itself is fascinating. If you don't believe me, look how Sneed presented these same details in this "showing" passage from *Reign of the Sea Dragons* (2008a):

> The elasmosaur *had long, elegant flippers to propel its turtle-shaped body, and a fifteen-foot neck that came in handy for sneaking up on its favorite food, squid. Soon, in fact, the elasmosaur spotted a school of squid and began swimming toward it. As it opened its jaws to strike, however, a thirty-foot-long* pliosaur *suddenly shot up out of the depths. With its massive, seven-foot long jaws, the pliosaur seized the elasmosaur and impaled it with dozens of cone-shaped teeth. The elasmosaur struggled and thrashed to free itself, but it was no use (12).*

As students compare these two passages, ask how drama adds not only to our reading enjoyment, but our understanding of factual information.

Afterward, have students scan their own drafts for any passage that "tells" readers facts without "showing" them in action. Challenge them to create an action sequence that makes information memorable. Here is a tip for doing that: have them choose one character—human or otherwise—from their nonfiction writing, and confront that character with one of the following:

- *a crisis or conflict*
- *a challenge*
- *a hard decision*
- *an opportunity.*

Have volunteers read their "facts in action" revisions aloud. Do they show more than tell? By the way, we will talk more about "showing versus telling" under "Sentence Revision."

Vary Sentence Length and Structure

6

> Energy is the movement of our words, the cadence, the rhythm, the music, the beat, the syntax, the electricity. Energy is what moves the reader through the text, creating mood and bringing variety to the eye and ear.
>
> —**Jeff Anderson**, *10 Things Every Writer Needs to Know* (2011, 173)

Take a moment to reread the original paragraph from "Smartphone = Smart Kids" from the last chapter:

> Parents, have you ever been so worried about your child when they are home alone? Or so worried that you don't even let your child stay home by themselves at all? Well, if you get your child a smartphone, you won't have to be as worried as you were before. With this smartphone, you can keep in touch with your child whenever you need to.

Now stare at the middle of the paragraph and try to take in the entire thing without moving your eyes. Do you notice anything about its structure?

Yes! Most of the sentences are the same lengths. For experienced writers, this raises a flag. It tells them, "Your piece needs more varied pacing."

Don't get me wrong. Uniform sentences are not the literary equivalent of the *Hindenburg*, consuming your paragraph in a deadly fireball. It's just that they prevent a paragraph from really rocking. They do this by hypnotizing the reader into a steady carriage-horse cadence, ultimately putting him to sleep. Good writers spot these uniform sentences and take steps to mix things up. Fortunately, this is relatively easy to do. Here are six common strategies:

- Combine two shorter sentences into one.
- Cut a longer sentence into two.
- Throw in a one- or two-word sentence fragment.

- Vary the structure of sentences.
- Cut unneeded or redundant sentences or phrases.
- Replace an explanatory clause with a question.

Take a look at this persuasive paragraph, prompted by my own desire to eat less chocolate:

> *A healthy life plan should include exercise and good eating each day. You should get out and do some kind of exercise for at least thirty minutes. Make sure that some of this is vigorous exercise like running or tennis. You should also make sure not to eat too much sugar and fat like ice cream and soda pop. Instead, you could eat nuts, fruits, and green vegetables like broccoli. This will help you live a lot longer and not have as many health problems.*

Besides being as uninspiring as an empty Pop-Tarts wrapper, this paragraph suffers from two life-threatening problems. If you again do the "Zen stare" with your eyes, you'll notice that most of the sentences are similar *lengths*. This sets up a plodding pace that persists through the entire paragraph. A second issue is that the sentences tend to be the same *structure*. Almost every sentence is a command or suggestion, constructed with the modal verbs *should, could, would,* and *will* (and yes, I did have to look up "modal verbs"). This creates a paragraph both stilted and monotonous.

Strategies to the rescue!

A Writing Secret to Share with Students

Reading aloud is invaluable in assessing variety. The ear will pick up differences—or deadly, monotonous sameness—faster than the eye alone. Here's a little trick that will help your eyes *and* ears check for repetitive patterns. Underline or highlight the first four words of every sentence in your piece, and read *just those words* aloud. How much variety do you hear? In most cases, the more varied your sentence beginnings, the better! Of course, writers occasionally repeat words or patterns on purpose for emphasis. Julius Caesar's "I came, I saw, I conquered" is one famous example. Can you think of others? The point is . . . if you repeat, have a reason. And read the result aloud to make sure it creates the effect you desire.

Whipping out our list from the previous page, we can reshape our paragraph to read:

> *A healthy life plan should include exercise and good eating every day. At least thirty minutes of vigorous running, tennis, or other activity is a must. Replace sweet and fatty foods with nuts, fruits, and green vegetables. The payoff? You will live longer, feel better, and slash your medical bills.*

The first thing I did here was to combine the second and third sentences. Why? Because separating the "command" sentence from the "example" sentence served no useful purpose. They are part of the same thought so they easily fit together.

For the same reason, I combined the fourth and fifth sentences. However, I didn't want the new sentence to feel like the sentence before it, so I turned it into a short, assertive command. In the process, I axed my specific examples such as "ice cream" and "broccoli," but I didn't need them. Ninety-nine percent of my readers understand the concept of sweet, fatty foods—along with the concept of "nuts, fruits, and green vegetables."

For my final Big Move, I recast the last sentence. Instead of a sleep-inducing, forgettable conclusion, I tossed a sentence-fragment question to the reader. Then, I answered it with a short, snappy response that included the power verb *slash*.

Astute readers will note that even in my new paragraph, four of the five sentences are of similar lengths, but you know what? Here, that's okay—and there are two reasons why. The first is that the paragraph is short enough that inserting just *one* sentence fragment shakes things up enough to keep the reader alert. The second reason is that I have changed the structures of all of those other sentences, so that even though they are of similar lengths, they *read* like very different kinds of sentences.

My new paragraph is a vast improvement. Using every strategy on my list, I varied sentence length and structure and, in the process, gave the paragraph much more

! Something to try
Revising for Variety

Have students review their current drafts, checking specifically for sentence variety within paragraphs. Encourage them to read aloud, looking and listening for two things:

1. repetitious sentence structure or patterns, and

2. monotonous similarity in length.

Students can vary *structure* by changing the ways in which they begin sentences and by inserting an occasional command or question. They can vary *length* by combining sentences, cutting long or hard-to-follow sentences in two, and using an occasional very short sentence—or even a fragment, if it's effective. Be sure they read their revisions aloud, and take time to discuss differences they hear. It is especially helpful for the whole class to hear and discuss "before" and "after" versions of one or two pieces.

voice. The revision transformed "dead weight" into something a reader might actually feel like reading.

Now, some of you are going to ask, how do I know where to use which strategy and when? The answer: you don't. Part of a writer's job is to experiment and try things. When I am working, I tackle a paragraph, dicing and slicing and moving things around. Then I read the result, often aloud. If I like the rhythm I'm hearing inside of my head, I move on. If I don't, I take a breath and charge back in. Revising the paragraph previously mentioned took me four or five tries, but you know what? I didn't mind—and the reason, once again?

Paragraph work is fun.

IN CONFERENCE

Separating Effective from Confusing Fragments

Fragments offer an effective way of varying sentence rhythm—if they're carefully crafted. In his memoir *Winterdance* (1994), author Gary Paulsen writes about running the Iditarod race in Alaska under conditions few people could survive. In one scene, he falls from the sled as his dog team races out of control, dragging him through heavy brush and trees at breakneck speed. Unable to stop, he fears he will die, but later writes, "A deer saved me. A deer and luck" (104). The rhythm of "A deer and luck" is almost lyrical. Had Paulsen written "A deer and luck saved me," it wouldn't have been nearly as effective because the emphasis on "luck" would have been lost.

Note that a fragment can *only work* if the missing part is understood. In other words, the reader can mentally fill in the blank. In the example with Gary Paulsen, we know that "A deer and luck" means "A deer and luck *saved me*."

But consider this student example: "We should pick up paper, bottles, and trash from our beaches. It helps the environment. A good invention." Obviously, the writer doesn't mean the environment is a good invention. He probably means "recycling is a good invention," but there's no way to know for sure.

In a conference, you can help students understand the difference between effective and confusing fragments by asking them to fill in the understood part. If this is easy to do—as in the Paulsen example—then the fragment won't cause confusion, and may add appealing rhythm to the writing. If you can't be sure what goes in the blank, the writer needs to revise.

Connecting Rhythm to Meaning and Mood

In this chapter, Sneed emphasizes the importance of sentence variety. One notable exception to this rule occurs when a writer repeats length or structure deliberately for dramatic effect. In *Stung!* (2013), author Lisa-ann Gershwin uses sentence rhythm to underscore the rising menace of jellyfish taking over our oceans. Like drumbeats, her short sentences build up to a climactic longer sentence that erupts like a jellyfish bloom:

> *The climate is changing. Pollution is increasing. Fish stocks are vanishing. Oceans are becoming more acidic. Species composition is rearranging. And jellyfish populations are exploding into superabundances and exploiting these changes in ways that we could never have imagined—not only exploiting the changes but in some cases driving them. (2)*

Share this with students—minus my comments—and ask for their reaction to the rhythm of short, short, short, short, short . . . *long*. Is this kind of build-up effective? Why? Encourage students, as they're reading nonfiction, to watch for ways writers use sentence patterns to enhance meaning or mood.

7 Ferret Out Contradictions and Falsehoods

When my son joined Boy Scouts, I rashly signed up to be a merit badge counselor for about fifteen different merit badges. I don't know what possessed me, but I decided to focus on the nerdier merit badges that the more masculine adults in the troop tended to overlook. These included Reading, Scholarship, Public Speaking, and yes, Communication.

As one of the requirements for the Communication Merit Badge, Scouts have the option to write a letter to the editor of a newspaper or magazine. One Scout wrote the following:

> Dear Editor,
>
> I am inquiring about the pedestrian overpass being built over Reserve Street by Auto Zone. It will connect the trail from Lolo to Missoula, but I never see any pedestrians or bikers around the area. On the contrary I have seen some pedestrians almost get hit because motorists were not paying attention. The overpass would provide those people the comfort of crossing Reserve Street safely. I believe it provides a safe means of travel for others. Will it really be cost effective for this city project if hardly anyone uses it? And at what point each person saves does this overpass become paid for and cost effective to the city?

I enjoyed this letter. Pedestrian and bike safety is a subject dear to my heart, and the writer clearly understood that building the overpass posed an important question for the city. I had just one problem. By the end of the letter, I couldn't decide if the writer favored or opposed the overpass construction. Early in the letter, he seems to suggest that no pedestrians or cyclists use this part of the road, but then immediately observes that he's seen some people almost get squashed by traffic there. Similarly, in the middle of the letter, he extolls the advantages of the overpass, but then closes by suggesting that the whole thing just may not be worth the money.

These contradictions might not pose a problem if his purpose were to weigh the pros and cons of the issue—and if he presented these pros and cons a bit more clearly. However, the purpose of a letter to the editor usually is to voice a particular position. In such a letter, contradictions can leave readers confused and asking themselves, "What's this guy trying to say?"

Many writers, especially student writers, introduce similar contradictions into their work. That's often because they're not exactly sure what they're trying to say or even what they think. One of the beauties of writing, however, is that it helps one think more clearly. Having students take a dedicated pass through their work looking for contradictions, or having them search for these in writer's group, can lead to a better understanding of the connection between writing and thinking—something that will help them in all areas of their lives.

A Writing Secret to Share with Students

Contradictions like those in the Scout's letter about the overpass often occur because a writer begins an argument before thoroughly exploring an issue. When you write, you are asking readers to follow your thinking. If your thinking is still evolving, keeping pace with your constantly changing ideas may feel like tracking a confused mouse through a dark maze. More research, an interview with an expert, a conversation with a friend or coach, or even a list of pros and cons can help you make up your mind about a topic. This doesn't mean you can't rethink your position as you write. Revision gives you a chance to revisit your comments, reflect on what you've said, and reshape your conclusions. When drafting an argument, however, you must eventually take a stand, and make sure every sentence clearly supports that stand.

But let's say you're not writing an argument. Instead, suppose your purpose is to walk readers through the pros and cons of an issue—whether homework is or is not a good idea, for example. In that case, your job is to present both sides fairly and equally, helping readers to make up their own minds.

A similar problem I look for in my own work are statements that aren't true. When writing the introduction to this section of this book, I wrote the following excerpt:

> *Of all the levels of revision I do as a writer, I have to rank paragraph revision as my number one favorite. I'm not sure why. Perhaps it's because paragraphs are like little works unto themselves, but unlike other works, you can take in a paragraph all in one glance.*

I liked this excerpt. It felt friendly and flowed well. Reading through it for the fourth or fifth time, however, I realized something about the second sentence, "I'm not sure why."

It wasn't true!

I *did* know why I loved revising paragraphs, and went on to explain as much. So why did I put that line in there originally?

Pacing.

Especially with long sentences before and after it, I liked how that short second sentence varied the rhythm. I didn't include it to intentionally mislead you—honest! The statement was *enough* true that I didn't think much about it until later.

Many writers make similar mistakes, but as with contradictions, it's important to teach your students to challenge the truth of their own assertions. And because these statements cannot be understood except in the context of surrounding statements, the paragraph is the best place to correct them.

Author's Note: Perhaps the Boy Scout's letter to the editor was more persuasive than I recognized. The pedestrian overpass got approved!

Something to try

Resolving Contradictions

Following is an essay written by a sixth grader asked to explain whether dogs or cats make better pets. Share it aloud, using a document projector, and give students a few minutes to talk with a partner about whether the writer's position is clear—or whether he has yet to form an opinion on this issue:

> ### Dogs or Cats?
>
> Which one makes a better pet? I think dogs because they are far more active. You can take your dog for a walk by the river. Try doing that with a cat. Cats are playful, however, and entertaining because they're unpredictable.
>
> If you want to make a funny video to share with your friends, pick a cat. Give a cat a paper bag and it will play in there for hours. A dog will just look at you like you're crazy then walk away.
>
> Dogs can learn tricks like "roll over" or "shake hands" or "sit." Cats can also learn tricks, but will almost never perform for your friends when you want them to show off.
>
> Dogs are loyal. They interact with people, and will be your friend for life. Cats have their good points, though. They mostly take care of themselves, which makes them low maintenance.

Does the writer prefer cats or dogs? Can we tell? Talk about any contradictions that leap out at your students, and ask what they would do to revise this piece. Have each student frame a strong position for the writer, and then rewrite just the lead paragraph to make this position clear. By the way, it is not necessary for students to agree with one another about this—and likely they will not!

After sharing a few revised leads aloud, ask students to review their own writing, looking carefully for contradictions. Also remind them, as Sneed suggests, to challenge their own thinking: Do they mean what they say in each sentence? If not, have them revise to make their writing clear.

8 Eliminate Unnecessary and Redundant Information

I and other writers often bloat our early drafts with unnecessary or repetitive information. The most logical explanation for this is that as we write, our minds are processing and organizing, and we don't always know if something needs to be there until we try it out. Take this example from my memoir, *Snakes, Alligators, and Broken Hearts* (2015b):

> *Mr. Gambill stepped into our living room and studied the shelves around him. Besides holding an extensive library of my dad's biology books, these shelves displayed turtle shells, dried starfish, snake skins, and a host of other zoological specimens. Mr. Gambill closely studied both the books and the animal artifacts. I assumed he was thinking something like,* Yeah, just as we thought. These Yankees are damned animal freaks and en-vi-ro-mentalists. We'd better rub 'em out before they stir up any trouble.

During revision, I spotted a couple of repetitions here. I refer to the shelves more than once, and also to the fact that Mr. Gambill is studying them. To fix this, I couldn't just eliminate a sentence. I had to rework a couple of sentences:

> *Mr. Gambill stepped into our living room and studied the shelves around him. Besides holding an extensive library of my dad's biology books, these shelves displayed turtle shells, dried starfish, snake skins, and a host of other zoological specimens.* ~~Mr. Gambill closely studied both the books and the~~

A Writing Secret to Share with Students

Spotting repeated or unnecessary information can be one of revision's toughest challenges. Here's a way to think about it that may help. If someone showed you six photos of people you had never seen, but told you that two were of the same person, do you think you could pick those two out? Probably, right? In a way, each sentence you write is a "snapshot" of an idea. In revising, you need to ask of each sentence, "Is there a match for this thought anywhere else in my writing?" If you spot such a match, pick your favorite and cut the other—just as you might toss a duplicate photo.

~~animal artifacts.~~ I assumed ~~he~~ <u>Mr. Gambill</u> *was thinking something like,* Yeah, just as we thought. These Yankees are damned animal freaks and en-vi-ro-mentalists. We'd better rub 'em out before they stir up any trouble *(107).*

One of the special challenges of writing science books is making sure a reader understands challenging concepts or ideas. As a result, I often end up repeating myself or getting just a little too detailed in my descriptions during my early drafts. Here's a perfect example from a sidebar in *Hopping Ahead of Climate Change* (2016):

> *Hares can be mismatched in two ways. They can be white sitting on a brown background or they can be brown sitting on a white background. Is one mismatch more dangerous than the other? Scott's team lumped the two kinds of mismatches together for their study so they can't come up with a definite scientific answer. "We study brown on white, and white on brown," Scott says. "We call white on brown 'positive mismatch' and brown on white 'negative mismatch,' but it's hard to separate those things statistically. But just spending time out in the woods, we feel like white on brown is much more noticeable."*

IN CONFERENCE
Reading Aloud to Let Repetition Surface

Sometimes, the most useful thing to do in a conference is to read a student's work aloud as she listens. Students can read their own work, it's true, but many read so quickly, and with so little expressiveness, that subtle repetition simply doesn't jump out. When you read a student's work at an unhurried pace and with thoughtful inflection, a student hears her words in a whole new way. Still, don't expect miracles. As the reader, you can expect to hear a few redundancies that the student misses entirely. Be patient. If she misses something, reread *just* the key passage aloud, giving the writer a chance to hear it again. Few writers, including professionals, manage to do away with all excess baggage on the first pass. If the writer uncovers even one redundancy, that's a victory! With practice and coaching, she will eventually uncover them all.

Did you see anything that could be cut from this paragraph? The fourth sentence. Why? Because Scott basically says the same thing in the quote that follows it. This fourth sentence, by the way, also gives away the punch line before I get to it. I solved both problems by axing the sentence so that the paragraph reads:

> *Hares can be mismatched in two ways. They can be white sitting on a brown background or they can be brown sitting on a white background. Is one mismatch more dangerous than the other?* ~~Scott's team lumped the two kinds of mismatches together for their study so they can't come up with a definite scientific answer.~~ *"We study brown on white, and white on brown," Scott says. "We call white on brown 'positive mismatch' and brown on white 'negative mismatch,' but it's hard to separate those things statistically. But just spending time out in the woods, we feel like white on brown is much more noticeable (28)."*

See how much cleaner—and simpler—the paragraph becomes? Vicki pointed out that cutting the first part of Scott's quote, "We study brown on white, and white on brown," would make the paragraph even *easier* to understand, and she may be right. However, my instincts told me to leave it in—a decision that may incite generations of future readers to curse my name and spit on my tombstone!

Learning to make these kinds of revisions takes experience and practice, and even so, it took me several attempts to revise the paragraphs above. The vital first step is to help students recognize superfluous and redundant information in their own work—and try to do something about it.

Something to try
Cutting Redundant Lines

Have a look at this fifth-grade student's paragraph on zoos. Share it aloud, asking students to look and listen for repeated ideas or unnecessary information. Give them a few minutes to talk with partners about what they would cut. Then have students work within writing groups to see which group can come up with the shortest revision. Have them compare the final length to the writer's original 132 words.

> Eliminate Zoos Now!
>
> Zoos are really fun for people. But how do the animals feel? They are in an enclosed space while people are banging on the glass or taking pictures. Some animals start going crazy, which they call zoochosis. Also, they have to put up with people taking pictures and banging on glass. Some feel so stressed they pace or bang their heads on walls. If you were taken away from your home would you be happy? You'd have to live in an enclosed space and eat whatever they feed you. Also, little kids like to bang on the windows and this drives the animals crazy. People love to get out their cameras and click away. The noise and constant flashes make the animals crazy. In conclusion, we should eliminate zoos. (132 words, including the title)

Just how long is the shortest revision your students came up with? Did most groups cut whole sentences? Did any group begin the essay differently? Did any group change the order of sentences?

When you finish discussing the zoo paragraph, have students look for one paragraph in their own writing that contains redundant or unneeded information. Ask them to revise, and discuss the impact of making writing more concise. Is it stronger? Why?

9 Eliminate Word and Phrase Repeats

Repeated words and phrases happen at both the paragraph and sentence levels, and are a pervasive issue in early drafts. Unlike the redundant and unnecessary information we tackled in the last chapter, repeats are more of a technical problem—and as a result, are easier to resolve. In fact, excising repeated words and phrases is *so* simple and makes such a positive impact on my own writing, I almost feel guilty about correcting it!

Phrase and word repeats generally fall into four categories:

- repeated adverbs such as *really*, *very*, *just*, or *kind of*
- repeated adjectives such as *enormous*, *huge*, *scary*, or *awful*
- repeated transitions such as *however*, *though*, *in fact*, or *but*
- forms of repeated nouns or verbs that have been used immediately beforehand.

The first three categories are easy to locate. Just remind your students to check their work for them. The last category requires a sharper eye. Here's an example from a draft of my memoir, *Snakes, Alligators, and Broken Hearts* (2015b):

> Ancient cypress trees draped with Spanish moss still towered from the shorelines. I could hear the roar of a bull alligator from across the water. Most important, the tower lurked, every bit as tall and rusting and ominous as before.

Did you spot the repeat?

Towered and *tower*.

Because one is a verb and the other a noun, I overlooked this repeat numerous times. In fact, I probably subconsciously used the verb *towered* because I was actually writing about a tower! This kind of thing often happens in writing and is an interesting—and amusing—window into how our brains work.

Here is a trickier example from a seventh-grade student essay:

> A good novel has believable characters. Stacy, from *Roll of Thunder, Hear My Cry*, demonstrates this well. There are many characters like this in the book, but Stacy is the most believable character. He is believable because he is forgiving, protective, and quiet.

In this case, the repeats of the words *believable* and *characters* sprouted from the wording of the teacher's original assignment. However, that doesn't make them any less tiresome. Our goal? To reduce the use of each word to a single instance. As a first stab, we can simply cut the third use of *character* and replace "He is believable" with "He rings true." That gets us to the following:

> A good novel has believable characters. Stacy, from *Roll of Thunder, Hear My Cry*, demonstrates this well. There are many characters like this in the book, but Stacy is the most believable ~~character. He is believable~~ rings true because he is forgiving, protective, and quiet.

We're halfway there, but to complete the job we need to go beyond simple deletions and replacements. We need to restructure that third sentence, the one with the passive phrase, "There are many characters like this in the book." We can do this in several ways. The simplest is to turn that phrase into a dependent clause. When we do this, we end up with:

> A good novel has believable characters. Stacy, from *Roll of Thunder, Hear My Cry*, demonstrates this well. ~~There are many characters like this in the book, but Stacy is the most believable.~~ <u>Of all the people in the book, Stacy is the most authentic.</u> He rings true because he is forgiving, protective, and quiet.

As is so often the case in paragraph revision, when we fix one problem, we also fix others. Here, we not only eliminated the repeats, but we improved the overall voice of the piece by axing two weak *to be* verbs—an *is* and an *are*.

Cool, huh?

A Writing Secret to Share with Students

In revising the passage from the essay on *Roll of Thunder, Hear My Cry* (Taylor 1976), Sneed makes a critical change to the third sentence: he gets rid of the words *There are*. The expressions *There is* and *There are* could well win the medal for Weakest Sentence Openers on the Planet. Why? They push the subject clear to the end of the sentence, causing impatient readers to think, "Get to the point!" Let's say I want to write about my love of travel. I could write, "There are many terrific things about travel!" Or I could be direct: "Travel rocks!" Hear the difference? Avoid *There is* and *There are* sentence openers any time you want to sound sure of yourself.

Something to try
Revising to Eliminate Repetition

The following short passage comes from a fifth-grader's passionate essay on treating immigrants fairly. Read it aloud using a document projector so that students can follow along. When you finish, have them count the repetitions they spot:

> You and 20 other sweaty workers are crammed into the back of a restaurant kitchen trying to make dishes as fast as you can. You came into this country for the American Dream and you finally think that you accomplished your goal, but is this the life you dreamed of in your childhood? Everyone wants to have the life of their dreams. It may not turn out to be what you dreamed, but your real life should be close to the dream, right? Instead of living your dream, you live in a room that is 5 feet by 9 feet and you have no money left over to help your family back home.

Eliminating repetitions will make this already strong essay even more powerful, but here's the trick: While spotting repetition is easy, it's challenging to come up with other ways to talk about living or fulfilling one's dream. As a class, brainstorm alternatives and reread parts of the passage aloud so students can hear how much stronger an argument becomes when a writer refuses to fall back on repetition.

Following this warm-up, have students read through their own drafts aloud, searching out repeated words, forms of words, or phrases. Remind them to also listen for repeated use of

- *adverbs such as* very *or* really
- *adjectives like* good, huge, special, *or* awful
- *transitions such as* so, then, in fact, *or* next.

Listening for repetition makes an outstanding writing group activity because most writers, as Sneed and I have discovered, have a far easier time hearing repeats in the work of others!

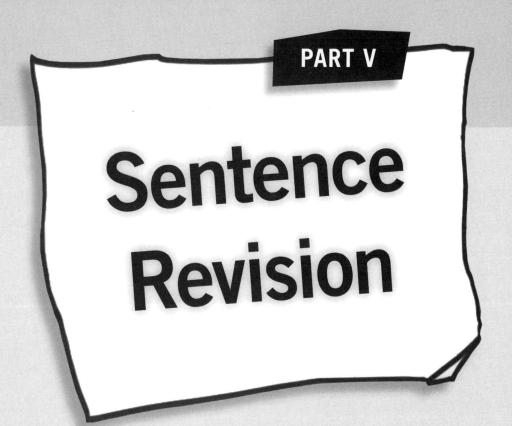

PART V

Sentence Revision

Okay, I lied. In the introduction to Part IV: Paragraph Revision, I indicated that paragraphs are my favorite writing chunks to revise. Now I have to come clean and admit that I enjoy working on sentences just as much. Sentence work differs from paragraph revision in important ways, however. When you work on a paragraph, you are still considering a bigger organizing unit and must constantly evaluate the relationships of individual elements to the scene or manuscript as a whole. That's only partly true for sentences, which often can be treated independently, without regard to what surrounds them.

Pretend that a complete manuscript is a '69 Camaro with a big block engine (sorry, I'm a guy—I can't help myself). In this metaphor, a scene might be a major system such as an engine, and a paragraph might be a major assembly within the engine such as a piston. A *sentence*, in this testosterone-filled scenario, would be a part of the piston assembly such as a piston ring or connecting rod. You can pick up the piston ring or connecting rod, examine it from different angles, and see if it's well made. It doesn't really make sense or do work all by itself, but that's okay. It can still be refined and perfected.

Sentences are the same way. By themselves, they usually have minimum utility—but just try driving anywhere without them! What's more, a well-crafted sentence is a thing of beauty, like a finely polished piston head that has been cast and milled to the tightest specs. Creating that finely polished piston head not only takes an artistic sense, it demands specific skills that must be learned and cultivated.

Sentences also offer an undeniable bonus for teachers: they are fun and fast to work with! Because sentences are short, discrete units that won't by themselves make or break a draft, students find them less overwhelming to revise than longer chunks of text. Like paragraphs—and unlike a '69 Camaro—sentences are also easy to tear down and rebuild. That can make sentence revision a favorite classroom activity.

Trim the Fat

1

> Vigorous writing is concise. A sentence should contain no unnecessary words, a paragraph no unnecessary sentences, for the same reason that a drawing should have no unnecessary lines and a machine no unnecessary parts.
>
> —**William Strunk Jr. and E. B. White**, *The Elements of Style* (2000, 23)

If you've been reading this book straight through, you already know that I love cutting almost as much as I love chocolate chip cookies. We talked about large-scale cuts in Big-Picture Revision and Scene Revision, but chopping down sentences can be a real executioner's delight! Cuts to sentences generally involve one of four strategies:

- eliminating unnecessary information
- tightening phrases
- distilling explanatory phrases
- combining sentences.

Let's look at some examples.

Eliminating Unnecessary Information

The search for needless information yields almost endless treasure troves of word-cut booty. Read the following sentence I wrote in a "factional" autobiography of a great white shark:

> *After leaving the Farallones, me and the Boys again cruised south along the California coast for a month or two.*

Do you see any obvious candidates for cutting? When rereading this sentence, the phrase "a month or two" struck me as superfluous, especially since I was telling the story as a sequence of events that would unfold naturally. Cutting that phrase produced a much tighter sentence and saved words:

> *After leaving the Farallones, me and the Boys again cruised south along the California coast ~~for a month or two~~.*

Depending on how much information I want in the sentence, I also could axe "along the California coast." Either way, we're left with a crisper, sharper result.

Tightening Phrases

Almost all sentence first drafts contain phrases that can be tightened. The following sentence is from the same shark story:

> *Unfortunately, just as he was about to hit it, the people on the boat hauled the cage back up to the surface.*

Here, "it" refers to a shark cage, which you would know by reading previous sentences. With that in mind, do you see anything you'd like to tighten? I sure did. Here's my revision:

> *Unfortunately, ~~just as he was about to hit it~~ right before impact, the people on the boat hauled the cage back ~~up~~ to the surface.*

I especially like this example not only because *right before impact* eliminates five very dull words—it makes the sentence punchier and more consistent with the tone of the action. Note that the deletion of the word *up* makes the sentence even tighter.

Condensing and Moving Phrases

Often, a phrase or even an entire sentence can be condensed to a word or two and relocated for a cleaner result. See what you can do with this example:

> *He tried to carry the bag, which was big and heavy.*

A simple revision yields:

> *He tried to carry the big, heavy bag.*

Specifically, what we've done here is eliminate a dependent clause and relocate the information—as two adjectives—to immediately before the object.

Try another example:

She had difficulty revising the sentence because it was complicated.

Here, two easy modifications yield this version:

She struggled to revise the complicated sentence.

As in the previous example, we first cleaned up the sentence by killing off the dependent clause, but we also made the sentence more active—and less cumbersome—by changing the phrase "had difficulty revising" to "struggled to revise."

Combining Sentences

In my workshops for young writers, I often ask students to revise an entire short story or essay. After they dive in, I provide an important hint: instead of always considering each sentence individually, read several at a time to unearth precious cutting opportunities. Ask your students what they would do with the following introduction to the Galápagos Islands (I've put each sentence on its own line to make it easier to view and consider):

There are twenty islands in the Galápagos.
These islands are volcanic.
The volcanoes started on the sea floor.
The youngest island is only .7 million years old.
The oldest is South Plaza Island.
It is about 4.2 million years old.

After a few tries, students discover that they can combine sentences to cut length and make the writing a whole lot snappier. The ultimate result may look something like this:

The twenty Galápagos Islands began as volcanoes on the sea floor.
The youngest broke the ocean surface .7 million years ago.
The oldest, South Plaza Island, dates back 4.2 million years.

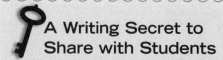

A Writing Secret to Share with Students

Even an ace word-slasher like Sneed usually needs more than one run through a passage to trim it effectively. To make your writing lean, take a first run, pencil in hand, cutting what you don't need. Then go through that same passage again, reading aloud this time, and listening for additional words or phrases you can cut. You'll get far better results with this two-times-through approach!

Combining sentences to cut words may at first sound counterintuitive, but as you can see, doing so here allows us to deftly eliminate extra words—and three of six sentences. It also makes this nonfiction story flow much more smoothly. That, in fact, is a benefit with all of the previous strategies. In the process of trimming words, they help writers dramatically improve the readability of sentences—part of what makes this kind of work so rewarding.

A NOTE TO THE TEACHER

Take One Approach at a Time

In this chapter, Sneed shares four strategies for trimming wordy sentences:

- *cutting unnecessary words*
- *tightening phrases*
- *moving phrases*
- *combining sentences.*

Invent examples—or borrow some from your own writing—to model each of these strategies for students. Your modeling will be even more effective if you do three things.

First, make the problems in your model sentences obvious so that even struggling writers have a good chance at achieving success. Sneed uses a scalpel to remove words many a writer would leave behind, but you don't have to be that subtle in showing students how to revise for wordiness. Try an example like this one: "Since it looked like it might rain, we took our umbrellas in case it rained." Most of your writers will readily spot the repetition in that sentence.

Second, remind students that they may need more than one try to achieve the result they want:

- ~~Since it looked like it might rain,~~ *We took our umbrellas in case it rained*.
- *We took our umbrellas.* (Unless the umbrellas are being used to smuggle secret documents, their purpose is obvious.)

Third, have students revise on their own. *Then* have them coach you. If you jump into modeling before they try revising on their own, many students will sit back and observe while you and a few eager revisers do all the work. The goal is to get everyone participating.

Revising a Wordy Passage

Sneed suggests eliminating words we don't need, tightening phrases, and sometimes combining sentences to make writing more concise. Ask students to use everything they know about paring down sentences to revise this passage from Sneed's book *The Prairie Builders* (2005c). (He didn't write it this way originally. I fattened it up for this exercise while he was off somewhere obsessing over revision.)

> *In 1997, the very first bison calf was born on the refuge. During the period of the next five years or so, more than two dozen additional baby bison were born, and a number of elk calves were born during this time as well. By the time 2001 rolled around, a total of seventy-four bison lived at the refuge—and as it turned out, that was way too many for the enclosure they lived in. Refuge managers came up with what they thought was a pretty good idea. They reduced the herd by donating extra bison to Native American tribes so that the people in those tribes could start their own herds. Even to this very day, managers continue to keep the refuge herd at a reasonable size so that the prairie meadows can support it.*

The "fattened" passage above is 136 words, but Sneed's final version from *The Prairie Builders* is a lean 85 words:

> *In 1997, the first bison calf was born on the refuge. During the next five years, more than two dozen additional baby bison were born, along with a number of elk calves. By 2001, seventy-four bison lived at the refuge—too many for the enclosure they lived in. Refuge managers reduced the herd by donating extra bison to Native American tribes so they could start their own herds. Today, managers continue to keep the refuge herd at a size that the prairie meadows can support (37).*

For comparison, ask students to count the number of words in their revision. Was their count closer to my fat 136-word version or to Sneed's lean final? As a follow-up, have students do a word count on one of their own current drafts, then revise to tighten sentences, and recount the number of words for comparison. Discuss your results as a class and ask your champion cutters to share the secrets of their success.

2

Eliminate Passive Voice

In crafting sentences, most skilled writers strive to write in *active voice*. That is, we try to write sentences in which the main subject performs the action. Here are some examples:

> *The boy tossed the ball.*
> *Rudy finished the test.*

Both sentences are straightforward and easy to understand. *A* does—or acts upon—*B*, right?

The term *passive voice*, on the other hand, refers to a specific sentence construction in which the object of the action becomes the subject of the sentence. Here are passive voice versions of the above sentences:

> *The ball is tossed by the boy.*
> *The test was finished by Rudy.*

In these sentences, the *real objects*—the ball and the test—pose as the subjects by appearing first. Meanwhile, the *real subjects*—the boy and Rudy—are exiled to the far reaches of the Sentence Galaxy in the object positions. The result? Anemic, awkward sentences.

Scientific and academic writing traditions have especially emphasized passive voice over the centuries. Recently, many academics have begun to shed this stilted style, but I still encounter passive voice almost everywhere, including in student work.

The good news is that even beginning writers can easily transform passive voice to active. How?

A NOTE TO THE TEACHER

The Key to Understanding Active Voice

Even after careful explanation, the difference between active and passive voice remains mysterious to many students. The secret to unlocking this door lies in identifying sentence subjects. Without this critical information, it is impossible to tell passive from active because the difference, contrary to what many readers think, has nothing to do with how powerful or weak the verb itself is. It has to do with whether the subject *does* the action—or is *acted upon*. It's the difference between "Bob watched the TV" and "The TV was watched by Bob." In the first example, *Bob* is the subject. In the second, the subject is *The TV*. Take some extra time to ensure that students can identify sentence subjects, using sentences from your own or any writing as models. This will make your discussion of active and passive voice simpler and more productive.

First, underline the verb to identify what needs changing. Then, figure out the real sentence subject; i.e. the person, place, or thing that truly performs the action. Flip or recast subject and object to create a stronger, more direct sentence.

For fun, try this "outpatient procedure" on the following sentence:

The trip was planned by Helen.

What's the verb here? *Was planned.* Is it active or passive? Passive. How do we make it active? Start by asking, "Who is performing the action of planning the trip?" Answer: *Helen.* To write an active sentence, therefore, we need to make Helen, the person doing the work, our subject by placing her at the beginning of the sentence. Once we do that, the entire sentence turns active almost automatically:

Helen planned the trip.

When eliminating passive voice, don't let an introductory clause or phrase throw you. Check out this example:

Throughout the tropics, diseases are being spread by mosquitoes.

Right now, the subject is *diseases*—but what should it be? *Mosquitoes.* In revising, you can leave the introductory clause as is to yield:

Throughout the tropics, mosquitoes spread diseases.

You'll note that a significant bonus of this revision is that the weak verb phrase *are being spread* becomes the much stronger verb *spread.* We'll talk more about replacing weak verbs under "Word Revision."

Here's one final example for you to present to your class:

I was chased for miles by a vicious dog.

What did your students come up with?

Be sure to explain to your young writers that not all sentences have to be active. Sometimes we don't know who did the action: "Thousands of dollars were stolen." There's little point in making this sentence active if we can't identify the thief. We'd

> ## 🔑 A Writing Secret to Share with Students
>
> Remember, you don't need to revise every passive sentence. Some work beautifully. Here's an example from Sneed's book *Fire Birds* (2015a): "Northern flickers can often be spotted in urban areas, feeding on ants and other insects" (41). The phrase "can often be spotted" is passive, but there's little point changing it because we don't know who is doing the spotting, and it doesn't matter. Use passive voice when the thing being acted upon—in this case, the flickers—is more important than the thing or person performing the action.

only wind up with something like "Someone stole thousands of dollars." In other cases, it really doesn't matter who did the action: "The actor was arrested for hurling a prop at the director." Did Sergeant X or Officer Y make the arrest? No one cares! In general, however, the more a writer can replace passive voice with active voice, the more exciting and visual her writing will become.

! Something to try
Turning Passive into Active

The following four sentences are expiring under the weight of passive voice. Have students come to the rescue by turning these sentences from passive to active. Point out that this revision calls for changing the sentence subject—and that requires figuring out who is really performing the action. Students can rearrange words, but should not add details or alter the meaning. Tip: Many students find it helpful to first *identify* the subjects and verbs. You may wish to do this sentence by sentence as a class before students revise.

1. The kite was flown as high as possible by a small boy on the beach.

2. An enormous ice cream sundae was consumed by the woman in three bites.

3. Before heading into the sleet, a snug scarf was wrapped around her neck by Edna.

4. Just at sunrise, a breaching whale was spotted in the bay by two tourists.

Once students finish this activity, have them look through their own writing for examples of passive voice. For each one they find, have them underline the verb, then decide whether the sentence should be revised to give it a new subject—and active voice. Ask volunteers to share their revision examples.

Show, Don't Tell

3

Compare the following two sentences:

> *Construction of the wildlife refuge began in spring, 1992 near Prairie City, Iowa.*

> *In the spring of 1992, architects, engineers, and construction workers swarmed over corn and soybean fields near the small town of Prairie City, Iowa.*

Are these sentences showing or telling? You and I know the answer: the first sentence is an example of telling while the second one demonstrates showing. Until you pose the question, however, most of your students will never think about this difference. A few may intuitively write with rich imagery that shows instead of tells—especially if they are writing about vampires—but most beginning writers need to be taught the "show, don't tell" concept.

So what does it mean to show instead of tell? If you've discussed it at all with them, your students will come up with a variety of answers, including:

- using more descriptive phrases
- choosing better words
- making it more exciting
- using metaphors and similes.

All of these answers are correct—partly. The essence of show-don't-tell, however, boils down to *placing a picture of events in the reader's mind without ever telling him explicitly what is occurring.* Yes, this can involve better descriptions or metaphors and similes, but it doesn't have to. The key is to make the picture of events accurate enough that a reader can quickly draw her own conclusions about what's going on. One young writer I recently worked with described it as "watching a movie of what is happening."

In our opening example, drawn from my book *The Prairie Builders: Reconstructing America's Lost Grasslands* (2005c, 17), the second sentence plays a movie reel in our heads. We can actually watch different types of workers scurrying like ants across richly plowed farm fields. In the first version, we are given only the basic facts. From our own experiences we *may* assemble a vague picture of events from the phrase "Construction of the wildlife refuge began," but in this version, I'm taking a shortcut by dropping readers straight to the bottom line. If there's a movie at all, it's one we might walk out of!

To better understand "show, don't tell," I usually give students this simple sentence:

> *The boy is sad.*

Is this showing or telling? Telling, of course. The author again takes a shortcut, giving us the summary instead of letting us watch it for ourselves.

Sad??!! Where's the evidence?

But what *makes* this telling instead of showing? The weak verb *is* presents a big part of the problem here. We'll talk more about this later, but getting rid of weak verbs often proves a key to transforming "telling" sentences into "showing." A second problem is the word *sad* which, *ahem*, sadly skips to the bottom line instead of placing a rich image in readers' minds.

Armed with these two insights, I ask students to come up with an alternative that shows instead of tells. A typical sequence of suggestions often looks something like:

> *The boy seems sad.*
> *The sad boy got very upset.*
> *The boy looked sadly.*
> *The boy was crying sadly.*
> *The boy had tear drops on his face because he was so sad.*

You can see that some of these suggestions offer traces of a solution, but once again, it's important to let students struggle with the process. After each suggestion, I ask, "Is this telling or showing?" After a few tries, most of them begin to get it. They circle closer and closer until one offers something such as:

> *Tears rolled down the boy's face.*

I seize on this breakthrough sentence, writing it on the board, and ask, "In this revision, do we ever *say* that the boy is sad? Then, how do you know that he is?" Students happily tell me. With your own students, hammer home the point that simply using strong, active verbs often helps facilitate showing. Also emphasize that they don't have to bury their sentence with details to show instead of tell. Writing:

> *The boy walked around very upset with tears coming from his eyes because his favorite llama just died during the Great Depression.*

does *not* make this sentence better. Simply sticking to the essence of the matter and projecting one powerful image into the readers' minds generates the best results.

Confession: I almost always take one separate pass through my own manuscripts specifically seeking opportunities for showing. That's because I often fail to do it in my early drafts. In *Snakes, Alligators, and Broken Hearts* (2015b), I related my excitement at having Bobby Kennedy running for president in 1968. In my first version, I wrote:

> I still clearly remembered the tragic assassination of his brother, President John F. Kennedy, five years earlier. The national trauma of that event imprinted itself deeply on me, along with the sense that something very special had been lost.

These aren't terrible sentences, but I realized that they *told* instead of *showed*—and missed an opportunity for powerful imagery. I rewrote the sentences to read:

> The image of horses pulling his brother's flag-draped coffin up Pennsylvania Avenue five years earlier remained fresh in my brain, along with the sense that something very special had been lost (50).

In the revision, I never say that I remembered Kennedy's funeral, but readers know it just the same. More important, readers can now watch a "movie" in their heads instead of pondering a dry account of events. What are they watching? The horses and the flag-draped coffin. Learning to "show" takes practice, but writers who master it wield a powerful tool that vastly improves their writing.

! Something to try
Act It Out

In this chapter, Sneed describes showing as "playing a movie reel." So . . . why not hold some "auditions"? Have six or more students each choose an adjective to act out: e.g., *thoughtful, joyful, nervous, menacing, suspicious, angry, confident*—or anything of their choice. Print a few options on cards ahead of time for students who can't immediately come up with something. "Actors" must not reveal their adjectives to the rest of the class, nor should they speak during their one- or two-minute audition. When they finish, discuss their expressions, movements, and body language. Could students determine what each actor was trying to portray? Which "showing" clues proved most helpful? How might students apply what they learned to their writing?

Something to try
Distinguishing Showing from Telling

Following is a brief passage from Sneed's book *Science Warriors* (2008b). Share it aloud with students and discuss their response. What mood does this passage create? What contributes to that mood? Is this more of a telling or showing passage, and why?

> *Under the watchful eye of her handler, one terrier walks toward a large military truck. The dog's sensitive nose filters the air for the tiniest odors. Suddenly, the hair on her neck stiffens and she sits down.*
>
> *The agent steps forward, his heart racing. "Find it," he tells the terrier. Sniffing vigorously, the dog makes her way toward the front of the truck and holds her paw out toward the engine compartment (3).*

After discussing the preceding passage, let students know it is from "Chapter One: Enemy at the Gates," and is about the capture of a brown tree snake, one of Guam's most treacherous invaders. The episode closes with these lines:

> *Working quickly, the agent unwraps the struggling serpent from the brake cylinder. After placing the hissing reptile into a bag, the agent's heartbeat begins to return to normal and relief washes through him (3).*

What verbal clues does Sneed incorporate into this conclusion, and what do they show about the snake? About the agent? By the way, that closing passage contains one "telling" moment. Can your students find it? Can they revise to create a "showing" moment?

One of the most common sentence revisions I make is moving a phrase from the end of a sentence to the beginning. In "Eliminate Passive Voice," we saw how flipping sentences around can help transform a passive voice sentence to an active one, but there are other reasons for this type of revision. At the end of a sentence, a phrase often sounds weak, confusing, or out of place. Switched to the beginning, that same phrase might help draw in the reader, establish a time sequence, and set up a main idea. More important, it won't detract from the main point of the sentence.

Below is a sentence from an early draft of *Snakes, Alligators, and Broken Hearts* (2015b). Look carefully at the phrases I underlined, and read the entire sentence aloud. Ask yourself where you would place the underlined phrases. (This is another good exercise to do with your students!)

> *By coincidence, my mother decided to take me and Spencer to the island of Nantucket <u>a few days later</u>.*

What did you decide? When I first read this sentence, it sounded okay, but not great. After playing around with it, I decided to swap the order to read:

> *<u>A few days later</u>, by coincidence, my mother decided to take me and Spencer to the island of Nantucket.*

What prompted these changes? A couple of things. Moving "a few days later" to the front sets up a logical time sequence in the reader's mind. More important, if you boil this sentence down to its essence, or key point, you end up with one word: "Nantucket." Going

A Writing Secret to Share with Students

Does every single sentence need to end with a *kapow*? Probably not. But if none of your sentences end with a punch line, you could be camouflaging the most important things you mean to say. Here's an easy way to check it out. As you read through one of your drafts, highlight the final four or five words of each sentence. Then, skim through the whole draft quickly and ask yourself, "Am I emphasizing my most important points?"

to Nantucket is the whole point of this sentence. The timing of the trip holds much less importance. And here's the thing—you want the most important part of your sentence at the end. Why? It's like the punch line of a joke. If you told the punch line first, no one would laugh—and no one would want to hear the rest of the joke. In writing, always lead up to what matters most.

! Something to try
Relocating Trailing Phrases

The idea of completely flipping a sentence around or relocating a "trailing phrase" can sound confusing, so you may need to model this for a student or small group. Pull a sentence from your own writing or try revising one or more of the examples below. First, ask students as a class to identify the trailing phrase—or phrases—in each sentence. Second, have them revise the sentences on their own. And finally, ask them to coach you sentence by sentence while the whole class watches you revise:

- *The disgruntled golfer hurled his golf club across the fairway with some angry words.*

- *The student finally turned in her manuscript following several weeks of heavy revision last Tuesday.*

- *The heart rests between beats so it is actually still for nearly twenty years over the course of a normal lifetime.*

- *The cat pounced on the mouse as it tried to run away with blinding speed.*

Notice that there may be more than one viable revision for a given sentence. Take the cat and mouse sentence. A revision might look like one of these:

With blinding speed, the cat pounced on the fleeing mouse.

As the mouse tried to escape, the cat pounced with blinding speed.

If you think the mouse was the speeding bullet, you might change the wording and write something like, "The fleeing mouse was a blur—but no match for the cat." After warming up on these examples, have students scan their own drafts for trailing phrases that could be relocated. Even if they don't find any, the search will help them realize how word order affects sentence power and logic.

Consider these three variations on a sentence:

The dog walked around with a painful-looking limp.

The dog walked around with a limp that looked very painful.

Having a limp that looked painful, the dog walked around.

Which sentence do you prefer? I'm guessing that 99 percent of us prefer the first version. If you distill this sentence to its essence, it's *the limp* that matters most, not the pain or the walking around. So that limp is the punch line—the part you want at the end of the sentence. Similar examples—and Vicki's tips—will help students learn to recognize this useful strategy for improving their own work.

Use "Real Language"— Even If It's Wrong

Anyone who cares deeply about the proper use of the English language probably ought to move to her own island, unplug the television, cancel her cell phone service, and stick to reading properly vetted books from the nineteenth century. We all know why. It's because English is not merely being abused; it is being massacred as never before.

In an age when even highly educated people say things like, "He gave the money to him and I," who would blame anyone for sinking into a pit of literary despair? & DEGT abt txting & emails!

(Okay, I made up DEGT—Don't Even Go There.)

For a writer, the bastardization of our language presents a dilemma: stick to the *Chicago Manual of Style* and sound like a nut, or write like people actually speak. Now, I don't claim to have the goodest understanding of English grammar, but I have always done my best to write correctly. In the past few years, however, my attitudes have loosened. This stems from a recognition that the English language has *always* changed, and changed rapidly.

Consider the Norman conquest of England in 1066. BAM! Overnight, these Vikings-*cum*-Frenchmen introduced *ten thousand words* to the English language! What's more, the Normans did us a favor. One of the real beauties of our language is how it has evolved and adapted to changing times and technologies.

That said, I believe in knowing the rules before breaking them, and fully support your efforts to make sure students know their grammar. As you do your best with that, however, it's important to recognize

A Writing Secret to Share with Students

How many words are in the English language? Estimates range from half a million to well over a million. No one can say for sure. Why? Well, for one thing, some words are ambiguous. For instance, is *cut* really two words since it can be a verb or noun? Is *hotdog* a word—or just a combination of two other words? Furthermore, it isn't as if English is holding still while we do the tally. It changes daily—hourly—with additions from diverse cultures and our ongoing need to label new inventions and our ways of interacting with them. *The Oxford English Dictionary*—perhaps the most comprehensive listing of English words— is updated quarterly and claims to add about 500 words per update. Recent additions include *waybread, hot mess, blazar, phablet,* and *Bank of Mom and Dad.* Check out *www.oed.com* to find other new words, learn their origins, and even hear pronunciations.

Just how much *does* grammar change as we write for different audiences? Here's a fun way to find out. Have students draw numbers—1 or 2—from a hat without showing them to anyone. Then ask everyone to write a short review of any film, TV show, or book they have enjoyed. Reviews should run no more than four or five sentences. Here's the trick:

- *Students who draw a 1 should write something that will be read only by adults.*

- *Students who draw a 2 should write something that will only be read by friends their own age.*

When they finish, collect the papers and read a few aloud—anonymously. Ask students to identify the likely audience and discuss what they base that decision on. Is it grammar, tone, or other factors? In general, how different are the pieces for the two audiences? Do some writers tend toward the formal—or informal—no matter *who* the audience is? If you made a continuum for your class from least to most formal writing style, where would your students place themselves?

that professional writers usually go with what sounds better, even if it gives grammar a black eye. Perhaps the most common case of this occurs in an exchange such as:

"Who wants an ice cream?"

"Me!"

As most of us know, the answer should be *I*, not *me*. Unfortunately, answering *I* sounds extremely odd—to the point that even I usually answer *me*. Please forgive I.

Here's another example from my memoir:

> *Bill said nothing, but the furrowed look on his face made me think that this was one man from whom I wouldn't dare steal a catfish.*

In this example, I obviously tried to go with what was correct, but guess what? It sounded stilted, especially from the viewpoint of a thirteen-year-old boy. Reluctantly, I changed the passage to:

> *Bill said nothing, but the furrowed look on his face made me think that this was one man I wouldn't dare steal a catfish from. (2016b, 132)*

I have come to view these kinds of corruptions not as the end of the world, but as part of the inevitable progression of the language. And OMG, it ain't gonna stop. Under the onslaught of smartphones and similar devices, it will be a miracle if, fifty years from now, 10 percent of the population can write a complete sentence. Don't let it keep you up at night. All you can do is make sure your students know how to construct grammatically correct sentences and, with the help of Vicki's suggestions, explore when it might be better to break the rules.

Something to try

Correcting Errors

One way to help students recognize errors in grammar and usage is by sharing real-world examples. The following sixteen sentences all come from comments shared in newspapers and on television by professional writers or journalists. How many errors can your students spot and correct? After revising, talk about when it's important to be *absolutely* grammatically correct—and when some informalities could be allowed. Does it depend on what you're writing and who will read it?

1. Me and him will appear on stage together.

2. The use of cameras in the theater are forbidden.

3. The high school team was successfuller this year than last year.

4. The outcome of events in Egypt, which will affect numerous people, are hard to predict.

5. We need to eat good to stay healthy.

6. No one wants this more than me.

7. Him and others in Congress are still in disagreement.

8. We are seeing less shoppers at the mall this week.

9. Being really salty, I couldn't eat the soup they served at the dinner.

10. This is just between you and I.

11. I had to move so you could see the stage.

12. Everybody had their tickets by then.

13. I want to vote for whomever seems most qualified.

14. This is an important issue, irregardless of who wins.

15. He and myself could not agree about the best show on TV.

16. Hopefully, we will know the outcome soon.

Don't stop here! Continue, with your students, to collect errors you see or hear and to discuss which might be "allowable" in some contexts. Try to hunt up at least three or four per week.

Correct versions appear on the following pages.

Corrected Sentences

Following are the sixteen sentences from "Something to Try," each revised for grammar and usage. Would the original versions be acceptable in everyday conversation? How about in written dialogue? A report? A speech given at a conference? A TV newscast?

1. <u>He and I</u> will appear on stage together. Neither *him* nor *me* can be a sentence subject.

2. The use of cameras in the theater is forbidden. The subject is *use*, not *cameras*.

3. The high school team was <u>more successful</u> last night. *Successfuller* is not a standard English word.

4. The outcome of events in Egypt, which will affect numerous people, <u>is</u> hard to predict. The subject is *outcome*, not *people*.

5. We need to eat <u>well</u> to stay healthy. *Good* is an adjective or noun, never an adverb. Therefore, it cannot modify a verb like *eat*. Hey, I see a hand going up out there . . . In the sentence "That cake looks good," the word *looks* is a linking verb, linking the noun *cake* to the adjective *good*. Isn't it fun to know that?

6. No one wants this more than <u>I</u>. Meaning "more than I want it."

7. <u>He</u> and others in Congress are still in disagreement. *Him* can never be a sentence subject.

8. We are seeing <u>fewer</u> shoppers at the mall this week. *Less* modifies things in bulk or mass—*less flour, less wind, less humor. Fewer* modifies things that can be counted—*fewer cookies, fewer storms, fewer jokes.*

9. <u>Because it was so salty</u>, I couldn't eat the soup they served at the dinner. It's the soup that's salty, not the writer—though with some writers, it's debatable.

10. This is just between <u>you and me</u>. *Me* and *I* are both pronouns, but *I* works as a subject while *me* works as an object—as in this sentence. "Between you and I" is just as wrong as "Me can keep a secret." Even "*I* can keep a secret" isn't always correct. As when Sneed writes it, for example.

11. I had to move so I could see the stage. If you start with first-person *I*, stick with it. *I* and *you* refer to two different people, so the original sentence makes no sense. This could be revised to read, "You had to move so you could see the stage." But that's probably not what the writer means.

12. Everybody had his or her tickets by then. *Everybody* is singular, so it calls for singular possessive pronouns *his* and *her*. This is one of those cases Sneed talks about, though, where the "correct" version sounds a bit stilted. Most people these days go with "Everybody had their tickets," even if it is incorrect. Don't do this in a formal report or on a writing test—but when you're attending a movie with friends, it's up to you!

13. I want to vote for whoever seems most qualified. It's surprising how many people think *whom* or *whomever* is always right. They just sound more grammatically impressive, right? Not necessarily. Here's a little trick: Use *who* when you would use *he*, as in "Who is at the door?" Use *whom* when you would use *him*, as in "Whom did you hire?" You wouldn't say, "Him seems most qualified." You'd say, "He seems most qualified." So *whoever* is correct.

14. This is an important issue, regardless of who wins. At last—an easy one! *Irregardless* is not a word, so you can just run that one through the shredder. The word *regardless* says it all.

15. He and I could not agree on the best TV show. *Myself* is a reflexive pronoun that can be used in several ways—but never as the subject of a sentence. Here are some correct uses: "I myself detest Brussels sprouts." "I took a good look at myself." "I treated myself to more popcorn."

16. We hope we will know the outcome soon. Sticklers cringe at the use of *hopefully* to mean "I hope" or "It is hoped." However, this usage is now so popular that no doubt the word *hopefully* will soon be as widely accepted as, say, *luckily*.

6 | Use Similes

For me, using similes is like adding patches to my son's Boy Scout uniform. With the basic uniform, yeah, people still get the point: "He's a Boy Scout." Adding the extra merit badge, rank, and event patches, however, both jazzes up the uniform and gives the observer greater insights into exactly what kind of Scout my son has become.

In writing, adding similes accomplishes the same thing. It makes a manuscript more enjoyable *and* helps impart additional insight and understanding to the reader. With these benefits, it's no wonder that writing teachers hit similes hard with their students. When I give writing workshops, I find that by the fourth or fifth grade, kids understand similes and metaphors better than almost any other writing concepts. They also have fun using them—an added bonus when working with reluctant writers!

That said, before I launched into this tip, I asked myself, "When do I actually use similes?" To find out, I read through a handful of my nonfiction books and articles. I discovered that I tend to use similes in two situations. The first is when I want to add drama to an especially exciting or fast-paced section. Consider this description of a cowboy's ride from *The World Famous Miles City Bucking Horse Sale* (2010):

> *The rider's boots fling skyward while his torso slams back hard onto the horse's rump.*

We get it, right? It's a rough ride. What's missing is a visceral *feel* of what's happening. To impart that gut "ugh" to the reader, I revised this sentence to read:

🔑 A Writing Secret to Share with Students

Similes and metaphors are much alike, but not quite the same. A *metaphor,* as we'll discuss in the next chapter, refers to one thing as if it actually *were* another. A *simile* describes one thing as being *like* something else—often using the words *like* or *as.* Here are two similes that show how comparisons can enrich our understanding of an idea. In describing Einstein's vision of space, Carolyn Cinami DeCrostofano explains that space is not rigid, but "more like a flexible mat or stretchy knit blanket" (*A Black Hole Is Not a Hole,* 2012). In *Years of Dust* (2009), author Albert Marrin wants us to feel the horror of the giant 1930s dust storms that blotted out the sun and tortured everything in their paths. "The windblown dust," he tells us, "acted as sandpaper, scraping paint off cars, shredding crops, and rubbing skin off faces." (72)

The rider's boots fling skyward while his torso
slams back <u>like a feed sack</u> onto the horse's rump.

Using "like a feed sack" makes us *feel* that dead weight of the rider's body hitting the horse, doesn't it? Astute readers will note that I easily could have used "bag of cement" here, but not only is this phrase trite, it wouldn't fit the book's image system of cowboys and rodeos. Here, "feed sack" fits perfectly.

"But whoa, pardner!" you might be saying. "What's this newfangled term *image system* you're slingin' at me?"

It's worth pulling our ponies up under the shade of a cottonwood tree to jaw on that a spell. An *image system* is basically a selection of descriptions and word choices that repeatedly reinforce the *feeling* the writer is trying to evoke in the reader. In the example above, I am obviously writing about the West. My work ends up stronger if, whenever possible, I use words and phrases that help readers *feel* that setting and theme. Similes and metaphors are powerful devices in this regard. They can go beyond just helping improve descriptions. Chosen well, they reinforce a piece's image system, creating a richer—often subconscious—reader experience.

Okay, let's mosey on.

A second place I employ similes is to help readers grasp an unfamiliar or difficult concept or situation. Not long ago, I wrote an article for *Highlights for Children* about the endangered Ethiopian Wolf. This wolf inhabits a unique environment that most readers might have a hard time imagining. To help them out, I wrote sentences such as:

Strange, tree-like plants called giant lobelias poked up like silent sentries.

Scattered around Ethiopia are a series of very high plateaus, like islands.

Here, "silent sentries" and "islands" both deliver familiar images to help readers visualize this strange, far-away habitat.

! Something to try
Refreshing Overused Similes

Many similes fall flat because we've heard them so often they've become clichés: "ran like the wind," "busy as a bee," "crazy as a loon." Have your students work in pairs to replace the following clichés with more original similes. They can use one word or a phrase:

- *Jack's room was clean <u>as a whistle</u>.*
- *Those kids fought <u>like cats and dogs</u>.*
- *The runner flew down the track <u>like lightning</u>.*
- *He was big <u>as a mountain</u>.*
- *That explanation was about as <u>clear as mud</u>.*

When students finish, have them check their own drafts for any tired similes and replace them with something more creative.

Of course, similes aren't restricted to the above two situations. Writers can use them to describe almost anything. They are powerful tools that can enliven writing, make it more fun to read and help writers "show, not tell."

Despite all of their advantages, I have yet another confession to make: just as I have to remind myself—or my wife—to add patches to my son's Scout uniform, I have to remind myself to go back through my work and look for places to use similes. Especially in first drafts, I often forget to use them. It's worth encouraging your students to make a special pass through the sentences they've written with the sole purpose of adding similes and their cousins, metaphors.

Which, like an electric rabbit at a racetrack, happens to lead us to our next chapter . . .

! Something to try
Using Similes to Create an Impression

Similes work best when the comparison creates a striking impression or helps us see something differently. If I say, "The coffee was as hot as steaming water," I'm not suggesting anything you wouldn't think of on your own. But if I say, "It was as hot as Old Faithful," that's enough to curl your tongue. In his memoir, Sneed uses a simile to help readers picture his handwriting when he was in fifth grade. See if your students can decide which of the following similes he chose. Which one helps them picture how that handwriting really looked?

"I was no slouch in other subjects, either, though I scrawled the ugliest handwriting since . . ."

   a. my friends and I first started writing in cursive.

   b. our next-door neighbor's kids scribbled words in chalk on the sidewalk.

   c. my father made out a grocery list that nobody else could read.

   d. Neanderthals had penned pictographs on cave walls thirty thousand years before.

This excerpt comes from *Snakes, Alligators, and Broken Hearts* (2015b 80), and the simile Sneed chose is, of course, d—the Neanderthal pictographs. Talk with your students about why option d is a good choice. Ask them to find one place in their own working drafts where a simile could help readers appreciate a character, setting, or concept in a new way.

Consider Metaphors—Sparingly

ike a bake show contestant making a soufflé, I almost folded the use of metaphors into the tip on similes, but I knew Vicki wouldn't let me get away with it. She's right, too. Metaphors clamor for their own attention, even though they usually play a smaller role in nonfiction than they do in poetry and literary fiction.

Poetry and literary fiction, of course, are all about metaphor. My friend, award-winning poet Rebecca Kai Dotlich, shares, "A poet spends an inordinate amount of time comparing one thing to another and imagining what else that might look like" (Dotlich, pers. comm.).

For nonfiction writers, the situation is much different. For us, metaphors are bears in the woods. We don't see them often, but when they appear, they usually make a powerful impression.

As with similes, I use metaphors sparingly, saving them for especially dramatic or humorous situations. Here's one from *Shep: Our Most Loyal Dog* (2006b) in which Shep watches the train carrying his master's body pull away from the station:

> *Then, with a loud hiss of steam and the labored panting of a thousand horses, the train slowly chugged east into the shadows cast by the afternoon sun.* (5)

Here, the metaphor of panting horses accomplishes so much. It

Metaphor National Forest.

helps create a dramatic, unforgettable scene. It gives the reader that visceral, sensory understanding of an event. It helps reinforce the western setting and image system. Most notably, it firmly establishes the narrative voice.

Yet you won't find another metaphor in the entire book. Why not? Well, there are no hard-and-fast rules here, and some types of nonfiction—adventure and outdoor writing, for instance—seem to lend themselves to metaphor more than others but personally, I find it distracting to have too many metaphors in nonfiction. I read nonfiction to discover real things and events, yet metaphors often pull readers more into a world of fantasy and imagination. For those reasons, a good approach with your students might be to encourage them to look for that *one spot* where a metaphor not only fits, but will have a significant impact on their writing.

"But how do we know where to put a metaphor?" your students will ask.

Good question. For me, a metaphor is called for *when it can express the essence or underlying emotion better than a literal description.* Is a person's gut all twisted up or is a volcano about to explode inside of her? Was the choral concert heavenly or did the voices of legion angels stun the audience? Was the astronaut really scared or did he stare into the eyes of his Maker?

When I was researching fire ants for *Science Warriors* (2008b), I came across a wonderful metaphor for the dominance of the newer multiqueen fire ant colonies that have ravaged Texas. Instead of just saying how numerous and dense the colonies were, one scientist described them as a "sheet of fire ants through the earth." I loved that—and quoted it in the book. Once again, it's probably the only metaphor I included, but like a bear, it leaves a strong impression.

A Writing Secret to Share with Students

Like similes, metaphors create comparisons. Unlike a simile, though, a metaphor doesn't merely say one thing is *like* another—it refers to one thing as if it actually *is* another. In *World Without Fish* (2011), author Mark Kurlansky calls the jellyfish "the cockroach of the sea" (13). Metaphors can be subtle, too. In her memoir *I Am Malala* (2014), author Malala Yousafzai confesses, "In a country where women aren't allowed out in public without a man, we girls traveled far and wide inside the pages of our books" (34). The books become, in this metaphor, her world.

! Something to try

Thinning the Bears—or Adding One

Without solid rules to guide us, we have to rely on our writers' instincts to tell us when we have just the right number of "bears in our woods." The following passage from Sneed's book *The Prairie Builders* (2005c 8) originally contained one vivid metaphor. I added another—plus a simile. What would you keep or cut?

> *Fanned by the day's gentle breezes, a crackling orange wall five, ten, fifteen feet high quickly climbs toward the sky. Men and women carrying tools called "flappers" rush along the line like eager shoppers at a yard sale, smothering stray embers that threaten to burn in the wrong direction. Two fire engines and their crews also stand by, waiting to leap into action if the blaze turns into a fire-breathing dragon.*

Once you've discussed this passage, compare Sneed's original passage to see if your writers made the same decisions about what to keep:

> *Fanned by the day's gentle breezes, a crackling orange wall five, ten, fifteen feet high quickly climbs toward the sky. Men and women carrying tools called "flappers" rush along the line ~~like eager shoppers at a yard sale~~, smothering stray embers that threaten to burn in the wrong direction. Two fire engines and their crews also stand by, waiting to leap into action if the blaze ~~turns into a fire-breathing dragon~~ gets out of control.*

Calling the fire a "crackling orange wall" helps us picture and feel how menacing it truly is. The "eager shoppers" comparison doesn't work because fire fighting is serious, dangerous business. And "fire-breathing dragon" is a cliché.

After sharing this example, have students look through their own writing for examples of metaphors to share in their writing groups. See if each group can identify one "bear in the woods"—in other words, a metaphor with real impact. Students whose woods are bear-free might search for an opportunity to help readers appreciate a person, event, place, or natural phenomenon by thinking of it as something else. Help them rehearse metaphorical thinking by brainstorming metaphors for a rough assignment, wild weather, a good friend, a great (or terrible) meal, an old bus or automobile, a traffic jam—or anything else your class can dream up.

8

Choose Good Quotations

Skillful and timely use of quotations can work wonders in raising the quality of nonfiction writing. Experts, characters, and "witnesses" not only provide valuable information, they tell it *in their own words*—and that can make any manuscript eminently more interesting. Quotations, though, also can:

- break narrative monotony
- punctuate a point
- reveal and develop characters
- show instead of tell
- add authority
- add voice
- inject humor.

And much, much more. In fact, it's hard to think of another tool that can transform a piece of writing so quickly and dramatically as a good quotation.

To be honest, we could have discussed quotations under paragraphs instead of sentences. In my own work, I often include quotes that extend an entire paragraph. Like most student writers, however, I frequently quote a single sentence, too, so discussing quotations under "Sentence Revision" fits here as well. Let's look at a few examples of how quotations can help bring nonfiction writing to life.

Quote for Variety

One place I especially like to use quotations is to break up long descriptions or narratives. In *Fire Birds* (2015a), I wrote a five-paragraph scene describing scientist Dick Hutto going out to use a game caller to try to "call in" an elusive Black-backed Woodpecker. After describing Hutto walking to a likely location and the device he intended to use, I could have just written, "Next, he turns on the game caller and waits." Instead, I decided to quote Dick directly:

> *"Okay," he says. "Let's see if anyone's home." (11–12)*

This is the only quote in the entire scene, but it accomplishes a lot. It breaks up the monotony of my own narrative voice. It reinforces the immediacy of the scene, helping readers feel like they are part of what's going on. It helps establish Dick as a character by revealing how he talks and thinks. The choice of the quote also helps build suspense, leading the reader to wonder, "What exactly *is* going to show up here?"

Quote for Authority

Quotations are especially important when writing about controversial topics. In *Hopping Ahead of Climate Change* (2016), I tackle the highly politicized issue of our warming planet. In Chapter Two, "Hares in a Warming World," I have to firmly establish not only what is causing climate change, but the impacts of resulting higher temperatures. To do so, I present a lot of statistics, but I recognized that readers would accept statements from *bona fide* experts more than they would from me. Because of this, I include this quote from professional climate scientist Steve Running:

> The winter season, with snow on the ground, is on average two to three weeks shorter than the snow cover period fifty years ago. (17)

By lending the weight of a real expert to the discussion, this quote makes the book's arguments much more convincing. It also presents climate change in terms that anyone can understand. Also, because the quote is so simple, it breaks down the barriers between skeptical readers and the scientific community. When I read this quote, I think to myself, "This is just another guy like I am, repeating an observation that is sitting right in front of him. How can I argue with that?"

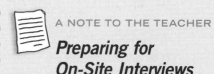

A NOTE TO THE TEACHER

Preparing for On-Site Interviews

Have students consider two things when preparing for an interview. First, if possible, encourage them to conduct the interview in their expert's working "habitat." Observing a trainer working with horses, a nurse drawing blood, or a photographer struggling to get the perfect shot of a squirmy toddler adds authenticity you just can't match on the phone or in an office.

Second, have them list questions in advance—considering what readers most want to know. If I were to interview Sneed for a bio piece, I wouldn't ask who his favorite coauthor is. Too obvious. But I think readers would eat up his answers to questions like these:

- *What was your all-time favorite nonfiction topic?*
- *Did your field research ever put you in danger?*
- *Which is harder to write—fiction or nonfiction?*
- *Who's your favorite nonfiction writer—and why?*

Good interviews—and quotations—come from good questions.

Humorous Quotes

I don't know about you, but I am a sucker for humor. I'll read anything from a cereal box top to a book about croquet if it's funny. In nonfiction, though, humor isn't just an indication that something is funny; it is the mark of strong writing. Skilled writers tirelessly search for places to insert levity, and one of the simplest ways to do that is to find and use humorous quotes.

Also in *Hopping Ahead of Climate Change* (2016), I have to discuss the disturbing fact that snowshoe hares are eaten by almost every imaginable kind of predator. Fortunately, Professor Scott Mills offered a hilarious quote to help me deal with this unsavory statistic:

> *I call hares the candy bar of the forest, but my students call them the cheeseburger of the forest. (8)*

This quote provokes a laugh in most readers, making the text more entertaining, but it also helps readers handle the gruesome reality that these adorably cute little fur balls rarely live more than a year. (FYI, this is the quote that book reviewers most often focused on, reinforcing the power of humor to make a point.)

You'll note that in each of the previous examples, a quote accomplishes multiple tasks—a key to what makes quotes so valuable. Of course, finding good quotes takes work. My favorite way to obtain quotes is to interview experts myself. If you haven't yet done so, assign your students the task of interviewing a friend or family member, then have them write a nonfiction piece about that person using the best quotes from the interview.

What if a writer can't conduct his own interviews? In such cases, it's perfectly acceptable to quote other authors or borrow from other interviews, such as those found in a book, magazine, or talk show. When writing my American Heroes biography series, I specifically looked for autobiographies or in-depth biographies that would provide a wealth of quotations from my subjects. These quotes always helped bring my writing alive—just as they will for your own students.

One final point about quotes: writers should not use quotations as a replacement for their own writing. I've seen writers quote paragraph after paragraph of an interview as a substitute for writing their own narrative. I've done it myself! Quotes, though, should only be used when they provide a special accent, emphasis, or insight to a draft—or when they help prove a point by adding an expert's authority to a discussion. Used too often or indiscriminately, quotes weaken a writer's own narrative voice and lead to a less satisfying result.

A Writing Secret to Share with Students

Quotations can't just be dropped into your text like supplies from a helicopter. Help readers understand why you chose each quotation and how it connects to the text as a whole.

Before quoting biologist Larry Gilbert (2008b 8), Sneed tells us that Dr. Gilbert is director of the Brackenridge Field Laboratory at the University of Texas. Knowing he is an authority on the topic—fire ants—gives his words even more weight. In addition, Sneed carefully links each quotation to the discussion at hand. Here, he quotes Dr. Gilbert explaining how a red ant invasion was anything but random: "Instead," Larry describes, "it was more like Patton's tank invasion of Europe during World War II" (11). Those little words—"Larry describes"— are critical. They tell us that this quotation from Dr. Gilbert is included to provide information as well as create an unforgettable image.

Just drop 'em anywhere!

You can use many expressions to connect a speaker's words to your discussion. Following are just a few examples:

- *As Jordan explains,*
- *Raul recalls,*
- *Wildlife expert Marie Frederick adds,*
- *Professor Smith disagrees, offering this argument:*
- *Dr. Butler sees it this way:*

Without an introduction, quotations read like interruptions. Help your readers understand whether each quotation offers an explanation, description, contradiction, humor—or something else.

Something to try

Choosing a Winning Quotation

A winning quotation has to make a point so effectively that the author thinks, "I couldn't have said it better myself."

Following are two strong quotations about climate change. Share both with students and discuss the main point each makes. Which one—if either—might your students incorporate into their own writing? Would they use the entire quotation—or only part of it? Would it be possible to use both quotations in the same report?

1. "Climate change is happening but we're *not* doomed. We can't stop it, but we could slow it down and we could prepare for its effects. It's going to be a big job, and it'll mean changing almost everything about the way we live now—how we light and heat our homes, what transportation we use, how we design buildings, how we grow food, how we handle disasters and diseases, and even how people and countries decide, together, what's fair and what isn't" (Davies 2011, 14).

2. "During the last century, the average temperature of the earth's surface and the air near the surface rose between 0.6 and 0.9 degrees Centigrade. The temperature appears to be continuing to rise, and most scientists agree that a rise of two degrees would bring about catastrophic changes. Polar ice caps would melt and sea levels would rise enough to overflow many coastlines, ports, and major cities" (Kurlansky 2011, 136).

Once you finish discussing these quotations and when or how a writer might use each one, have students review any quotations they have collected for use in their own work. Ask them to identify the specific purpose behind each quotation: to inform readers, challenge common knowledge, introduce a startling fact, make readers laugh, add voice to the discussion, or something different. Suppose a writer cannot identify any particular purpose for a given quotation. Should she use it anyway—or discard it? Discuss this.

9

As I contemplated writing this chapter, I worried, "How am I ever going to approach this subject? After all, crafting sentences that make just the right impact on the reader is one of a writer's most difficult challenges." Then I had an epiphany. I realized that *all* of our other sentence chapters in this section deal with this topic. Employing active voice, real language, similes, quotations—all of these strategies converge on a common goal: creating a precise impact.

And yet, following all of these tips still may not be enough. Even a good reviser often ends up looking at a sentence she's written several ways and thinks, "This just isn't doing the job I want."

What's a writer to do?

The first thing to ask her is, "Well, what exactly do you want readers to experience or learn here? Do you want them to feel something? Understand something? Picture something? Follow a complicated sequence of events?" Many student writers never even think about this as they write, but defining their intention for a sentence gives them a revision compass heading.

With this intention dialed in, it's time to begin ruthless experimentation: adding a word, swapping phrases, deleting a couple of extra words, even dividing or combining sentences. Tell your students, "You might not hit on the exact solution right away. Just keep trying things—until you're close to achieving what you want."

In *Snakes, Alligators, and Broken Hearts* (2015b), I often had to wrestle with finding exactly the right phrasing. In the following example, I try to convey the turmoil I experienced summoning the courage to jump off of a thirty-foot diving platform. A stranger shows up and admits that he also is scared by the prospect of jumping. I wrote:

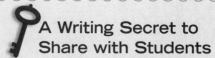

A Writing Secret to Share with Students

The urge to revise starts with a vague feeling of discomfort—like a pebble in a shoe. People with tough feet might tune out the irritation for a time. But that won't make it go away. When you sense that something in your writing isn't quite right, pay attention to that feeling. It shows you are developing a good instinct about when to revise—and that's a sign you are growing as a writer. Skilled revisers don't put up with "sore feet." They go after the problem.

Hearing him—a grown adult—say that, made me feel better about my own cowardice. It also gave me an idea.

The problem with this draft lies in the second sentence. Yes, the stranger *did* give me an idea, but this sentence does not reinforce the extreme agitation I felt throughout the scene. After several tries, I realized that adding a few choice words would solve my dilemma:

Hearing him—a grown adult—say that, made me feel better about my own cowardice. It also gave me one final, desperate idea. (96)

Changing the last words to "one final, desperate idea" gives readers the sense that I was at the end of my rope—exactly my goal.

Not all problems are so easy to remedy. Harkening back to an example we discussed in Part II, Chapter 6, in the dramatic introduction to *Hopping Ahead of Climate Change* (2016), I describe the death of a white snowshoe hare that thinks it is camouflaged, but instead sticks out like a glowing lightbulb against the brown forest floor. A great horned owl notices the mismatched hare and swoops in for the kill. To wrap up the passage, I wanted a sentence that emphasized how ominous this situation is for the species—but without getting hysterical about it. I quickly hit upon a beginning that I liked, one that precisely conveyed the immediate situation. It was the rest of the sentence—in this case, the ramifications—that gave me fits. Here are just a few of the twenty-plus variations that I tried:

- For the hare, it is a disaster—a disaster that may be happening more and more frequently throughout the hare's Rocky Mountain range.
- For the hare, it is a disaster—one that casts a shadow over the hare's future survival.
- For the hare, it is a disaster—one that could threaten its survival in its Rocky Mountain home.
- For the hare, it is a disaster—one that casts a shadow across the animal's very survival.
- For the hare, it is a disaster—one that raises serious questions about the species' ability to survive.
- For the hare, it is a disaster—one that throws the species' very survival into question.

And here's the one I finally settled on:

For the hare, it's a disaster—one that casts doubt on the species' future survival. (2016, 5)

You'll notice that to reach my goal, I tried myriad ideas and phrasing. Sometimes I combined two ideas. Sometimes I backtracked. Sometimes I simplified. Other times, I made it more complicated. Did I arrive at the best solution? I may never know, but I do know that the struggle of *trying* brought me closer to what I wanted.

> **! Something to try**
>
> ## Defining Purpose
>
> Sneed tells us that revision depends on purpose, on what we want readers to learn or feel. Share the following two-sentence passage from Nicola Davies' book *What's Eating You?* (2006):
>
> *Almost every free-living animal on the planet is just a walking habitat—a "host" to many parasites—and that includes us humans! There are more than 430 different kinds of parasites that can live on a human body (ectoparasites) or in one (endoparasites). (8)*
>
> Consider the purpose behind each of these two sentences, discussing one at a time. What is Davies trying to do with the first sentence? What about the second? Do the two purposes work in harmony—and if so, how?
>
> After talking about these two sentences, have students look at any sentence—or combination of sentences—from their own writing and define the purpose behind each one: Are they trying to teach readers something? Make them feel a particular way? Help them picture something? Have them share their sentences in writing groups and see if listeners can identify the intended purpose behind each one. If listeners' responses don't match what the writer had in mind, writers should revise to make the purpose behind the sentence more clear.

Modeling Multiple Revisions

Revising a single sentence several times is a relatively manageable task, but students can still benefit from seeing it in action. You can model this with any sentence from your own writing—or one you make up, like this: "Warts are caused by viruses, not frogs." Share the sentence and have students guess how many revisions you can come up with in three minutes—then let them time you. Ask them to notice how one revision leads into another, creating a kind of revision momentum. Here are seven revisions of my original sentence:

- *Contrary to popular myth, warts come from viruses, not frogs.*

- *When you think of warts, think of viruses, not frogs.*

- *If you think frogs cause warts, think again. The culprits are viruses.*

- *Frogs don't cause warts—but viruses do!*

- *Can frogs cause warts? Never. Think viruses.*

- *Viruses, not frogs, cause warts.*

- *What causes warts? Viruses— not frogs.*

Maybe warts cause frogs. Did you ever think of that?

When you finish your own revisions, ask students to choose one or two favorites. Maybe one has better rhythm or creates some suspense or contrast. Perhaps another has more voice or is more direct.

Then have them choose one sentence from their own writing that they're not quite happy with. Ask them to create at least six new versions of the sentence, choosing the best one to include in their writing. Remind them to follow Sneed's advice about "ruthless experimentation"—start the sentence differently, change words, cut, add, turn a statement into a question, or even make two sentences.

By the way, students can have some fun sharing their revisions in writing groups to see if listeners and writers agree about which sentences work best. Listeners may also have additional revisions to suggest.

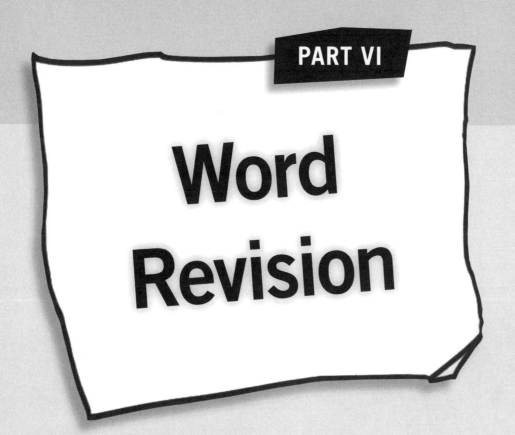

PART VI

Word Revision

With word revision we finally arrive at the smallest unit of text that a writer can revise. In formulating the chapters for this section, I wondered about separating word revision from sentence revision. "Are they really worth distinguishing?" I asked myself. Like word revision, sentence revision often involves changing only a single word or two. I concluded, however, that word revision does deserve its own place in the sun—or at least on the teacher's smartboard.

Why?

Because word revision takes a writer down to a level of thought required for deep, quality work. The choice of one word over another can totally change the meaning or tone of a sentence, or even an entire paragraph. It can erase confusion, add drama, enhance voice, and much more. And while most word revision tips fall into the "easy" category, actually *using* these tips helps distinguish the average writer from one who really knows what she is doing.

The following word revision tips fall into one of two categories: eliminating needless or confusing words, and searching for *better* words. A writer is not Isaac Newton here, trying to derive complex equations to describe the motions of celestial bodies. Like an archer, she instead focuses on very specific tasks. If she shoots a bull's-eye, she usually knows it immediately. If she hits one of the target's outer rings, well, that may be harder to figure out. Experience plays a huge role in word work. How much a student has read and written especially helps program that inner alarm system that flashes the words *delete* and *replace* in her brain.

the perfect word

Even an advanced writer, though, benefits from instruction and examples on this topic. Like paragraph and sentence work, word target practice is a lot of fun, but it doesn't overtax the intellect. It's something you may want to save for a late Friday afternoon when you and your students need something worthwhile to do, but aren't quite up to solving global warming, war in the Middle East, or the problems of Third World debt.

You'll note that we include only half a dozen word revision tips in this section. We considered adding more, but they would have been variations of the ones that follow. If you think of other indispensable word revision strategies you'd like to use, go for it—and let Vicki and me know for the next edition!

Cut Unnecessary Descriptors

Most of us would agree that descriptive writing is a good thing, but I find that it carries too much weight in student writing—perhaps because it's such a simple concept for young writers to grasp. After all, just tell students to load up on the five senses and they dive right in! Whatever the cause, most young writers burden their work with adjectives, adverbs, participles, and other words aimed at describing objects, situations, and events. Here's an opening paragraph from a short fifth-grade memoir:

> One steaming summer day our family went hiking. As we were hiking around we encountered a nice flat open field. That is where we sat down to chow down some lunch.

Do you see any extra descriptive words the passage could do without? Taking pen in hand, I would slash as follows:

> One steaming summer day our family went hiking. As we were hiking ~~around~~ we encountered a ~~nice~~ flat open field. That is where we sat ~~down~~ to chow down ~~some~~ lunch.

My exact reasons for cutting vary with each word. I cut *around* because few people hike *around*. They hike. Period. I cut *nice* because if they stopped for lunch there, it is implied they found the field inviting in some way. I cut *down* and *some* because if the family was hiking,

A Writing Secret to Share with Students

Two types of adjectives can nearly always be slashed from your writing. The first are the redundant descriptors: green grass, slimy slug, flowing river, fragrant roses, small children. Don't waste adjectives telling readers what the noun itself makes obvious. Of course, if the river is stagnant or the children gigantic, you need to point that out. The second group of adjectives to cut are the annoyingly vague words: *wonderful, special, awesome, nice, great, terrific, cool, epic,* and any of their cousins that come to mind. Here is where Sneed's advice to "show, don't tell" (Part V) comes into play. For example, instead of telling readers someone is a "special friend," show them why: "Henry could always sense when something was bothering me. But he would wait for me to talk instead of prying me with questions." You might want to make a list in your writing journal of overused words—*nice, good, wonderful*—that you'd like to avoid in your writing. Then congratulate yourself each time you find a way to avoid them!

they couldn't sit *up*, and does anyone eat *some* lunch? I don't think so. Even if you eat only a bite, that's your lunch. Lunch is binary: you either eat it or you don't.

In every case, these words weigh down the passage with useless, unnecessary information. You will observe, however, that I left the word *steaming*. Why? It gave me a visceral feel for the situation. I liked that. I also left *flat* and *open*, reasoning that not all fields are flat and open—but you could easily convince me to cut those, too. All of the other words—the ones that I crossed out—undermined what the writer was trying to accomplish, which was to succinctly set the scene for a story.

❗ Something to try
Playing with Wording

Have students revise the following fifth grader's passage by eliminating or replacing vague adjectives—or just finding other ways to say things. Tip: Most students will find it helpful to look up "Port Jackson Shark" to see a photo or read a few facts before revising:

> *A Port Jackson shark is weird. It is awesome, but not better than a Great White Shark. A Port Jackson is not that scary. But it is dangerous to be next to any shark.*

When students finish, discuss the revision process. Does changing one word—such as *weird*—sometimes lead to additional revisions, such as adding details or reshaping a whole sentence? After discussing the "Port Jackson Shark" piece, have students check their own drafts, deleting or revising words that fall into one of these categories:

- *unnecessary words (like* pleasant *spring morning)*
- *redundant adjectives (like* huge *mountains)*
- *vague adjectives (like* cool *or* special)
- *adverbs that can be cut by strengthening verbs* (raced *instead of* ran quickly)*.*

Take a look at this next example from my own memoir:

I quickly snapped some pictures on my little Kodak Instamatic camera—proof
to Eric and other friends back home in California . . .

See any possible cuts? *Quickly* can go because when you snap something—anything—
it always happens quickly. *Little* also can go because all Instamatic cameras are small.
Finally, I cut *back home* because by now the readers already knew that California was
my home for most of the year.

The lesson here is that a committed writer should take at least one pass through
her work, challenging every modifying and descriptive word she has written. Once
she gets the hang of it, she'll be astonished at how many words she can dump into the
recycling bin.

Something to try
Eliminating Adverbs by Strengthening Verbs

Many adverbs can be eliminated simply by making the verbs they modify stronger.
For instance, instead of writing, "The man walked slowly down the sidewalk," a
writer might say, "The man strolled down the sidewalk." This eliminates the adverb
slowly, and also creates a more vivid picture because *strolled* is more precise
than *walked*. Model this for students using one or two of the following examples,
or some you make up yourself. Then ask students to eliminate adverbs in the
remaining examples by making the verbs stronger. When they finish revising these
four sentences, students should check their own drafts to see if they can eliminate
any adverbs simply by making each verb stronger.

1. Tall grasses moved gracefully in the wind.

2. The growling dog came quickly toward me.

3. "Keep out means keep out!" Julie said forcefully to her pesky brother.

4. Rain fell heavily on the skylight.

2 Eliminate Intensifying Words

Continuing our theme of "word search and destroy," all writers—myself included—throw extra modifying words into their initial drafts. The most common include *really, very, extremely, sort of, quite, kind of,* and in my own case, *pretty much.* At least I sort of think that pretty much covers the very common ones. When I began this tip, I didn't actually know the official name for these words, but a little Internet digging reveals that they fall under the category of "intensifiers" or "intensifying words."

If you're J. D. Salinger, intensifiers can help add voice to a character or narrative. Consider the opening paragraph of *The Catcher in the Rye* (1951):

> *If you really want to hear about it, the first thing you'll probably want to know is where I was born, and what my lousy childhood was like, and how my parents were occupied and all before they had me, and all that David Copperfield kind of crap, but I don't feel like going into it, if you want to know the truth (3).*

Here, Salinger masterfully slings a fusillade of intensifying words at us in such a way that the voice of Holden Caulfield embeds itself immediately and permanently into our brains.

Unfortunately for the rest of us, frequent use of intensifiers weakens our writing. When I revise, I do a special flyby to hunt down and eliminate these words. Take this sentence from an early draft of *Hopping Ahead of Climate Change* (2016):

> *Scott's observation of hare "light bulbs," or mismatched hares, led him to ask three very important questions.*

IN CONFERENCE

You Go First!

Ideally, a conference provides an opportunity to share writing, thoughts about writing, and ideas for revision. For struggling students, though, it can feel more like a critical review of everything that isn't working. Take the pressure off by opening the conference with a look at your own writing or an anonymous piece. This helps the student focus on the problem—such as unwanted intensifiers—rather than on how well she is doing. It also puts her in the empowering position of being the assessor and advisor. Once a student becomes adept at spotting problems in someone else's work, it becomes much easier, and less threatening, to find parallel problems in her own writing.

Did you spot the intensifying word? Yep—*very*. A quick cut yields:

> *Scott's observation of hare "light bulbs," or mismatched hares, led him to ask three ~~very~~ important questions*

Do you agree that *very* could go? More important, do you know why? It's worth spending a paragraph to ponder, because the answers aren't all obvious. I came up with three reasons for eliminating this word. First, I didn't need it. *Important* means "important." It does. What else could it mean? Writing *very important* dilutes the meaning of this, *ahem*, important word. Second, eliminating modifying words gives my writing a stronger, more confident tone. It subtly tells the reader, "This guy knows what he's talking about. He's not trying to snow me with extra, empty words." My last reason for cutting this and other intensifying words may be the most interesting: if I cut most of these words in my work, it allows me to use one when I want to make a special impact.

In Chapter Four of *The World Famous Miles City Bucking Horse Sale* (2010), I wanted to emphasize how different it is for cowboys down by the ring than for spectators in the stands. I relied on the simple intensifier *much*:

> *Watching the events from the stands is a much different experience than being down by the corrals. (42)*

What makes *much* work here is that I had eliminated every other intensifying word within a couple of pages fore and aft. This made my use of this word stand out in the reader's mind. If I had riddled my writing with *kind of, very*, and so forth, I would have lost my opportunity to make *much* mean something.

Really.

! Something to try

Checking Personal Drafts for Intensifier Overload

After they have warmed up by revising Sneed's doctored passage (page 181), ask students to look at their own drafts to see if they have overdone intensifying words. You might start by making a list of words or expressions that can almost always be excised from writing: *very, really, more or less, pretty much, kind of, sort of*, and so on. Glancing at this list will give students a place to begin, but they need to rely on the sound of the text to know whether they've trimmed enough, so remind them to read aloud continuously as they work. Sharing work in a writing group enhances this exercise. Good listeners pick up unneeded intensifiers many writers overlook!

A Writing Secret to Share with Students

It's easy to imagine that words like *very* or *really* boost voice. Actually, the opposite is true. These adverbs make a writer sound as if she's working overtime to convince us of something—and if she has to work that hard, maybe we shouldn't be too quick to agree with her. If you feel the need to write, "It was very hot" instead of, "It was hot," try saying it differently: "The heat was intense." Hear the confidence there? Another way to avoid intensifiers is to take Sneed's judicious advice to show, not tell: "Relentless sun made the pavement so soft and sticky it pulled the shoes right off our feet."

Dear Aunt Dedra, I really truly totally love the very nice hat you knit me...

Something to try
Trimming the Intensifiers

Sneed tells us that he took most intensifiers out of his manuscript for *The World Famous Miles City Bucking Horse Sale* (2010). That way, when he used the word *much*, it stood out. See if your students can edit text as ruthlessly. To offer them a challenge, I've doctored the following passage from that book by adding intensifying words I know Sneed would not approve of. He won't mind, though, because I have also included his original, modifier-free version so you can compare the two:

> *In very recent decades, Miles City has really suffered through pretty much the exact same struggles as most other rural farming and ranching communities throughout the entire West. As ranches and farms have truly grown way more efficient and needed a whole lot fewer hands, young people in search of education and jobs have more or less left their communities. While other areas of the country have definitely gained population over the past half-century, most eastern Montana towns have actually shrunk or just about disappeared altogether. No kidding.*

And here is Sneed's original passage, *sans* tinsel. Read both versions aloud to hear how much stronger his original sounds:

> *In ~~very~~ recent decades, Miles City has ~~really~~ suffered through ~~pretty much~~ the ~~exact~~ same struggles as ~~most~~ other rural farming and ranching communities throughout the ~~entire~~ West. As ranches and farms have ~~truly~~ grown ~~way~~ more efficient and needed ~~a whole lot~~ fewer hands, young people in search of education and jobs have ~~more or less~~ left their communities. While other areas of the country have ~~definitely~~ gained population over the past half-century, most eastern Montana towns have ~~actually~~ shrunk or ~~just about~~ disappeared altogether. ~~No kidding~~. (31)*

3

Remove Redundant Words— Again and Again!

I n "Paragraph Revision," we zeroed in on eliminating word repeats. It's worth revisiting the topic again now, but with an added twist. Instead of just cutting or revising repeated words (remember *tower* and *towered*?), a sharp reviser weeds out different words that actually mean the same thing—and, in some instances, can distort the meaning of a sentence. As an example, reread the second sentence of this current paragraph:

> *It's worth revisiting the topic again now, but with an added twist.*

Can you find a word that not only repeats the meaning of another word, but actually undermines its meaning? You bet—*again*. I drafted this sentence with little scrutiny. Being the recursive writer that I am, however, I circled back to it and noticed something—that if I used the word *revisit*, I didn't need the word *again*. In fact, if I kept the word *again*, I would imply that we had already *re*visited this topic!

A NOTE TO THE TEACHER

Identifying Writing Specialists

As Sneed points out, writers—especially in their role as listeners—have "specialties." Some listen for big-picture ideas like clarity or organization, while others are detail people. Have writers within each group spend a session identifying one another's specialties. They may think they already know—but give them a chance to revisit the specialty question by responding to any piece written by someone outside the group. See what specialties emerge: Who's good at dialogue? Does someone have a knack for leads—or endings? How about rooting out passive voice? Who always seems to come up with a strong verb or precise noun? Does anyone have an ear for sentence fluency, eye for detail, or talent for organizing information? During writing workshop, students can use what they learn about one another's specialties to ask for precisely the kind of help they need to move forward.

Catching these kinds of missteps takes a sharp eye and experience. It requires thinking about every single word in a sentence and asking yourself, "Do I need this and is it accomplishing what I want? Are there other words in this sentence that already fill the role of this one?" I probably miss a lot of redundancies. Yet again, a writer's group can come to the rescue because different readers catch different things. In my own writer's group, we have one or two members with particular skills at this kind of detailed revision. Others are more "big-picture" people. Having four to six other readers helps a writer catch a broad range of issues, including redundancies.

Let's try one more example that could come from any writer:

> I stopped to admire the beautiful, gorgeous flower.

Here, *beautiful* and *gorgeous* are obviously redundant. Most writers would simply cut one of them. Alert writers, however, might seize the opportunity to use one of these "word placeholders" to tap into another one of the reader's senses:

> I stopped to admire the ~~beautiful~~ fragrant, gorgeous flower.

Now, instead of repeating himself, the writer brings the scene more fully alive. Vicki also noted that it's in the nature of flowers to be attractive, so we could also take the opportunity to replace *gorgeous* with something more useful:

> I stopped to admire the fragrant ~~gorgeous~~ purple flower.

This simple example showcases an unexpected bonus to word revision work. By fixing word problems, a writer also notices opportunities to improve his work in other subtle, but important ways. When I am revising on this level, I am surprised—and delighted—by how often this happens.

Something to try

Holding a Revision Competition

Following is a short passage from a fifth grader's persuasive essay about the evils of wearing high heels. Read it aloud, asking students to listen for redundancies. Challenge writing groups to see which can come up with the most concise revision. Students should feel free to make any changes to wording, length, or sentence order—and even delete or add new sentences—so long as they retain the essential meaning of the passage:

> Women shouldn't have to wear high heels. They cause a ridiculous amount of health problems if you wear them too much, and some just look completely stupid. Heels also hurt your feet, are horrible for getting around in, and after a long day wearing them, it would feel like heaven to take them off. I doubt anyone would wear them for comfort. They were invented only for fashion. Women shouldn't feel like they have to wear high heels. High heels are painful. Have you ever heard someone sigh with relief while taking their heels off after a long day? Many women are tired of high heels, but wear them anyway.

Later, have students review their own writing for similar redundancies. Eliminating even two or three redundant passages can transform a draft.

Swap Weak Verbs for Strong Ones

4

While writing this book, no topic ignited more heated discussion than weak verbs. Surprised? Me too. Replacing weak verbs with stronger ones is not only a basic tenet of my own revision process, it's a strategy I focus on with students during writing workshops. "What's to think about?" I asked myself. "Some verbs are weak and some are strong. A good writer strives to replace weak verbs with stronger ones."

And that's when both Vicki and our editor, Katie, called the Joint Chiefs of Staff, scrambled the F-22 attack aircraft, and went to DEFCON 1.

The issue, it turns out, was not the strategy itself. Both Katie and Vicki agreed that replacing weak verbs with strong ones constitutes good writing. The issue was how I *defined* weak verbs.

Check out my favorite list of weak verbs in the box below:

Common Weak Verbs to Watch Out For

  To Be—is, was, were, am, are

  To Have—have, has, had, having

  To Get—get, got, gets, gotten, getting

  To Do—do, did, does, doing

During my writing workshops I encourage students to hunt down these words and, whenever possible, delete them or replace them with stronger, more active verbs. This simple exercise can totally transform a piece of writing, helping a writer "show, don't tell," assume a stronger voice, and focus her message. So what's the problem?

The problem, both Katie and Vicki insisted, is that no verbs are weak *by themselves*. They are only weak in how they are used in *particular situations*.

I gotta admit that at first, this smacked of PC overload—akin to calling a cat a "quadruped nonhuman associate" or dead people "living impaired." My first response was to consider declaring a kind of Verbal Mason-Dixon Line. People in the west (where I live) could teach about "weak verbs" while those in the east (where my publisher is located) could refer to "action-impaired verbs." After sulking for the next few days, however, I grudgingly began to acknowledge Vicki's and Katie's point of view. Even more, their input helped me understand a conundrum I've had difficulty articulating—that my list of weak verbs actually works well in many situations. Just look at how many times I've used the words *is* and *was* in this chapter!

By taking into account the *context* in which a verb is used, we can recast this chapter's strategy as follows: Replace weak verbs with verbs that are stronger *for a particular situation.*

And that—finally—allows us to discuss how to teach it . . .

I loved you guys in Still Life II—*but see, we're shooting an action film here!*

A Crash Course in Replacing Weak Verbs

A first step in teaching how to replace weak verbs is to remind students what a verb's job is. I find that by fourth grade, most kids understand that a verb expresses action in a sentence. Once you remind them of that, it's time to talk about the two features that make a verb strong—power and precision. Let's consider power first.

A strong verb radiates vigor, decisiveness, and expression. It puts a sharp picture of what's going on in a reader's mind—and, conveniently, often helps a writer "show, don't tell."

In my book *Teeth* (2008c), I write about the hyena's formidable jaws and fearsome teeth. "Hyenas use these teeth," I explain, "not only to eat meat but also to crack and crush up the bones of zebras and other large animals" (8). The verbs *crack* and *crush* allow readers to see and hear—almost feel—the power of those jaws. If I had written "*eat* the bones of zebras," that drama would have been lost.

Well-chosen verbs don't always derive their strength from swift action or athleticism, however. Equally important is precision—expressing exactly what you mean in a given situation. *Ponder* is a wonderful strong verb that describes a delicate, measured action. So are *hesitate, throw, exchange, tell, surmise, inhale,* and thousands of other verbs.

In *Hopping Ahead of Climate Change* (2016), I write about how snowshoe hares blend in with their surroundings by changing color to white each fall and to brown in the spring. This allows them to stay camouflaged during radically different seasonal conditions. "As snow cover decreases over time," I point out, "hares that molt later in the fall and earlier in the spring will most likely survive better than other hares" (42). In this sentence, consider the two verbs *molt* and *survive.* Neither suggests vivid, heart-stopping action, but each has a precise meaning that few, if any, other verbs could convey. For this particular situation, therefore, *molt* and *survive* constitute extremely strong verbs.

In contrast to strong verbs, a weak verb is like a patient lying on an emergency room table. The verb has a pulse, but it's faint. Even worse, doctors might lose it at any moment.

IN CONFERENCE

 Simplifying Verb Revision

How will students figure out which verbs need strengthening? Here's a step-by-step approach to give writers both confidence and choice. First, working together, identify *all* the verbs within a passage of three or four sentences. Second, have the student choose two verbs she feels could be stronger or more precise. Third, ask the student—with respect to each verb she has chosen to revise—"What do you want the reader of this sentence to see or feel?" With this purpose in mind, work together to brainstorm two or three alternative verbs that match the writer's intent. After choosing the strongest verbs for the passage at hand, the student can pursue these same steps on her own with another paragraph.

Take another look at my list of "weak verbs" at the beginning of the chapter. In due deference to Vicki and Katie, I have to agree that these verbs often fit a particular situation perfectly. For many other situations, however, they comprise poor substitutes that can and should be replaced by stronger alternatives. Here's the catch: *a writer can rarely dump a weak* is *or* am *by popping another verb into its place.* During writing workshops, I demonstrate this to students by giving them a simple sentence, such as:

> *The rocks were very large.*

This sentence contains the ultimate "suspect" verb, "to be"—in this case in its past plural form, *were.* Asking students to replace it with a strong, active verb usually leads to convoluted—sometimes hilarious—results:

> *The rocks were extremely large.*
> *The rocks seemed very large.*
> *The rocks looked extremely large.*
> *The extremely large rocks were giant.*
> *It is true that the rocks were large.*
> *The large rocks sat there.*

. . . and so forth.

As you can see, most of these sentences simply move the weak verb from one spot to another or replace the original weak verb with another that is just as weak (*seemed* and *looked*). One sentence adds a second weak verb, *is.* Not only that, most of these efforts add in superfluous details and some change the meaning of the original sentence—breaking the rules of the exercise and inciting the wrath of the judges! Still, the struggle students go through trying to replace *were* helps them understand the issue, and most of them quickly think of the process as a fun game.

In workshop, I let students smack around a sentence like this for several minutes. I write down each of the kids' suggested revisions on a whiteboard, letting the class point out the flaws in each one. If the students come up with a sentence such as "The rocks sat there," however, I raise my hands and shout "Halleluja!" Well, not quite. I *do* point out

🔑 A Writing Secret to Share with Students

Strong verbs add life to writing, but if you turbocharge *every* verb, readers feel as if they're caught up in an Arizona windstorm. As Sneed reminds us, it's intent that determines what verb is right for the moment. In her book *Seabiscuit* (2001), author Laura Hillenbrand recounts the 1940 Santa Anita Handicap in which twelve thoroughbreds competed. Just prior to the race, Hillenbrand uses verbs that convey the restrained prerace energy: "stepped onto the track," "looked up," "walked to the gate." Moments later, the horses leave the gate and the verbs explode with them: "Whichcee screamed along the rail." "Wedding Call tracked them." "Seabiscuit shook free and hurtled into the home stretch" (320–322). Matching power to intent, Hillenbrand saves the dynamics for those moments when she wants to get readers' hearts pumping.

that the verb *sat* is stronger and more active than *was*, and I encourage the group to use this better verb to create an even stronger alternative.

One thing that makes this revision exercise challenging is that students don't know the context or point of the original sentence, and this can be important to finding exactly the right verb replacement. If I give students a hint, such as, "Imagine yourself staring up at this rock," they more easily come up with a strong alternative. Here are a few:

> *The rocks loomed over us.*
> *The rocks cast a giant shadow.*
> *The rocks towered over the landscape.*

 A NOTE TO THE TEACHER

Collecting Examples of Strong Verbs

A good way to encourage use of strong verbs is by sharing examples you find striking. The following examples contain several verbs—*collided, disengage, blundered, suspended*, and *porpoised*, for example—that are strong because they are precise, visual, and original. One is the writer's own invention! After sharing these examples, invite students to find favorites they can add to their writing journals:

1. "The mountain lion collided with the vegetation below." (Childs 2007, 49)

2. "Corn kernels do not spontaneously disengage from their cobs, so unless they are deliberately stripped and planted, no corn will grow." (Bryson (2010, 39)

3. "A blister beetle has blundered into a spiderweb, and now it waits, suspended in silk, for the spider to come and release it." (Daubert 2009, 133)

4. "Ichthyosaurs may have porpoised through the water, chasing their prey and then leaping out of the water to catch a deep breath." (Collard 2008a, 21)

One more . . . In *Hopping Ahead of Climate Change* (2016), Sneed writes, "Every time we ride in a car, flick on a computer, or turn on a heater, we contribute to global warming" (58). I was struck by the precision of the word *flick*. True, it's a little less muscular than *boot up, light off,* or *launch*. A flick is casual, almost flippant, and that makes it perfect in the context of a discussion on global warming. The message is clear: We can no longer afford to be nonchalant.

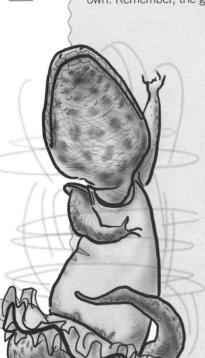

whirl

! Something to try

Finding the "Just Right" Verb

The following short passage from Sneed's book *Hopping Ahead of Climate Change* (2016, 5) describes a snowshoe hare out for breakfast. Share the passage with students, asking them to think about the image and mood Sneed is likely trying to create here. With this in mind, ask them to choose one of the alternative verbs provided to go in each blank—or they can come up with an original verb of their own. Remember, the goal is finding the verb that's "just right" for the moment:

Dawn ___ 1 ___ across the northern Rocky Mountains and a showshoe hare ___ 2 ___ through the forest in search of food. It ___ 3 ___ frequently to ___ 4 ___ on grasses, leaves, and the twigs of low-growing fir trees.

1. explodes, arrives, breaks, turns up

2. bounds, hops, crashes, creeps

3. grinds to a halt, stops, takes a breather, pauses

4. nibble, chow down, gnaw, snack.

Discuss students' choices, thinking about the impression each verb conveys. Then have students look through their own writing for two or three verbs to revise. Encourage them to brainstorm alternatives, working with partners or in writing groups. By the way, Sneed's choices for the passage above are, respectively, *breaks, hops, pauses*, and *nibble*. Notice how relatively calm and quiet these verbs are, just right for an early morning glimpse into the life of a snowshoe hare.

Again, my point is that a writer often can't just swap a weaker verb for a stronger one. She may have to restructure the offending sentence.

But wait—even after doing this, her work may not be finished! Once a sentence is in a form that works, the writer needs to examine it again to see if she can find an even *better* verb than the one that she's just come up with. This poses a fun challenge—one that both student and professional writers eagerly embrace. Take this example from a picture book I am working on about bird migration:

> *They push against the wind, fighting to stay above the deadly waves.*

In crafting this original sentence, *push* worked fine, but I felt it was too bland. In searching for a stronger replacement, I considered *battle*, but as a reader, I still didn't feel the desperation of the situation. Finally, I revised it to read:

> *They claw at the wind, fighting to stay above the deadly waves.*

Boo-yah! I knew that I had hit the bull's-eye with that one. Why? Because *claw* gives me a visceral feel for what the bird is up against.

Here's another example from *The World Famous Miles City Bucking Horse Sale* (2010):

> *The bucking horse bursts out of its holding pen, hooves flying, and jumps into the air.*

In this example, *bursts* nails what I mean. It's that second verb, *jumps*, that needs work. Why? Because it is ordinary and nonspecific. It fails to precisely capture the action and drama of the scene I am trying to describe.

In searching for an alternative, I tried all the usual suspects. *Leaps* was a good thesaurus option, but proved just as ordinary and nonspecific as *jump*. *Flies* had more action—but gave a strange, incorrect vision of what's happening. *Bounds*? Hm . . . sounded like something a kangaroo would do. Finally, I settled on:

> *The bucking horse bursts out of its holding pen, hooves flying, and catapults into the air (5).*

Saunter

A gal can't just flit and dart all the time.

Catapults fits just right here. It may not be technically what happens, but here that doesn't matter. What matters is that this word allows readers to picture the explosive violence of the rodeo ring.

To recap, revising verbs is a multistep process. The first step is to identify the verbs in a sentence. Step two is to figure out if the verbs you've chosen fit your purpose and achieve your desired effect. The final—and most fun—step is to track down the best verbs for the action and situation. This last step may require restructuring your original sentence and may take a writer several tries. Chances are, however, that she will enjoy doing it—especially in a classroom setting where other "verb-mongers" are one-upping each other as they go along!

Get Specific!

5

One of the word revision tasks I enjoy most is identifying and replacing general words. We touched on weak and imprecise verbs in the last chapter, but general nouns, adjectives, and adverbs such as *stuff, enormous*, and *happily* also give a ho-hum, hazy feeling to a writer's work. They don't provide the explicit detail or meaning that a writer looks for—and a reader craves.

Recently, I read over the chapter titles I'd originally written for a book on climate change. I titled one of the chapters "Effects of a Changing Climate"—which sounded fine, but something about it bothered me. A moment's reflection revealed the problem: the word *effects* was too general. Effects can be good, bad, or in between, but my chapter focused specifically on climate change's *negative effects*. As a result, I revised the title to "Impacts of a Changing Climate," a title that captured exactly what I wanted.

In revising my memoir, I found dozens of places where my early drafts could use more specifics. In recounting a relatively carefree time with my father, I wrote:

> *When my dad wasn't working, we'd go get pizza or drive over San Marcos Pass*
> *to a placed called Red Rocks to go swimming in the river there.*

This sentence has a couple of nice specifics—San Marcos Pass and Red Rocks—but I also missed an important opportunity with "the river there." I revised to:

> *When my dad wasn't working, we'd go get pizza or drive over San Marcos Pass*
> *to a place called Red Rocks to swim in the ~~river there~~ Santa Ynez River. (47)*

This replacement helps cement the writing in a real place for the reader. Revisiting the sentence for this chapter, however, I realized that even this second version doesn't go far enough. If I revised this sentence again now, I'd also reconsider *pizza* and *drive* to render an even better version:

> *When my dad wasn't working, we'd pick up a pepperoni pizza or roar over San*
> *Marcos Pass to a place called Red Rocks to swim in the Santa Ynez River.*

A Writing Secret to Share with Students

Teachers often write "Be specific" on students' writing. If this happens to you, do you know what to do? Here are a few tips based on Sneed's advice in this chapter and others.

- *First, use names. If you mention a river, city, country, ship, person, pet, or anything else with a name, include that name in your writing.*

- *Second, avoid meaningless nouns like* stuff *and* things. *What stuff? Which things?*

- *Third, watch out for those vague adjectives that seem to say something but really don't: "He was a great friend." "We had a wonderful time." "It was a special day." Use details to show readers what made this friend different, why a particular time stands out, or what made a certain day unforgettable.*

- *Finally, remember that details are based on senses. If you're writing a how-to piece on hiking, help readers hear the rush of the river, smell the cedar, taste the canteen water, feel the blisters on their tired feet, or see that dangling spider that's about to drop right on top of their s'mores.*

The reason for adding *pepperoni* is obvious—it puts a better picture in the reader's mind. In considering the replacement of *drive* with *roar*, however, our editor, Katie, asked the very good question, "Why would *roar* necessarily be better than *drive*? *Drive* gave me the feeling of a lazy, Sunday afternoon sort of adventure. *Roar* makes me think you were on a Harley or at least driving something really loud and fast." Her point was that *drive* could be perfect for this sentence.

She's absolutely right—except for one thing. My dad and I happened to be riding in a Sunbeam Tiger sports car with a ridiculously oversized engine. We didn't *drive* anywhere in that car! We *roared*—making that word the better choice.

Could I improve the sentence even more? Maybe, but with this last revision, I think I've finally come close to milking what I can from it.

Consider a more challenging example from *Hopping Ahead of Climate Change* (2016):

> *By the late twentieth century and into the twenty-first century, our use of fossil fuels reached giant proportions.*

Here, *giant* gets the point across—sort of. It lets readers know that our fossil fuel use was extensive, but then again, so were the uses of wood, hydro, and nuclear energy. What I needed here was a word that specifically captured just *how* extensive fossil fuel use had become, a word that left an emotional impact on the reader.

I experimented with a variety of options. *Huge* was no more specific than *giant*. *Extensive*, while accurate, failed to capture the magnitude of the situation. It also sounded too academic and non-threatening. *Unbelievable* could have meant almost anything—and sounded too much like I was talking to friends while drinking a beer: "Man, that global apocalypse is just *unbelievable*, isn't it?"

I finally hit on:

> *By the late twentieth century and into the twenty-first century, our use of fossil*
> *fuels reached astonishing proportions. (13)*

Here, *astonishing* creates the impact I'm looking for. It leaves no doubt that our use of fossil fuels reached enormous proportions, but it takes it a step further and emphasizes that the extent can be viewed as incredible *by any possible standard*.

 A NOTE TO THE TEACHER

Modeling the Path from Vague to Specific

Getting specific is foundational in nonfiction revision, but precision takes effort. A student who doesn't yet fully understand her topic may write, "Reading makes cool stuff happen in your brain." It's easier to fall back on a generality than to explain how reading triggers sensory and neurological responses that mimic real life.

Model the transition from vague to specific by revising your own writing as students watch. If you don't have a good example handy, make one up. Fill your draft with fluffy words like *ways, things, fun, super, stuff, wonderful, special,* and others that bug you. For inspiration, check out the vague words or expressions that pop up in your students' own writing! After sharing your foggy draft, invite hard questions that push you closer and closer to your core meaning. Tell your students, "Don't let me get by with generalities. Make me work!" Their questions—the same ones they need to ask themselves—can help you make the leap from vague to precise: e.g., from "The hummingbird was amazing" (Why?) to "The hummingbird was tiny" (How tiny?) to "The hummingbird was smaller than my thumb."

Like other aspects of word revision, "getting specific" requires examining each word in a draft and asking, "Is this really the best word for the job?" If the answer is no, then a writer must put on his scientist hat and begin experimenting until he hits on the best alternative. This can take time, but approached with the right attitude, it becomes one of the most enjoyable tasks in the revision process.

Something to try
Revising for Precision

Following is a short passage from a student essay about the power of books to inspire us and change our moods. Have students read and discuss the passage, looking for vague words or phrases that cry out for revision. Challenge your students to come up with precise words that will make the writer's message clear and compelling:

> When you feel sad, read something happy. If you are angry, read something smooth. If you read a lot, it can turn into a habit! If you can just get some time and open that book, you will express lots of character.

When they finish, have students look at their own drafts—slowly, line by line. Ask them to identify a few words or phrases that could be more clear or specific, and come up with two alternatives for each. After sharing potential revisions with partners or in writing groups, students should incorporate final choices into their drafts.

Use the Language of the Territory

6

Enjoy the following excerpt from a fifth-grade student's essay:

> The Porsche 918 has 4 wheel drive and 4 wheel steering, so it can practically drive sideways! It can also go ¼ of a mile in 9.8 seconds, which is about the size of BV's track. And with its 887 horsepower it can produce a gnarly 944 pounds of torque (the tendency of a force to rotate an object about an axis).

All through this book, I've been looking for a place to excerpt this essay, but I just couldn't find the right spot. The piece is too good! Sure, it has punctuation and reference problems, but it infected me with its enthusiasm. The single best thing the writer does to sell me on the essay? He uses what Vicki calls "the language of the territory." He immerses us in his world by using words and expressions that can only come from a real car nut—terms such as *4 wheel drive*, *horsepower*, and *torque*. He refers to a quarter-mile track, a standard for race-car drivers—even though we don't know who or what the heck BV is! Then, he throws in that one perfect word to convey his unmitigated passion for his topic—*gnarly*.

All great writers use the authentic language of their topic. Cooking writers use cooking words such as *palate*, *brazier* (not to be confused with *brassiere*), and *reductions*. Military writers use *deploy, zone of action*, and *dope on a rope*. Science writers use *sample, half-life*, and *ecological succession*. Using this kind of language not only establishes the writer's qualifications

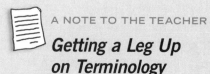

A NOTE TO THE TEACHER

Getting a Leg Up on Terminology

Students whose research hasn't yielded the right term for something specific can check an online glossary for help. For example, Wikipedia's *Glossary of Firefighting* offers clear definitions for terms like *A-side, accelerant, backdraft, charged hose, fire wall, hotshot crew*, and dozens of others that can give a young student an edge in writing knowledgeably about the topic. A writer doesn't want to sound like a walking dictionary, but using the right term at the right moment gives readers confidence in the message. (See "Something to Try" for suggestions on teaching students to make use of this resource.)

A Writing Secret to Share with Students

You may be wondering how you will learn this language of the territory. The answer is simple, and it's one we've emphasized throughout the book: research. If you don't know enough about cell phones, the galaxy, black holes, jellyfish, or any topic, you cannot write about that topic convincingly. And the surest way to expose your lack of knowledge is by struggling to come up with things to say: "Jellyfish are so cool! The way they move is awesome!" You do not have to speak like a professional to be convincing, but you do need to master enough basic terminology to write authentic nonfiction that readers trust: "Jellies, the dominant phyla in the sea, lack the muscular or skeletal structure necessary to swim, and simply float on currents, periodically stinging and absorbing their prey." Remember that in writing nonfiction, you are creating a resource on which others will depend for the truth. Using appropriate terminology correctly encourages readers to trust you in that role.

to write about a topic, it helps immerse the reader in the unique world that she desires to explore.

Read the following passage that *could have* appeared in *Hopping Ahead of Climate Change* (2016):

> *Scott asked for money to study snowshoe hares in Montana and other places where lynx live. He especially wanted to find out if logging and other human actions might affect hares—and, in turn, harm lynx.*

This passage does its job, but doesn't impart any particular "scientific feel" to the reader, does it? In its place, I crafted a paragraph that kept readers in the world of this scientist and his subject:

> *Scott ~~asked~~ applied for and received grant money to study snowshoe hares in Montana and other ~~places where lynx live~~ parts of the lynx's US range. He especially wanted to ~~find out~~ discover ~~if~~ whether logging and other human activities might affect ~~hares~~ hare numbers—and, in turn, harm lynx populations.*

Do you feel a difference? The introduction of the terms *grant money, range, activities, numbers,* and *populations* all add a "science-y" feel to the piece. They help sell my qualifications as the writer. More important, they make the passage more interesting for the reader.

Some would argue that the second version makes it more difficult for the reader to understand, but what really happens is that it makes the reader eagerly *reach* for new vocabulary. Part of the satisfaction of reading is that it makes you feel as one with the narrator and the topic. By reading words unique to a topic, a reader feels like she's on the "inside," privy to knowledge and experience no one else has.

This extends even to language that could have originated with aliens in the Horseshoe Nebula. If a skateboarder is writing about a particularly memorable run, a line such as, "I rolled down the ramp, jumped onto the bar, and slid down it before performing a complete circle at the bottom" will leave a reader flat. Instead, we expect something such as, "I carved the ramp, ollied, and grinded down a rail goofy-foot before nailing a 540 landing in front of one righteously delicious babe."

Authentic language renders this line all but incomprehensible to the average reader, but it doesn't matter. It's so full of action and life that we will happily look up the definitions of "ollie" and "goofy-foot"—or just accept that they mean something good and enthusiastically finish carving the writer's "totally sick" word run.

What if your students don't have the vocabulary to employ specialized language in their work? As is so often the case, the solution is *more research*! Which, for the final time in this book, provides the perfect segue into one of Vicki's special features . . .

! Something to try

Making Good Use of an Online Glossary

Online glossaries are a terrific resource for anyone who wants to write with confidence. The trick is narrowing a big list down to the terms needed for your particular discussion. Model this process for the whole class before students begin their individual searches.

First, ask the class to choose a topic you will look up online together. Adding the word "terms" or "glossary" will take a searcher right to the site. For example, suppose my topic is "sharks." Under "shark terms" I find a long list of precise names and expressions—far more than I need for a short report.

How do I handle this? By narrowing my topic to something like "shark anatomy." Giving my topic focus helps me zero in on relevant terms like *dorsal fin, caudal fin, gill, bioluminescence,* and *countershading.* Five or six terms are enough to get me started. I can always return for additional words later if I want to expand my discussion.

When students feel confident about using a glossary on their own, have them scan their writing, searching for places where more precise terminology would add credibility. Then have them check an online glossary for two, three, or more terms that will take readers inside their chosen topic.

By the way, on a scale of 1–10, how important do your students think correct terminology is to authenticity? In answering this question, have students look at any nonfiction source they trust. How far can they read without encountering specialized terminology?

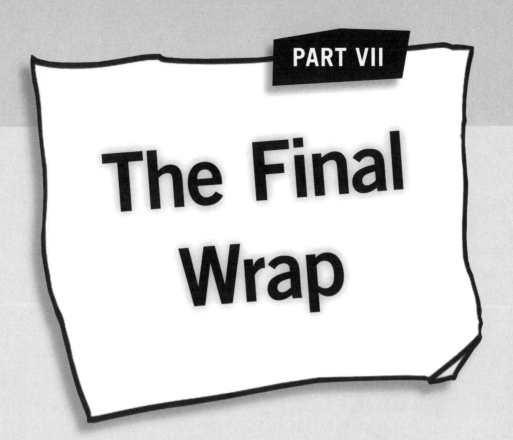

PART VII

The Final Wrap

By this point, you have incorporated each of our strategies into your classroom teaching. Your students are turning out scintillating prose and, because your classroom test scores have set new records for national achievement, Congress has awarded you the same pay increases, health insurance, and retirement benefits they award themselves! Time to sit back, relax, and congratulate yourself on a job well done.

Just kidding.

If you've read this book straight through, what's more likely is that you are taking a deep breath right now, thinking "Whew! This is a lot to take in!"

And you're right. Even Vicki and I feel that way. But please, don't get too worked up. Kindly recall that we have never intended this book to be a rigid regimen to be pursued with Navy SEAL-like determination. As we said before, we wrote this book for you. We created it as a resource to help you recognize where and why your students are having trouble, offer experience and tools for you to assist them, and help you establish reasonable expectations for their revision progress. Sure, you may wish to incorporate every one of our strategies into your classroom, but as we noted in our introduction, it's more likely that you will pick and choose those you find most helpful.

Regardless of your approach, goals, and expectations, you and your students will eventually arrive at that all-important step in the revision process: the final pass.

All writers must tackle a final review of their writing. Given their druthers, even your best students might interpret this to mean quickly skimming through their drafts, nodding their heads and mumbling, "Looks good. Awesome. Where do I turn it in?"

It's no surprise that Vicki and I believe that this final pass should involve just a *little* more activity than that. Here are six suggestions to share with your students that will help make their closing revisions powerful and effective.

Well, that was easy.

Let It Sit

Some students do their final revising while riding the bus to school on the day an assignment is due. Unfortunately, that allows no time for one of the most effective revision strategies in the history of writing—letting something sit.

As we have emphasized throughout this book, time away helps a writer see her work more objectively, and provides the mental break needed to sharpen revision skills. Writing is intense work. Thinking of something else for a time can open the writer's mind to fresh ideas.

Remember Part VI: Word Revision, "Swap Weak Verbs for Strong Ones"? You can probably guess that I felt a bit overwhelmed by Vicki's and Katie's diverging viewpoints on this topic. If I had immediately dived into revision, I would have done so with muddied thoughts and only a vague idea of how to handle them. My solution? To take a day off. Instead of hammering away, I went birding with my son. I took our new dog, Lola, for a walk. I broke out a jigsaw puzzle to work on with my daughter.

That mental break helped me process Vicki's and Katie's feedback. Even better, it gave me new ideas for how to approach it—namely, by bringing our opposing viewpoints into the open and even injecting a bit of humor (though that part about Vicki and Katie calling the Joint Chiefs of Staff really did happen!).

The point is to not have your writers sitting idly, staring into space. Good mental break activities engage the mind with things like reading, conversing, taking a walk, playing sports, or doing anything that helps a writer reflect—even subconsciously. When they return to their writing, your students can ask, "What will make this even stronger? What will readers look for that's missing from this piece?" Often, because of the break, new answers will leap to mind.

Caution students that allowing for time away prior to final revision takes planning. It might help to set some tentative deadlines with them to help factor in that "productive break."

Correct Spelling and Grammar

Once a writer feels confident that she will not make additional major revisions, it's time to get out the spyglass and track down details that trip up even the sharpest readers: misspelled words, wayward commas and quotation marks, grammatical errors, missing periods, faulty capitals, unwanted bold or italic print, incomplete references, and so forth.

Though spell-check and grammar-check programs have improved in recent years, they our far form infallible, as this sentence reveals. Sometimes they can be a real pain in the backside. Such programs not only miss numerous errors, but often find—and correct—fault where none exists. Encourage your writers to use computer programs, but not rely on them exclusively. Students also should make use of dictionaries, handbooks, and if possible, the eyes and ears of skilled friends or family members.

We have talked extensively about how reading aloud helps writers revise effectively. It's equally helpful with editing. It's too easy to skim when reading our own writing since we already know—or think we know—what we have said. Urge writers to read slowly as they edit so that mistakes can register in their brains. Dwelling on each word and punctuation mark is the essence of good editing. Speaking of which . . . some students find it's beneficial to look for spelling errors while reading up from the bottom of the page, holding a ruler beneath each line. This helps focus the reader's attention on spelling instead of getting distracted by meaning and content.

Revisit Your Title

Revise the title at the end of revision? Doesn't that run contrary to common sense? Actually, no. That's because most writers don't know precisely what they are going to write until a piece is finished. I almost never choose a final title until I have finished a book or article. That's because what I intended a piece to be at the beginning almost always shifts at least slightly during the writing process. You'll remember that this book you are reading began as a simple list of tips for writing students—yet look what it has become! Not surprisingly, figuring out our title constituted one of the last steps Vicki, Katie, and I discussed.

That said, it's a good idea to give any piece a "working title" at the beginning of the writing process, even prior to doing initial research. This gives direction to the writing and revision process. Students can think of their working title as a best guess about the document's final core message. During final revisions, each writer can zero in on the precise words that define what he has written and will attract a prospective reader.

Ask Yourself, "Am I Satisfied?"

Feedback from trusted listeners can be enormously helpful during the revision process. The final and most important critic, however, ought to be the writer.

My son and daughter often ask me to read stories and assignments they have written. In early drafts, I may offer them suggestions or point out trouble spots. For a final draft, though, I usually read it, hand it back to them, and ask, "Are *you* happy with it? As a reader, is this something you like and are excited about?"

The first time I asked this of my son, he looked at me, surprised. I don't think it had ever occurred to him to view his own work as a reader would. The more I've posed these kinds of questions, though, the higher he has raised his own standards for what he writes.

My guess is that this will also be true for your students. The problem, of course, is making sure that your students have the reading and writing skills to be able to critically evaluate their work. Students who read a lot usually do a better job of self-critiquing. Big surprise, huh? Beyond that, the more experience your students gain writing and revising, the more their evaluating skills will grow.

Don't be afraid to ask "the question," though, even to beginning students. As you place the standard of quality writing on their shoulders, most will take responsibility for their own expectations—and work hard to meet them.

Know When to Stop

Author Bernard Malamud once said that "revision is one of the exquisite pleasures of writing" (1988). You can hear the passion for his work in that line, but it reveals a truth that most writers eventually discover—revision can go on forever because there is no such thing as a perfect manuscript. At some point, however, revision becomes more trivial than substantive. Writers replace a word here, tighten a sentence there, but they are no longer reworking the foundation by changing meaning, voice, organization, or flow. They're tinkering.

And that's a good time to stop.

Here are some questions students can ask themselves to see if they have reached that "tinkering divide":

- Does my writing make sense to other readers as well as myself?

- Is it easy to follow, beginning to end—or does it feel as if I'm going in circles or leaping over crevasses?

- Do I hear the voice so clearly that I can easily find a word to describe it? A word like *authoritative, humorous, knowledgeable, passionate, determined, curious, caring* or *courageous*? Is that voice consistent?

- Can I honestly say that this piece leaves no vital questions about my topic unanswered?

- Do I like the sound of it when I read it—or hear it read—aloud?

- Have I done justice to this topic by teaching readers something important, fascinating, or memorable?

The more "yeses" a writer racks up, the closer he is to calling it a day.

Apply What You've Learned

Almost all professional writers read their published work and wish they had said something—or a lot of things—differently. This is not a mark of inferior writing. It's the sign of someone dedicated to improving his skills and growing as a writer. If your students experience this feeling, congratulate them. Recognizing need for improvement, even after it's too late to revise a particular draft, is a good thing. It means the writer has learned something she can use next time.

Especially for student writers, perfection should never be the goal. *Learning* and *improvement* should be the priority. Tell your students that each draft they write is a stepping-stone to becoming more competent. The more steps they take, the farther they will travel on the road to becoming a clear, persuasive, compelling—even entertaining—writer.

Vicki and I can both attest that it is a journey worth taking. With your encouragement and guidance, many students will discover the joy of turning their first rough ideas into something readers cannot put down.

APPENDIX A

Checklist of Revision Possibilities for Nonfiction Writers

Following is a list of reminders—things you *might* do when revising. We don't imagine any writer systematically going down the list and doing everything on it, lockstep fashion. If an item prompts you to go back for one more look, this list has done its work. As you gain experience in revising nonfiction, we hope you will add your own ideas to ours.

In revising my nonfiction piece, I:

____ Marked spots where I need more information or research

____ Did additional research

____ Added important details

____ Changed or sharpened the message

____ Deleted words, sentences, or whole paragraphs I didn't need

____ Got rid of repeated words or phrases

____ Replaced weak verbs with strong ones

____ Strengthened or changed my voice

____ Made my voice more consistent through the piece

____ Added drama

____ Made a "character" (person, place, object) more interesting

____ Moved a detail or sentence to a better spot

____ Reorganized the whole document

____ Reorganized information within paragraphs or sections

____ Came up with a stronger lead

____ Came up with a stronger ending

____ Rewrote sentences to add variety, clarity, or logic

____ Varied sentence length by combining some sentences—or splitting others

____ Came up with a new title

____ Other: _____

APPENDIX B

Recommended Nonfiction Books for Students

We hope that as a teacher you will explore these books, too—and share whole books or passages aloud. Keep in mind that even if you work with older students, picture books are ideal for illustrating such concepts as formatting and presentation, organization, voice, strong verbs, sentence variety, engaging leads and conclusions, the crafting of scenes, character development, and more. An asterisk marks books written at a slightly easier reading level.

Abeel, Samantha. 2003. *My Thirteenth Winter.* New York: Scholastic.

Anderson, M. T. 2015. *Symphony for the City of the Dead: Dmitri Shostakovich and the Siege of Leningrad.* Somerville, MA: Candlewick.

Aronson, Marc, and Marina Budhos. 2010. *Sugar Changed the World: A Story of Magic, Spice, Slavery, Freedom, and Science.* Boston: Houghton Mifflin Harcourt.

Bartoletti, Susan Campbell. 2005. *Hitler Youth: Growing Up in Hitler's Shadow.* New York: Scholastic.

Barton, Chris. 2016. *Whoosh! Lonnie Johnson's Super Soaking Stream of Inventions.* Illustrated by Don Tate. Watertown, MA: Charlesbridge.*

Bascomb, Neal. 2016. *Sabotage: The Mission to Destroy Hitler's Atomic Bomb.* Young Adult Edition. New York: Arthur A. Levine Books.

Brimner, Larry Dane. 2007. *We Are One: The Story of Bayard Rustin.* Honesdale, PA: Calkins Creek Publishing.

———. 2014. *Strike! The Farm Workers' Fight for Their Rights.* Honesdale, PA: Calkins Creek Publishing.

Brown, Daniel James. 2016. *The Boys in the Boat: The True Story of an American Team's Epic Journey to Win Gold at the 1936 Olympics.* Young Readers Adaptation. New York: Puffin.

Brown, Don. 2014. *America Is Under Attack: September 11, 2001: The Day the Towers Fell.* New York: Square Fish.*

———. 2015. *Drowned City: Hurricane Katrina & New Orleans.* Boston: Houghton Mifflin Harcourt.*

Bryan, Ashley. 2016. *Freedom Over Me.* New York: Atheneum Books.

Burns, Loree Griffin. 2007. *Tracking Trash: Flotsam, Jetsam, and the Science of Ocean Motion.* Boston: Houghton Mifflin Harcourt.

————. 2010. *The Hive Detectives: Chronicle of a Honey Bee Catastrophe*. Boston: Burns, Loree Griffin.

————.2014. *Beetle Busters: A Rogue Insect and the People Who Track It*. Illustrated by Ellen Harasimowicz. Boston: Houghton Mifflin Harcourt.

Carson, Mary Kay. 2017. *Mission to Pluto: The First Visit to an Ice Dwarf and the Kuiper Belt*. Photographed by Tom Uhlman. Boston: Houghton Mifflin Harcourt.

Castaldo, Nancy F. 2016. *The Story of Seeds: From Mendel's Garden to Your Plate, and How There's More of Less to Eat Around the World*. Boston: Houghton Mifflin Harcourt.

————. 2017. *Beastly Brains: Exploring How Animals Think, Talk, and Feel*. Boston: Houghton Mifflin Harcourt.

————. 2017. *Sniffer Dogs: How Dogs (and Their Noses) Save the World*. Boston: Houghton Mifflin Harcourt.

Cerullo, Mary M. 2012. *Giant Squid*. Washington, D.C.: Smithsonian.*

Collard, Sneed B. III. 1997a. *Animal Dads*. Illustrated by Steven Jenkins. Boston: Houghton Mifflin.*

————. III. 1997b. *Monteverde: Science and Scientists in a Costa Rican Cloud Forest*. London: Franklin Watts.

————. 1999a. *Birds of Prey: A Look at Daytime Raptors*. London: Franklin Watts.*

————. 1999b. *1,000 Years Ago on Planet Earth*. Illustrated by Jonathan Hunt. Boston: Houghton Mifflin.*

————. 2000. *The Forest in the Clouds*. Illustrated by Michael Rothman. Watertown, MA: Charlesbridge.*

————. 2003. *The Deep-Sea Floor*. Illustrated by Gregory Wenzel. Watertown, MA: Charlesbridge.*

————. 2005. *A Platypus, Probably*. Illustrated by Andrew Plant. Watertown, MA: Charlesbridge.*

————. 2005. *The Prairie Builders*. Boston: Houghton Mifflin.

————. 2006. *Benjamin Franklin: The Man Who Could Do Just About Anything*. Singapore: Marshall Cavendish Corporation.*

————. 2006. *Shep: Our Most Loyal Dog*. Ann Arbor, MI: Sleeping Bear Press.*

————. 2007. *Pocket Babies and Other Amazing Marsupials*. Plain City, OH: Darby Creek Publishing.

————. 2008. *Reign of the Sea Dragons*. Illustrated by Andrew Plant. Watertown, MA: Charlesbridge.

———. 2008. *Science Warriors: The Battle Against Invasive Species.* Boston: Houghton Mifflin Harcourt.

———. 2008. *Teeth.* Watertown, MA: Charlesbridge.*

———. 2010. *The World Famous Miles City Bucking Horse Sale.* Missoula, MT: Bucking Horse Books.

———. 2011. *Global Warming: A Personal Guide to Causes and Solutions.* Kalispell, MT: Lifelong Learning, Inc.

———. 2012. *Sneed B. Collard III's Most Fun Book Ever About Lizards.* Watertown, MA: Charlesbridge.*

———. 2015. *Fire Birds: Valuing Natural Wildfires and Burned Forests.* Missoula, MT: Bucking Horse Books.*

———. 2015. *Snakes, Alligators, and Broken Hearts: Journeys of a Biologist's Son.* Missoula, MT: Bucking Horse Books.

———. 2016. *Hopping Ahead of Climate Change: Snowshoe Hares, Science, and Survival.* Missoula, MT: Bucking Horse Books.

———. 2017. *Catching Air: Taking the Leap with Gliding Animals.* Thomaston, ME: Tilbury House.*

———. 2017. "Damper Ball 101!" *Highlights for Children,* January.*

———. 2017. *Insects: The Most Fun Bug Book Ever.* Watertown, MA: Charlesbridge.*

Dahl, Roald. *Boy.* 1984. Illustrated by Quentin Blake. New York: Penguin.*

Daubert, Stephen. 2009. *The Shark and the Jellyfish: More Stories in Natural History.* Nashville: Vanderbilt University Press.

Davies, Nicola. 2006. *Extreme Animals: The Toughest Creatures on Earth.* Illustrated by Neal Layton. Somerville, MA: Candlewick Press.*

———. 2007. *What's Eating You? Parasites—the Inside Story.* Illustrated by Neal Davies, Nicola.

———. 2009. *Just the Right Size: Why Big Animals Are Big and Little Animals Are Little.* Illustrated by Neal Layton. Somerville, MA: Candlewick Press.*

———. 2011. *Gaia Warriors.* Somerville, MA: Candlewick Press. Layton. Somerville, MA: Candlewick Press.*

Davis, Kenneth C. 2016. *In the Shadow of Liberty: The Hidden History of Slavery, Four Presidents, and Five Black Lives.* New York: Henry Holt & Co.

DeCristofano, Carolyn Cinami. 2012. *A Black Hole Is Not a Hole.* Illustrated by Michael Carroll. Watertown, MA: Charlesbridge.*

Facklam, Margery. 2001. *Spiders and Their Websites.* Illustrated by Alan Male. New York: Little, Brown and Company.*

Fleischman, Paul. 2014. *Eyes Wide Open: Going Behind the Environmental Headlines.* Somerville, MA: Candlewick Press.

Fleischman, Sid. 2006. *Escape! The Story of the Great Houdini.* New York: Greenwillow Books.

Floca, Brian. 2009. *Moonshot: The Flight of Apollo 11.* New York: Atheneum.*

———. 2013. *Locomotive.* New York: Atheneum.*

Freedman, Russell. 2006. *The Adventures of Marco Polo.* New York: Scholastic.

———. 2013. *Angel Island: Gateway to Cold Mountain.* New York: Houghton Mifflin Harcourt.

———. 2016. *Vietnam: A History of the War.* New York: Holiday House.

———. 2016. *We Will Not Be Silent: The White Rose Student Resistance Movement That Defied Adolf Hitler.* New York: Clarion Books.

Golio, Gary. 2017. *Strange Fruit: Billie Holiday and the Power of a Protest Song.* Illustrated by Charlotte Riley-Webb. Minneapolis: Millbrook Press.

Grossman, Laurie, Angelana Alvarez, and Mr. Musumeci's 5th Grade Class. 2016. *Master of Mindfulness: How to Be Your Own Superhero in Times of Stress.* Canada: Raincoast Books.*

Hillman, Ben. 2008. *How Fast Is It?* New York: Scholastic.*

Hood, Susan. 2016. *Ada's Violin: The Story of the Recycled Orchestra of Paraguay.* Illustrated by Sally Wern Comport. New York: Simon & Schuster.*

Hooks, Gwendolyn. 2016. *Tiny Stitches: The Life of Medical Pioneer Vivien Thomas.* Illustrated by Colin Bootman. New York: Lee and Low Books.*

Hughes, Susan. 2010. *Case Closed? Nine Mysteries Unlocked by Modern Science.* Canada: Kids Can Press.

Ignotofsky, Rachel. 2016. *Women in Science: 50 Fearless Pioneers Who Changed the World.* Emeryville, CA: Ten Speed Press.

Isaacson, Philip. 2015. *A Short Walk Around the Pyramids and Through the World of Art.* New York: Alfred A. Knopf.

Jarrow, Gail. 2016. *Bubonic Panic: When Plague Invaded America.* Honesdale, PA: Calkins Creek.

Jenkins, Martin. 2011. *Can We Save the Tiger?* Illustrated by Vicky White. Somerville, MA: Candlewick Press.

———. 2014. *Eye to Eye: How Animals See the World.* Boston: Houghton Mifflin Harcourt.*

———. 2016. *Animals by the Numbers.* Boston: Houghton Mifflin Harcourt.*

———. 2017. *Exploring Space: From Galileo to the Mars Rover and Beyond.* Illustrated by Stephen Biesty. Somerville, MA: Candlewick Press.

Kamkwamba, William, and Bryan Mealer. 2015. *The Boy Who Harnessed the Wind*. New York: Puffin Books.

Kurlansky, Mark. 2001. *The Cod's Tale*. Illustrated by S. D. Schindler. New York: Puffin Books.*

———. 2006. *The Story of Salt*. Illustrated by S. D. Schindler. New York: G. P. Putnam's Sons.*

———. 2011. *World Without Fish*. Illustrated by Frank Stockton. New York: Workman Publishing.

Lehmann, Devra. 2014. *Spinoza: The Outcast Thinker*. South Hampton, NH: namelos.

Levy, Debbie. 2016. *I Dissent: Ruth Bader Ginsburg Makes Her Mark*. Illustrated by Elizabeth Baddely. New York: Simon & Schuster.*

Leyson, Leon. 2013. *The Boy on the Wooden Box: How the Impossible Became Possible . . . on Schindler's list*. New York: Atheneum.

Marrin, Albert. 2006. *Oh, Rats!* Illustrated by C. B. Mordan. New York: Dutton Children's Books.*

———. 2009. *Years of Dust: The Story of the Dust Bowl*. New York: Dutton Children's Books.

———. 2015. *FDR and the American Crisis*. New York: Knopf Books for Young Readers.

———. 2016. *Uprooted: The Japanese American Experience During World War II*. New York: Knopf Books for Young Readers.

Montgomery, Sy. 2009. *Saving the Ghost of the Mountain: An Expedition Among Snow Leopards in Mongolia*. Boston: Houghton Mifflin Harcourt.

———. 2015. *The Octopus Scientists: Exploring the Mind of a Mollusk*. Boston: Houghton Mifflin Harcourt.

Nelson, Kadir. 2011. *Heart and Soul: The Story of America and African Americans*. New York: HarperCollins.*

———. 2013. *Nelson Mandela*. New York: Katherine Tegen Books.*

Noyes, Deborah. 2016. *Ten Days a Madwoman: The Daring Life and Turbulent Times of the Original "Girl" Reporter, Nellie Bly*. New York: Viking Books for Young Readers.

O'Brien, Tony, and Mike Sullivan. 2008. *Afghan Dreams: Young Voices of Afghanistan*. New York: Bloomsbury Children's Books.

O'Conner, Patricia T. 2016. *Woe Is I Jr.: The Younger Grammarphobe's Guide to Better English in Plain English*. New York: Random House.*

Osborne, Linda Barret. 2016. *This Land Is Our Land: A History of American Immigration*. New York: Harry N. Abrams.

Pallotta, Jerry. 2014. *The Incredible Crab Alphabet Book*. Illustrated by Tom Leonard. Boston: Charlesbridge.*

Patent, Dorothy Hinshaw. 2012. *Dogs On Duty: Soldiers' Best Friends on the Battlefield and Beyond*. New York: Walker & Company.*

———. 2015. *The Call of the Osprey*. Photographs by William Muñoz. Boston: Houghton Mifflin Harcourt.

Paulsen, Gary. 2001. *Guts*. New York: Random House.

———. 2007. *Woodsong*. New York: Simon & Schuster.

Philbrick, Nathaniel. 2015. *In the Heart of the Sea (Young Readers Edition): The True Story of the Whaleship Essex*. New York: Puffin Books.

Potter, Beatrix. 2016. *A Celebration of Beatrix Potter: Art and Letters by More Than 30 of Today's Favorite Children's Book Illustrators*. London: Frederick Warne & Company.

Pringle, Laurence. 2012. *Ice! The Amazing History of the Ice Business*. Honesdale, PA: Calkins Creek.

———. 2016. *Owls! Strange and Wonderful*. Illustrated by Meryl Henderson. Honesdale, PA: Boyds Mills Press.*

Raczka, Bob. *More Than Meets the Eye*. 2003. Minneapolis: Millbrook Press.*

Rappaport, Doreen. 2012. *Beyond Courage: The Untold Story of Jewish Resistance During the Holocaust*. Somerville, MA: Candlewick Press.

Reich, Susanna. 2017. *Stand Up and Sing! Pete Seeger, Folk Music, and the Path to Justice*. Illustrated by Adam Gustavson. New York: Booomsbury.*

Robinson, Sharon. 2004. *Promises to Keep: How Jackie Robinson Changed America*. New York: Scholastic.

Ross, Stewart. 2014. *Into the Unknown: How Great Explorers Found Their Way by Land, Sea, and Air*. Illustrated by Stephen Biesty. Cambridge, MA: Candlewick Press.*

Roy, Katherine. 2014. *Neighborhood Sharks: Hunting with the Great Whites of California's Farallon Islands*. New York: Roaring Brook Press.*

Rusch, Elizabeth. 2012. *The Mighty Mars Rovers: The Incredible Adventures of Spirit and Opportunity*. New York: Houghton Mifflin Harcourt.

Schaefer, Lola M., and Adam Schaefer. 2016. *Because of an Acorn*. Illustrated by Fran Preston-Gannon. San Francisco: Chronicle Books.*

Schatz, Kate. 2016. *Rad Women Worldwide: Artists and Athletes, Pirates and Punks, and Other Revolutionaries Who Shaped History*. Illustrated by Miriam Klein Stahl. Emeryville, CA: Ten Speed Press.

Scieszka, Jon. 2008. *Knucklehead: Tall Tales & Mostly True Stories About Growing Up Scieszka*. New York: Viking.*

———. 2014. *Guys Read: True Stories*. New York: Walden Pond Press.

Scott, Elaine. 2015. *Our Moon: New Discoveries About Earth's Closest Companion.* Boston: Houghton Mifflin Harcourt.*

Sheinkin, Steve. 2008. *Two Miserable Presidents: The Amazing, Terrible, and Totally True Story of the Civil War.* New York: Macmillan.*

——. 2012. *Bomb: The Race to Build—and Steal—the World's Most Dangerous Weapon.* New York: Flash Point.

——. 2014. *The Port Chicago 50: Disaster, Mutiny, and the Fight for Civil Rights.* New York: Roaring Brook Press.

——. 2015. *Most Dangerous: Daniel Ellsberg and the Secret History of the Vietnam War.* New York: Roaring Brook Press.

——. 2017. *Undefeated: Jim Thorpe and the Carlisle Indian School Football Team.* New York: Roaring Brook Press.

Shetterly, Margot Lee. 2016. *Hidden Figures (Young Readers' Edition).* New York: HarperCollins.

Sidman, Joyce. 2010. *Ubiquitous: Celebrating Nature's Survivors.* Boston: Houghton Mifflin Harcourt.*

Simon, Seymour. 2006. *The Heart: All About Our Circulatory System and More!* New York: HarperCollins.*

——. 2007. *Our Solar System.* New York: HarperCollins.*

——. 2012. *Extreme Earth Records.* San Francisco: Chronicle Books.*

Sloane, Eric. 2005. *Eric Sloane's Weather Book.* New York: Dover Publications.

Smith, David J. 2014. *If . . . A Mind-Bending New Way of Looking at Big Ideas and Numbers.* Illustrated by Steve Adams. Toronto: Kids Can Press.*

Stelson, Caren. 2016. *Sachiko: A Nagasaki Bomb Survivor's Story.* Minneapolis: Carolrhoda Books.

Steptoe, Javaka. 2016. *Radiant Child: The Story of Young Artist Jean Michel Basquiat.* New York: Little, Brown Books for Young Readers.*

Stevens, Joseph E. 1990. *Hoover Dam: An American Adventure.* Oklahoma City: University of Oklahoma Press.

Stewart, Melissa. 2011. *A Place for Butterflies.* Illustrated by Higgins Bond. Atlanta: Peachtree.*

Stone, Tanya Lee. 2009. *Almost Astronauts: 13 Women Who Dared to Dream.* Somerville, MA: Candlewick Press.

Strauss, Rochelle. 2007. *One Well: The Story of Water on Earth.* Illustrated by Rosemary Woods. Toronto: Kids Can Press.

Swaby, Rachel. 2015. *Headstrong: 52 Women Who Changed Science—and the World*. New York: Broadway Books.

Swanson, Jennifer. 2016. *Everything Robotics: All the Photos, Facts, and Fun to Make You Race for Robots*. Washington, D.C.: National Geographic.

Sweet, Melissa. 2016. *Some Writer! The Story of E. B. White*. Boston: Houghton Mifflin Harcourt.*

Swinburne, Stephen R. 2014. *The Sea Turtle Scientist*. Boston: Houghton Mifflin Harcourt.

Tougias, Michael J., and Casey Sherman. 2014. *The Finest Hours (Young Readers Edition): The True Story of a Heroic Sea Rescue*. New York: Henry Holt & Co.

Turner, Pamela S. 2016. *Crow Smarts: Inside the Brain of the World's Brightest Bird*. Photographs by Andy Comins. Boston: Houghton Mifflin Harcourt.

———. 2016. *Samurai Rising: The Epic Life of Minamoto Yoshitsune*. Illustrated by Gareth Hinds. Watertown, MA: Charlesbridge.

Walker, Sally M. 2005. *Secrets of a Civil War Submarine: Solving the Mysteries of the H.L. Hunley*. Minneapolis: Carolrhoda Books.

———. 2009. *Written in Bone: Buried Lives of Jamestown and Colonial Maryland*. Minneapolis: Carolrhoda Books.

Yousafzai, Malala. 2014. *I Am Malala*. Young Readers Edition. New York: Little Brown and Company.

APPENDIX C

Recommended Nonfiction Books for Adults

Within the following books you will find countless short passages to share aloud with students as examples of strong word choice, nonfiction voice, showing versus telling, sentence variety, compelling leads, effective conclusions, creative paragraphing, and many other characteristics we have identified as goals for revision.

Aiken, Mary. 2016. *The Cyber Effect: A Pioneering Cyberpsychologist Explains How Human Behavior Changes Online.* New York: Spiegel & Grau.

Al-Khatahtbeh, Amani. 2016. *A Muslim Girl: Coming of Age.* New York: Simon & Schuster.

Anderson, Scott. 2013. *Lawrence in Arabia: War, Deceit, Imperial Folly and the Making of the Modern Middle East.* New York: Random House.

Birkhead, Tim. 2016. *The Most Perfect Thing: Inside (and Outside) a Bird's Egg.* New York: Bloomsbury Books.

Bourdain, Anthony. 2000. *Kitchen Confidential: Adventures in the Culinary Underbelly.* New York: Bloomsbury.

Brown, Daniel James. 2014. *The Boys in the Boat: Nine Americans and Their Epic Quest for Gold at the 1936 Berlin Olympics.* New York: Penguin.

Bryson, Bill. 2000. *In a Sunburned Country.* New York: Random House.

———. 2004. *A Short History of Nearly Everything.* New York: Broadway Books.

———. 2010. *At Home.* New York: Doubleday.

Cain, Susan. 2013. *Quiet: The Power of Introverts in a World That Can't Stop Talking.* New York: Broadway Books.

Capote, Truman. 1996. *A Christmas Memory, One Christmas, & The Thanksgiving Visitor.* New York: The Modern Library.

Carroll, Sean B. 2016. *The Serengeti Rules: The Quest to Discover How Life Works and Why It Matters.* Princeton: Princeton University Press.

Casey, Susan. 2005. *The Devil's Teeth: The True Story of Obsession and Survival Among America's Great White Sharks.* New York: Henry Holt.

———. 2011. *The Wave: In Pursuit of Rogues, Freaks, and Giants of the Ocean.* New York: Doubleday.

Childs, Craig. 2007. *The Animal Dialogues.* New York: Little, Brown and Company.

———. 2012. *Apocalyptic Planet: Field Guide to the Future of the Earth.* New York: Vintage Books.

Czerski, Helen. 2016. *Storm in a Teacup: The Physics of Everyday Life*. New York: W. W. Norton & Company.

de Waal, Frans. 2016. *Are We Smart Enough to Know How Smart Animals Are?* New York: W. W. Norton & Company.

Doidge, Norman. 2007. *The Brain That Changes Itself: Stories of Personal Triumph from the Frontiers of Brain Science*. New York: Viking Penguin.

Duckworth, Angela. 2016. *Grit: The Power of Passion and Perseverance*. New York: Scribner.

Gershwin, Lisa-ann. 2013. *Stung!* Chicago: Chicago University Press.

Glausiusz, Josie. 2004. *Buzz: The Intimate Bond Between Humans and Insects*. San Francisco: Chronicle Books.

Grandin, Temple. 2005. *Animals in Translation: Using the Mysteries of Autism to Decode Animal Behavior*. New York: Simon & Schuster.

Guerrero, Diane, and Michelle Burford. 2016. *In the Country We Love: My Family Divided*. New York: Henry Holt and Co.

Harari, Yuval Noah. 2016. *Sapiens: A Brief History of Humankind*. New York: Harper.

Harford, Tim. 2016. *Messy: The Power of Disorder to Transform Our Lives*. New York: Riverhead Books.

Hawken, Paul, ed. 2017 *Drawdown: The Most Comprehensive Plan Ever Proposed to Reverse Global Warming*. New York: Penguin Books.

Hillenbrand, Laura. 2001. *Seabiscuit*. New York: Ballantine Books.

———. 2010. *Unbroken*. New York: Random House.

Houston, Keith. 2016. *The Book: A Cover-to-Cover Exploration of the Most Powerful Object of Our Time*. New York: W. W. Norton and Company.

Jahren, Hope. 2016. *Lab Girl*. New York: Knopf.

Johnson, Steven. 2014. *How We Got to Now: Six Innovations That Made the Modern World*. New York: Riverhead.

Kaku, Michio. 2012. *Physics of the Future: How Science Will Shape Human Destiny and Our Lives by the Year 2100*. New York: Anchor.

Kamler, Kenneth. 2004. *Surviving the Extremes: A Doctor's Journey to the Limits of Human Endurance*. New York: St. Martin's Press.

Katz, Jon. 2015. *Saving Simon: How a Rescue Donkey Taught Me the Meaning of Compassion*. New York: Random House.

King, Stephen. 2000. *On Writing: A Memoir of Craft*. New York: Scribner.

Kitchen, Judith, ed. 2005. *Short Takes: Brief Encounters with Contemporary Nonfiction*. New York: Norton & Company.

Kolbert, Elizabeth. 2014. *The Sixth Extinction: An Unnatural History*. New York: Henry Holt and Company.

Krakauer, Jon. 1997. *Into Thin Air: A Personal Account of the Mount Everest Disaster*. New York: Villard.

Kurlansky, Mark. 2003. *Salt: A World History*. New York: Penguin.

Macfarlane, Robert. 2016. *Landmarks*. New York: Penguin Books.

Mazzeo, Tilar J. 2016. *Irena's Children: The Extraordinary Story of the Woman Who Saved 2,500 Children from the Warsaw Ghetto*. New York: Gallery Books.

McCullough, David. 2004. *Posterity: Letters of Great Americans to Their Children*. New York: Doubleday.

———. 2015. *The Wright Brothers*. New York: Simon & Schuster.

———. 2017. *The American Spirit: Who We Are and What We Stand For*. New York: Simon & Schuster.

Millard, Candace. 2006. *The River of Doubt: Theodore Roosevelt's Darkest Journey*. New York: Broadway Books.

Montgomery, Sy. 2006. *The Good, Good Pig*. New York: Random House.

———. 2010. *Birdology: Adventures with a Pack of Hens, a Peck of Pigeons, Cantankerous Crows, Fierce Falcons, Hip Hop Parrots, Baby Hummingbirds, and One Murderously Big Living Dinosaur*. New York: Simon & Schuster.

———. 2015. *The Soul of an Octopus: A Surprising Exploration into the Wonder of Consciousness*. New York: Simon & Schuster.

Moor, Robert. 2016. *On Trails: An Exploration*. New York: Simon & Schuster.

Mukherjee, Siddhartha. 2011. *The Emperor of All Maladies: A Biography of Cancer*. New York: Scribner.

Paulsen, Gary. 1994. *Winterdance: The Fine Madness of Running the Iditarod*. New York: Harcourt.

———. 1996. *Puppies, Dogs, and Blue Northers*. Boston: Houghton Mifflin.

Pollan, Michael. 2008. *In Defense of Food: An Eater's Manifesto*. New York: Penguin.

Ripley, Amanda. 2008. *The Unthinkable: Who Survives When Disaster Strikes*. New York: Harmony Books.

———. 2014. *The Smartest Kids in the World and How They Got That Way*. New York: Simon & Schuster.

Rovelli, Carlo. 2016. *Seven Brief Lessons on Physics*. New York: Riverhead Books.

Rude, Emelyn. 2016. *Tastes Like Chicken: A History of America's Favorite Bird*. New York: Pegasus Books.

Schwalbe, Will. 2016. *Books for Living*. New York: Knopf.

Seidenberg, Mark. 2017. *Language at the Speed of Sight: Why We Read, Why So Many Can't, and What Can Be Done About It.* New York: Basic Books.

Seife, Charles. 2000. *Zero: The Biography of a Dangerous Idea.* New York: Penguin.

Sims, Michael. 2012. *The Story of Charlotte's Web: E. B. White's Eccentric Life in Nature and the Birth of an American Classic.* London: Walker Books.

Tyson, Neil deGrasse. 2017. *Astrophysics for People in a Hurry.* New York: W. W. Norton & Company.

Vance, J. D. 2016. *Hillbilly Elegy: A Memoir of a Family and Culture in Crisis.* New York: Harper.

Weiner, Jonathan. 1994. *The Beak of the Finch.* New York: Alfred A. Knopf.

White, E. B. 2003. *Farewell to Model T* and *From Sea to Shining Sea.* New York: The Little Bookroom.

Wilkerson, Isabel. 2011. *The Warmth of Other Suns: The Epic Story of America's Great Migration.* New York: Vintage Books.

Wohlleben, Peter. 2016. *The Hidden Life of Trees: What They Feel, How They Communicate—Discoveries from a Secret World.* Vancouver, BC: Greystone Books.

Zinsser, William 2006. *On Writing Well.* 30th anniversary ed. New York: HarperCollins.

REFERENCES

Anderson, Jeff. 2005. *Mechanically Inclined: Building Grammar, Usage, and Style into Writer's Workshop.* Portland, ME: Stenhouse.

———. 2011. *10 Things Every Writer Needs to Know.* Portland, ME: Stenhouse Publishers.

Brimner, Larry Dane. 2014. *Strike! The Farm Workers' Fight for Their Rights.* Honesdale, PA: Calkins Creek Publishing.

Brown, Don. 2015. *Drowned City: Hurricane Katrina & New Orleans.* Boston: Houghton Mifflin Harcourt.

Bryson, Bill. 2010. *At Home: A Short History of Private Life.* New York: Doubleday.

Childs, Craig. 2007. *The Animal Dialogues: Uncommon Encounters in the Wild.* New York: Little, Brown and Company.

Clark, Roy Peter. 2006. *Writing Tools: 50 Essential Strategies for Every Writer.* New York: Little, Brown and Company.

Collard, Sneed B. III. 1997. *Monteverde: Science and Scientists in a Costa Rican Cloud Forest.* London: Franklin Watts.

———. 1999a. *Birds of Prey: A Look at Daytime Raptors.* London: Franklin Watts.

———. 1999b. *1,000 Years Ago on Planet Earth.* Illustrated by Jonathan Hunt. Boston: Houghton Mifflin.

———. 2000. *Animal Dads.* Illustrated by Steve Jenkins. Boston: Houghton Mifflin.

———. 2003. *The Deep-Sea Floor.* Illustrated by Gregory Wenzel. Watertown, MA: Charlesbridge.

———. 2005a. *In the Deep Sea.* New York: Marshall Cavendish.

———. 2005b. *A Platypus, Probably.* Illustrated by Andrew Plant. Watertown, MA: Charlesbridge.

———. 2005c. *The Prairie Builders: Reconstructing America's Lost Grasslands.* Boston: Houghton Mifflin.

———. 2006a. *Benjamin Franklin: The Man Who Could Do Just About Anything.* Singapore: Marshall Cavendish Corporation.

———. 2006b. *One Night in the Coral Sea.* Watertown, MA: Charlesbridge

———. 2006c. *Shep: Our Most Loyal Dog.* Ann Arbor, MI: Sleeping Bear Press.

———. 2007–2010, "American Heroes" biography series (multiple titles). New York: Cavendish Square Publishing.

———. 2007. *Pocket Babies and Other Amazing Marsupials.* Plain City, OH: Darby Creek Publishing.

———. 2008a. *Reign of the Sea Dragons*. Illustrated by Andrew Plant. Watertown, MA: Charlesbridge.

———. 2008b. *Science Warriors: The Battle Against Invasive Species*. Boston: Houghton Mifflin Harcourt.

———. 2008c. *Teeth*. Illustrated by Phyllis V. Saroff. Watertown, MA: Charlesbridge.

———. 2009. *Lady Bird Johnson: Keeping America Green*. New York: Cavendish Square Publishing.

———.2010. *The World Famous Miles City Bucking Horse Sale*. Missoula, MT: Mountain Horse Publishing.

———. 2011. *Global Warming: A Personal Guide to Causes and Solutions*. Kalispell, MT: Lifelong Learning, Inc.

———. 2012. *Sneed B. Collard III's Most Fun Book Ever About Lizards*. Watertown, MA: Charlesbridge.

———. 2015a. *Fire Birds: Valuing Natural Wildfires and Burned Forests*. Missoula, MT: Mountain Press Publishing.

———. III. 2015b. *Snakes, Alligators, and Broken Hearts: Journeys of a Biologist's Son*. Missoula, MT: Bucking Horse Books.

———. 2016. *Hopping Ahead of Climate Change: Snowshoe Hares, Science, and Survival*. Missoula, MT: Bucking Horse Books.

———. 2017a. *Catching Air: Taking the Leap with Gliding Animals*. Thomaston, ME: Tilbury House.

———. 2017b. "Damper Ball 101!" *Highlights for Children*, January.

———. 2017c. *Insects: The Most Fun Bug Book Ever*. Watertown, MA: Charlesbridge.

Daubert, Stephen. 2009. *The Shark and the Jellyfish: More Stories in Natural History*. Nashville: Vanderbilt University Press.

Davies, Nicola. 2006. *Extreme Animals: The Toughest Creatures on Earth*. Illustrated by Neal Layton. Somerville, MA: Candlewick Press.

———. 2009. *What's Eating You? Parasites—The Inside Story*. Somerville, MA: Candlewick Press.

———. 2011. *Gaia Warriors*. Somerville, MA: Candlewick Press.

DeCristofano, Carolyn Cinami. 2012. *A Black Hole Is Not a Hole*. Illustrated by Michael Carroll. Watertown, MA: Charlesbridge.

Editors of the American Heritage Dictionaries. 2012. *The American Heritage Dictionary of the English Language, Fifth Edition*. Boston: Houghton Mifflin Harcourt.

Elbow, Peter. 1998. *Writing with Power*. New York: Oxford University Press.

Fleischman, Paul. 2014. *Eyes Wide Open: Going Behind the Environmental Headlines.* Somerville, MA: Candlewick Press.

Floca, Brian. 2009. *Moonshot: The Flight of Apollo 11.* New York: Atheneum Books.

Gantos, Jack. 1998. *Joey Pigza Swallowed the Key.* New York: Macmillan.

George, Twig. 2003. *Seahorses.* Brookfield, CT: The Millbrook Press.

Gershwin, Lisa-ann. 2013. *Stung! On Jellyfish Blooms and the Future of the Ocean.* Chicago: Chicago University Press.

Glausiusz, Josie. 2004. *Buzz: The Intimate Bond Between Humans and Insects.* Photographs by Volker Steger. San Francisco: Chronicle Books.

Gordon, Karen Elizabeth. 1993. *The Deluxe Transitive Vampire.* New York: Pantheon Books.

Gutkind, Lee. 2012. *You Can't Make This Stuff Up.* Boston: Da Capo Press.

Hale, Constance. 1999. *Sin and Syntax: How to Craft Wickedly Effective Prose.* New York: Broadway Books.

Hillenbrand, Laura. 2001. *Seabiscuit.* New York: Ballantine Books.

———. 2010. *Unbroken.* New York: Random House.

Hughes, Susan. 2013. *Case Closed? Nine Mysteries Unlocked by Modern Science.* Illustrated by Michael Wandelmaier. Toronto: Kids Can Press.

Ippisch, Hanneke. 1998. *Sky: A True Story of Resistance During World War II.* New York: Simon & Schuster.

Kamkwamba, William, and Bryan Mealer. 2015. *The Boy Who Harnessed the Wind.* New York: Puffin Books.

King, Stephen. 2010. *On Writing: A Memoir of the Craft.* New York: Scribner.

Kurlansky, Mark. 2001. *The Cod's Tale.* Illustrated by S. D. Schindler. New York: Puffin Books.

———. 2011. *World Without Fish.* Illustrated by Frank Stockton. New York: Workman Publishing.

Lopate, Phillip. 2013. *To Show and to Tell: The Craft of Literary Nonfiction.* New York: Simon & Schuster.

Leyson, Leon. 2013. *The Boy on the Wooden Box.* New York: Atheneum Books for Young Readers.

Malamud, Bernard. 1988. "Reflections of a Writer: Long Work, Short Life." *New York Times,* March 20. http://www.nytimes.com/1988/03/20/books/malamud-reflections.html.

Marrin, Albert. 2009. *Years of Dust: The Story of the Dust Bowl.* New York: Dutton Children's Books.

McCullough, David. 2015. *The Wright Brothers*. New York: Simon & Schuster.

Montgomery, Sy. 2014. "Tarantula Heaven." In *Guys Read: True Stories*, edited by Jon Scieszka. New York: Walden Pond Press, an imprint of HarperCollins.

———. 2015. *The Octopus Scientists: Exploring the Mind of a Mollusk*. Boston: Houghton Mifflin Harcourt.

Murray, Donald. 2004a. *Write to Learn*. New York: Holt, Rinehart and Winston.

———. 2004b. *A Writer Teaches Writing*, Revised Second Edition. Boston: Heinle.

National Writing Project and Carl Nagin. 2003. *Because Writing Matters: Improving Student Writing in Our Schools*. New York: John Wiley & Sons.

Newkirk, Thomas. 2014. *Minds Made for Stories: How We Really Read and Write Informational and Persuasive Texts*. Portsmouth, NH: Heinemann.

O'Conner, Patricia T. 2009a. *Woe Is I: The Grammarphobe's Guide to Better English in Plain English*. 3rd ed. New York: Riverhead Books.

———. 2009b. *Woe Is I Jr.: The Younger Grammarphobe's Guide to Better English in Plain English*. London: Puffin Books.

Paulsen, Gary. 1994. *Winterdance: The Fine Madness of Running the Iditarod*. New York: Harcourt.

Pringle, Laurence. 2016. *Owls! Strange and Wonderful*. Illustrated by Meryl Henderson. Honesdale, PA: Boyds Mills Press.

Roy, Katherine. 2014. *Neighborhood Sharks: Hunting with the Great Whites of California's Farrallon Islands*. New York: David Macaulay Studio.

Salinger, J.D. 1951. *The Catcher in the Rye*. New York: Little, Brown and Company.

Scieszka, Jon. 2008. *Knucklehead: Tall Tales and Mostly True Stories About Growing Up Scieszka*. New York: Viking.

Scott, Elaine. 2015. *Our Moon: New Discoveries About Earth's Closest Companion*. Boston: Houghton Mifflin Harcourt.

Sheinkin, Steve. 2008. *Two Miserable Presidents*. New York: Roaring Brook Press.

———. 2015. *Most Dangerous: Daniel Ellsberg and the Secret History of the Vietnam War*. New York: Roaring Brook Press.

Sidman, Joyce. 2010. *Ubiquitous: Celebrating Nature's Survivors*. Boston: Houghton Mifflin Harcourt.

Sims, Michael. 2012. *The Story of Charlotte's Web: E. B. White's Eccentric Life in Nature and the Birth of an American Classic*. London: Walker Books.

Smith, David J. 2014. *If: A Mind-Bending New Way of Looking at Big Ideas and Numbers*. Toronto: Kids Can Press.

Stevens, Joseph E. 1990. *Hoover Dam: An American Adventure.* Oklahoma City: University of Oklahoma Press.

Stone, Tanya Lee. 2009. *Almost Astronauts: 13 Women Who Dared to Dream.* Somerville, MA: Candlewick Press.

Strunk, William Jr., and E. B. White. 2000. *The Elements of Style.* 4th ed. New York: Pearson.

Taylor, Mildred D. 1976. *Roll of Thunder, Hear My Cry.* New York: Puffin.

White, E. B. 2003. *Farewell to Model T* and *From Sea to Shining Sea.* New York: The Little Bookroom.

Yousafzai, Malala. 2014. *I Am Malala.* Young Readers Edition. New York: Little Brown and Company.

Zinsser, William 2006. *On Writing Well.* 30th anniversary ed. New York: HarperCollins.